THE DURRELL L

ALSO BY BREWSTER CHAMBERLIN

Hiatus: Poems 1959. New York: privately printed, 1960.

A Piece of Paris: The Grand XIVth. Washington, DC: Masurovsky Publishing Company, 1996.

Paris Now and Then: Memoirs, Opinions, and a Companion to the City of Light for the Literate Traveler. Port Jefferson, NY: Vineyard Press, 2002; revised second edition, 2004.

Mediterranean Sketches: Fictions, Memories and Metafictions. Port Jefferson, NY: The Vineyard Press, 2005.

Situation Reports on the Emotional Equipoise: Collected Poems 1959–2006. Bloomington, IN: Xlibris, 2007.

Radovic's Dilemma: A Mediterranean Thriller. Bloomington, IN: Xlibris, 2009; revised edition 2012.

Travels in Greece and France and the Durrell School of Corfu Seminars: Travelogues and Lectures. Key West, FL: The New Atlantian Library (an imprint of Absolutely Amazing Ebooks), 2013, e-book; print version 2014.

The Hemingway Log: A Chronology of His Life and Times. Lawrence, KS: University Press of Kansas, Spring 2015.

Almost to the End: The Shorter Poems New and Old. Key West, FL: The New Atlantian Library (an imprint of Absolutely Amazing Ebooks), 2016, print and e-book.

Schade's Passage: A Novel of Berlin 1945–46, vol. 1 of *The Berlin Book.* Key West, FL & Corfu: The Garlic and Onion Press, 2017.

Schadow's Meditations or The Life Half-Lived, vol. 2 of *The Berlin Book.* Key West, FL and Corfu: The Garlic and Onion Press, 2017.

Peregrine's Island or The Pursuit of the Impossible, vol. 3 of *The Berlin Book.* Key West , FL and Corfu: The Garlic and Onion Press, 2018.

THE DURRELL LOG

A CHRONOLOGY
OF THE LIFE AND TIMES
OF
LAWRENCE DURRELL

BY

BREWSTER CHAMBERLIN

COLENSO BOOKS
2019

This third edition, revised, retitled and enlarged,
first published October 2019 by
Colenso Books
68 Palatine Road, London N16 8ST, UK.
colensobooks@gmail.com

ISBN 978-1-912788-04-0

First published as
*A Chronology of the Life and Times
of Lawrence Durrell, Homme de Lettres*
by the Durrell School of Corfu, 2007.

A second, online, edition was published as
Lawrence Durrell: A Chronology
on the website of the Durrell Library of Corfu, 2016.

The image on the cover shows the Shrine of St Arsenius
in its context, close to The White House at Kalami
where Lawrence and Nancy Durrell lived in the 1930s.
Photograph by Brewster Chamberlin.
See pages 27–28, 43 and 139.

CONTENTS

PREFACE AND ACKNOWLEDGEMENTS

In 2007, the Durrell School of Corfu published the first print edition of this *Log* (formerly *Chronology*). As with any chronology it became out of date as soon as it appeared because new facts are constantly dis-covered, and some interpretations must be adjusted because of the new facts. In 2016, the re-named Durrell Library of Corfu published a revised and expanded digital edition of the Chronology on its web site. Now (2019) an even further expanded, revised and retitled edition is published in print by Colenso Books in the UK. Much of the text of the original Preface and Acknowledgments remains relevant and should be repeated and updated here.

This is not a biography, nor is it a study of Durrell's writings. It is a list of events related to his life and the history of his times. It is as exhaustive and complete as I can currently make it. Given Durrell's genetic inability to properly date his correspondence with any regularity and the disparate information available in the public sources, this chronology can only be considered a work in progress. Nonetheless, it is to be hoped that this compilation will be useful and, in part, amusing to read.

Where there is divergent or contradictory evidence, footnotes to these instances, attempting to clarify the issues, have been added. The experience of researching and writing *The Hemingway Log: A Chronology of His Life and Times* (University Press of Kansas, 2015) has been of great help in this regard.

Persons mentioned in the text but not famously identified with Durrell are identified in the main text or footnotes on their first appearance as fully as possible in order to make clear their relationship to Durrell. Thus, Theodore Stephanides is not identified but Janina Martha Lepska is.

Unless otherwise noted, books by Durrell were first published in London by Faber and Faber through the good offices of the American-born British poet, T. S. Eliot, whose chosen personality (conservative, royalist, and Anglican) only partially paralleled that of Durrell, who was in most things a political and social conservative, did not rave against the royal house, but was not at all Anglican.

Where no day or month is known, the entry is placed at the start of the year; the same principle is applied where the month but not the day is known. In order to indicate the historical context in which Durrell lived and worked, entries concerning the publication of books and première performances of plays for each year of his adult life have been placed at the beginning of the year.

Several people have been helpful in the compilation of this work. Lynn-Marie Smith and Richard Pine read through both the original and the following revised versions (including this one) more than once and caught errors and infelicities in the text; all of the former and most of the latter have been corrected. I have also benefited from Mr Pine's second revised edition of his critical study, *Lawrence Durrell: The Mindscape* (Durrell School of Corfu, 2005). The text below has also greatly benefited from his thorough review and acute suggestions to extend and improve it.

Penelope Durrell Hope provided dates and other information I was unable to locate in printed sources. Fortunately, I was able to thank her personally before she died.

Because of prior commitments and the unavailability of his notes on Durrell, Gordon Bowker was unable to review the instances where his book differs from Ian MacNiven's biography. However, Mr Bowker's advice was to use MacNiven's work, which was twenty years in preparation with the authorization and assistance of the Durrell estate, whenever contradictory information appears. This advice I have, on the whole, but not always, followed.

I am grateful to Michael Haag — author of *Alexandria: City of Memory* (2004) and other relevant works such as *The Durrells of Corfu* (2017), and a new biography of Lawrence Durrell still in progress — for his review of the original manuscript and the suggestions he made to improve it. Joanna Hodgkin's book about her mother and Durrell, *Amateurs in Eden: The Story of a Bohemian Marriage: Nancy and Lawrence Durrell* (2012), was helpful in a number of instances.

No work on Durrell with any pretensions to completeness and accuracy can be written without constant and continuous referral to Ian MacNiven's biography. I have been extremely fortunate in having benefited from Dr MacNiven's review of the original text and I am immensely grateful to him for his detailed critique and suggestions.

Lee Durrell has been most generous with her time and knowledge of various matters which have enriched this edition of the chronology.

The original print version of the chronology was shepherded through the printing process by my long-time friend Aphrodite Papastephanou in Athens and I thank her for that.

This project would never have begun, nor would it have gone through its various stages without the encouragement and assistance of Lynn-Marie Smith.

This edition of the Durrell Log is dedicated to Anthony Hirst and Richard Pine both of whom have done so much to make this publication possible.

Brewster Chamberlin
Key West and Avignon, 2019

ABBREVIATIONS AND BIBLIOGRAPHY

WORKS, PEOPLE AND ORGANIZATIONS
IDENTIFIED BY ABBREVIATIONS

*The most frequently cited works are identified by the author's initials
or by the initials (in italics) of the title.*

DB   Douglas Botting. *Gerald Durrell: The Authorized Biography*. New York: Carroll & Graf Publishers, 1999.

DML   *The Durrell–Miller Letters 1935–80*, ed. Ian S. MacNiven. London: Faber & Faber and Michael Haag, 1988.

DSC   The Durrell School of Corfu

GB   Gordon Bowker. *Through the Dark Labyrinth: A Biography of Lawrence Durrell*, second, revised edition. London: Pimlico, 1998.

GD   Gerald Durrell

ILDS   The International Lawrence Durrell Society

IMN   Ian S. MacNiven. *Lawrence Durrell: A Biography*. London: Faber & Faber, 1997.

JH   Joanna Hodgkin. *Amateurs in Eden: The Story of a Bohemian Marriage: Nancy and Lawrence Durrell*. London: Virago Books, 2012.

MH   Michael Haag. *The Durrells of Corfu*. London: Profile Books, 2017.

LD   Lawrence Durrell

TLS   *The Times Literary Supplement*

TS   Theodore Stephanides. *Autumn Gleanings: Corfu Memoirs and Poems*, ed. Richard Pine, Lindsay Parker, James Gifford and Anthony Hirst. Corfu: The Durrell School of Corfu; Pine Bluff, AR: The International Lawrence Durrell Society; 2011.

VM   Vartan Matiossian. "Kostan Zarian and Lawrence Durrell: A Correspondence". *Journal of the Society for Armenian Studies* 8 (1995).

WORKS CITED BY AUTHOR AND SHORT TITLE

Anon, (ed.). *The Happy Rock: A Book About Henry Miller* (various authors). Berkley, CA: Bern Porter, 1945.

Ansen, Alan. *The Table Talk of W. H. Auden.* Princeton, NJ: Ontario Review Press, 1990.

Bartlett, Lee (ed.). *Kenneth Rexroth and James Laughlin: Selected Letters.* New York: Norton, 1991.

Beaton, Roderick. *George Seferis: Waiting for the Angel: A Biography.* New Haven, CT and London: Yale University Press, 2004.

Beauman, Nicola. *Morgan: A Biography of E. M. Forster.* London: Hodder & Stoughton, 1993.

Bowen, Roger. *"Many Histories Deep": The Personal Landscape Poets in Egypt, 1940–45.* Madison, NJ: Fairleigh Dickinson University Press; London: Associated University Presses; 1995.

Braybrooke, Neville and June. *Olivia Manning: A Life.* London: Chatto & Windus, 2004.

Cardiff, Maurice. *Friends Abroad: Memories of Lawrence Durrell, Freya Stark, Patrick Leigh Fermor, Peggy Guggenheim and Others.* London: Radcliffe, 1997.

Coldstream John (ed.). *Ever, Dirk: The Bogarde Letters.* London: Weidenfeld & Nicolson, 2008.

Cooper, Artemis. *Cairo in the War 1939–1945.* London: Hamish Hamilton, 1989.

Cowling, Elizabeth (ed.). *Visiting Picasso: The Notebooks and Letters of Roland Penrose.* London: Thames & Hudson, 2006.

Deriaz, Diane. *La Tête à l'envers: souvenirs d'un trapéziste chez les poètes,* Preface by Lawrence Durrell. Paris: Albin Michel, 1988.

Doyle, Charles. *Richard Aldington: A Biography.* Carbondale IL: Southern Illinois University Press, 1989.

Durrell, Gerald. *The Corfu Trilogy: My Family and Other Animals; Birds, Beasts, and Relatives; The Garden of the Gods.* London: Penguin Books, 2006.

Durrell, Gerald. *The Picnic and Suchlike Pandemonium*. London: William Collins & Sons, 1979.

Durrell, Lawrence. *Key to Modern Poetry*. London: Peter Nevill, 1952. Simultaneous US edition entitled *A Key to Modern British Poetry*. Norman, OK: Oklahoma University Press, 1952.

————. *A Smile in the Mind's Eye*. New York: Universe Books, 1982.

————. *Bitter Lemons*. London: Faber & Faber, 1959.

————. *Collected Poems 1931–1974*, ed. James A. Brigham. London: Faber & Faber, 1985.

————. "Constant Zarian: Triple Exile". *The Poetry Review* 1 (1952).

————. *Endpapers and Inklings: Uncollected Prose 1933–1988*, 2 vols, ed. Richard Pine. Newcastle upon Tyne: Cambridge Scholars Publishing, 2019 (forthcoming at the time of going to press, hence cited without page numbers).

————. *From the Elephant's Back: Collected Essays and Travel Writings*, ed. James Gifford. Edmonton, Alberta: University of Alberta Press, 2015.

————. *Letters to Jean Fanchette 1958–1963*. Paris: Éditions Two Cities Etc., 1988.

————. *Spirit of Place: Letters and Essays on Travel*, ed. Alan Thomas. London: Faber & Faber; New York: Dutton; 1969.

————. "The Happy Rock", originally published in Anon, *The Happy Rock*; reprinted in Lawrence Durrell, *From the Elephant's Back*.

————. *The Placebo*, ed. Richard Pine and David Roessel. London: Colenso Books for the Durrell Library of Corfu, 2018.

————. "'Yorick's Column': Lawrence Durrell's Unsigned Humor Sketches in the *Egyptian Gazette*, 1941". *Deus Loci* NS5 (1997).

Evans, Tom. *With the SOE in Greece: The Wartime Experiences of Captain Pat Evans*. Barnsley, South Yorkshire: Pen & Sword Books, 2018.

Fedden, Robin, Lawrence Durrell, Bernard Spencer, Terence Tiller, et al. (eds). *Personal Landscape: An Anthology of Exile*. London: Editions Poetry London, 1945.

Fiedler, Leslie. *The Collected Essays of Leslie Fiedler*, vol 1. New York: Stein and Day, 1971.

Fraser, G. S. *A Stranger and Afraid: The Autobiography of an Intellectual.* Manchester, UK: Carcanet Press, 1983.

———. *Lawrence Durrell: A Critical Study,* with a Bibliography by Alan G. Thomas. New York: E. P. Dutton & Co, 1968.

Furbank, P. N. E. M. *Forster: A Life.* London: Secker & Warburg, 1979.

Gray, Marianne. *La Moreau: A Biography of Jeanne Moreau.* New York: Donald I. Fine Books, 1994.

Haag, Michael. *Alexandria: City of Memory.* New Haven, CT and London: Yale University Press, 2004.

Haller, Robert. "The Writer and Hollywood: An Interview with Lawrence Durell". *Film Heritage* 6, no. 1 (Fall, 1970).

Hamalian, Leo. "Companions in Exile: Lawrence Durrell and Gostan Zarian". *Ararat* 35, no. 2 (Spring 1994).

———. "Lawrence Durrell and the Armenian Poet". *Ararat* 13, nos. 1–2 (Winter–Spring 1972).

Hughes, David. *Himself and Other Animals: A Portrait of Gerald Durrell.* London: Hutchinson, 1997.

Jeffreys, Peter (ed.). *The Forster–Cavafy Letters: Friends at a Slight Angle.* Cairo and New York: The American University in Cairo Press, 2009.

Kenner, Hugh. *Mazes: Essays.* San Francisco, CA: North Point Press, 1989.

Kershaw, Alistair and Frédéric-Jacques Temple (eds). *Richard Aldington: An Intimate Portrait.* Carbondale, IL: Southern Illinois University Press, 1965.

Klüver, Billy and Julie Martin. *Kiki's Paris: Artists and Lovers 1900–1930.* New York: Harry N. Abrams Publishers, 1989.

Liddell, Robert. *Cavafy: A Biography.* New York: Schocken Books, 1976.

MacNiven, Ian S. and Harry T. Moore (eds). *Literary Lifelines. The Richard Aldington–Lawrence Durrell Correspondence.* New York: The Viking Press, 1981.

Miller, Henry. *Big Sur and the Oranges of Hieronymus Bosch.* New York: New Directions, 1957.

———. *The Colossus of Maroussi.* Norfolk CT: New Directions, 1941.

Miller, Henry. *Dear, Dear Brenda: The Love Letters of Henry Miller to Brenda Venus*. New York: William Morrow &Company, 1986.

———. *A Devil in Paradise*. New York: Signet Books, 1956. Reprinted as "Paradise Lost" in Miller, *Big Sur*.

———.*The Intimate Henry Miller*. Introduction by Lawrence Clark Powell. New York: New American Library, 1959.

———. *Nights of Love and Laughter*. New York: Signet Books, 1955.

———. *Sextet*. New York: New Directions, 1977.

Moore, Harry T. (ed.). *The World of Lawrence Durrell*. Carbondale, IL: Southern Illinois University Press, 1962.

Paipeti, Hilary Whitton. *In the Footsteps of Lawrence Durrell and Gerald Durrell in Corfu (1935–39): A Modern Guidebook*. Corfu: Hermes Press and Production, 1998.

Perlès, Alfred. *My Friend, Henry Miller*. New York: The John Day Company, 1956.

Pine, Richard. *Lawrence Durrell: The Mindscape*, second, revised edition. Corfu: The Durrell School of Corfu, 2005.

Plimpton, George (ed.). *Writers at Work: The Paris Review Interviews*, 2nd Series. Harmondsworth: Penguin, 1977.

Quadflieg, Will. *Wir spielen immer: Erinnerungen*. Frankfurt am Main: S. Fischer, 1976.

Rexroth, Kenneth. *Assays*. New York: New Directions, 1961.

Rowley, Hazel. *Richard Wright: The Life and Times*. New York: Henry Holt and Co., 2001.

Shimwell, David, ed. *Dining with the Durrells: Recipes from the Indian and Corfiot Cookery Archive of Mrs Louisa Durrell*. London: Hodder and Stoughton, 2019.

Stuhlmann, Gunther (ed.). *A Literate Passion: Letters of Anaïs Nin and Henry Miller 1932–1953*. San Diego, CA: Harcourt Brace Jovanovich, 1987.

Stephanides, Theodore. *Autumn Gleanings. Corfu Memoirs and Poems*, ed. Richard Pine, Lindsay Parker, James Gifford and Anthony Hirst. Corfu: The Durrel School of Corfu; Pine Bluff AR: The International Lawrence Durrell Society; 2011.

Stephanides, Theodore. "First Meeting with Lawrence Durrell; and, The House at Kalami". *Twentieth Century Literature* 33, no. 3 (Fall 1987): *Lawrence Durrell Issue*, Part I.

Thaniel, George. *Seferis and Friends*. Stratford, Ontario: Mercury Press, 1994.

Thomson, David. *A Biographical Dictionary of Film*, 3rd edition. New York: Knopf, 1995.

Tremayne, Penelope. *Below the Tide*. London: Hutchison, 1958.

Webb, Constance. *Richard Wright: A Biography*. New York: Putnam, 1968.

Williams, Gwyn. *Flyting in Egypt: The Story of a Verse War*. Port Talbot, Wales: Alun Books, 1991.

Willliams, Jane (ed.). *Tambimuttu: Bridge between Two Worlds*. London: Peter Owen, 1989.

Wilson, Edmund. *The Sixties: The Last Journal, 1960–1972*. New York: Farrar Straus Giroux, 1993.

Zetterling, Mai. *All Those Tomorrows*. New York: Grove Press; London: Cape; 1985.

THE

DURRELL

LOG

ANTECEDENTS : TO 1910

331 BCE

April. Alexander, son of Philip of Macedon, founds the city of Alexandria on the southern shore of the Mediterranean Sea.

1851

Samuel Durrell (LD's paternal grandfather) is born in Suffolk, England.

1863

April 29. Constantine P. Cavafy is born in Alexandria, Egypt.

1869

At the age of 18, Samuel Durrell enlists in the British Army.

1874

Having transferred to the Royal Artillery two years previously, Samuel Durrell marries Emma Cooper in Portsea, an event shortly followed by the birth of two daughters.

1876

Sergeant Samuel Durrell is posted to India and travels with his family by ship via the Suez Canal, a three week voyage aboard the troopship *Malabar*, in the equivalent of steerage. By the end of the year both daughters die.

1879

January 1. Edward Morgan Forster is born in London.

1881

Having given birth to two more children, only one of whom, a daughter, survives infancy, Emma Cooper Durrell dies in Allahabad.

1882

January 25. Virginia Woolf (née Stephens) is born in London.

February 2. James Joyce is born in Rathgar, Dublin.

1883

His first wife Emma having died two years previously, Samuel Durrell marries Dora Maria Johnstone at Lucknow.

1884

Lawrence Samuel Durrell is born in Calcutta to Samuel and Dora.

1885

September 11. David Herbert Lawrence is born at Eastwood, Nottinghamshire.

1886

January 16. Louisa Florence Dixie is born in Roorkee, India.

1887

July 20. Jack Kahane is born in Manchester, England.

1888

September 26. Thomas Stearns Eliot is born in St. Louis, Missouri.

1891

December 26. Henry Valentine Miller is born in Brooklyn, New York.

1892

July 8. Richard Aldington is born in Portsea, Hampshire.

1896

January 21. Theodore Stephanides is born in Bombay, India, of a Greek father from Thessaly and a Greek mother born in England.

1897

Alfred Perlès is born in Vienna to a Jewish businessman father and a French Roman Catholic mother.

September 25. William Faulkner is born in New Albany, Mississippi.

1899

George Katsimbalis is born in Athens, Greece.

July 21. Ernest Hemingway is born in Oak Park, Illinois.

1900

March 13. Yeoryios Seferiadis (George Seferis) is born in Vourla, now Urla, near present-day Izmir in Asia Minor, Ottoman Empire (now Turkey).

1903

February 21. Anaïs Nin is born in the Paris suburb of Neuilly.

June 23. Eric Arthur Blair (eventually known as George Orwell) is born in Motihari, Bihar, British India.

1904

October. The Swedish Academy awards the great Provençal poet and philologist, Frédéric Mistral (France) the Nobel Prize in Literature.[1] For some arcane reason it is jointly awarded to the Spanish writer José Echegaray y Eizaguirre.

1907

Upon his father's retirement, and following a period of residence in France, the eleven-year old Theodore Stephanides and his family settle in Corfu, where the youngster whose mother tongue is English begins to learn Greek for the first time.

October. The Swedish Academy awards Rudyard Kipling (UK) the Nobel Prize in Literature.

1910

Lawrence Samuel Durrell marries Louisa Florence Dixie in India.

---

[1] Richard Aldington wrote a fine biography of Mistral, which LD reviewed (see the entry for May 4, 1957).

INDIA AND ENGLAND : 1912-1934

1912

Thomas Mann's *Tod in Venedig* is published in Berlin and Paul Claudel's *L'Annonce fait à Marie* is published in Paris.

February 27. Lawrence George Durrell is born in Jullundur (Jalandhar), India, to Lawrence Samuel and Louisa Florence Durrell.

May 8. Nancy Isobel Myers is born in Eastbourne, England.

Early October. The Swedish Academy awards Gerhard Hauptmann (Germany) the Nobel Prize in Literature.

1913

D. H. Lawrence's *Sons and Lovers* is published in London and Marcel Proust publishes the first volume of *À la recherche du temps perdu* in Paris.

February 27. LD is one year old.

Early October. The Swedish Academy awards Rabindranath Tagore (India) the Nobel Prize in Literature.

1914

Now retired, Major Samuel Durrell, LD's grandfather, dies in Portsmouth having spent his entire working life serving in India and China.

February 27. LD is two years old.

March 25. Frédéric Mistral, Nobel 1904, dies at the age of 83 in his native Maillane, Provence, and is buried in the cemetery there. The house in which he was born is now a museum devoted to his life and works.

June 28. The Serbian terrorist (or martyred patriot, depending on one's *Weltanschauung*), Gavrilo Princip, assassinates the Austrian Archduke, Franz Ferdinand, and his morganatic wife, Sophie, in Sarajevo.

July 23. Austria presents an ultimatum to Serbia, noting that if its demands were not met in two days, it would declare war.

July 29. The Russian Tsar mobilizes troops on the border with the Austro-Hungarian Empire.

July 31. The Russians extend the mobilization to their border with the German Empire.

August 1. Germany mobilizes for war against Russia.

August 2. France mobilizes its armed forces against Germany.

August 3. Germany declares war on France.

August 4. Britain declares war on Germany, which refused to respect Belgian neutrality guaranteed by Britain, and the slaughter begins.

Early October. The Swedish Academy does not award a Nobel Prize in Literature.

1915

February 27. LD is three years old.

June. *Poetry* magazine in Chicago, edited by Harriet Monroe, publishes T. S. Eliot's "The Love Song of J. Alfred Prufrock", which changes the way twentieth-century poetry is conceptualized and written.

September. D. H. Lawrence's *The Rainbow* is published in London.

Early October. The Swedish Academy awards Romaine Rolland (France) the Nobel Prize in Literature.

November. English authorities suppress *The Rainbow*.

November 12. Margery Durrell is born to Lawrence Samuel and Louisa Durrell in Mymensingh, India, where Lawrence Samuel is executive engineer of the Mymensingh Bhairab Bazar Railway.

1916

Margery Durrell dies in India, probably of diphtheria, the exact date is uncertain.

February 27. LD is four years old.

February 28. Having lived in England for decades and after becoming a British citizen to show his solidarity with England at war, the aging American prosemaster Henry James dies in London at the age of 73 and is buried in the Cambridge Cemetery in Cambridge, Massachusetts.

Early October. The Swedish Academy awards Carl Gustaf von Heidenstam (Sweden) the Nobel Prize in Literature.

November 22. The American writer Jack London dies at the age of 40 of uremic poisoning, aggravated by an accidental dose of morphine, at his ranch in Glen Ellen, California, and is buried in the State Park Cemetery, Glen Ellen, subsequently named after him as the Jack London State Historic Park.

1917

In London, the Egoist Press publishes T. S. Eliot's *The Love Song of J. Alfred Prufrock.* Carl Jung's *The Unconscious* is published. Leonard and Virginia Woolf establish the Hogarth Press in London.

February 27. LD is five years old.

March 10. Leslie Durrell is born in Mymensingh, India.

Early October. The Swedish Academy jointly awards the Nobel Prize in Literature to Karl Adolph Gjellerup and Henrik Pontoppidan (both of Denmark).

October. The Bolsheviks take power in St Petersburg in a violent coup d'état.

1918

The first volume of Oswald Spengler's *Der Untergang des Abendlandes* (*The Decline of the West*) is published.

February 27. LD is six years old.

c. November. The Durrell family moves from Mymensingh to Kurseong where Lawrence Samuel becomes resident engineer of the Darjeeling–Himalayan Railway.

August 8. Yvette Cohen is born in Cairo, Egypt.

Early October. The Swedish Academy awards Erik Axel Karlfeldt (Sweden) the Nobel Prize in Literature, which, as a true gentleman and a scholar, he refuses because his work is unknown outside Sweden.

November 9. The republic is proclaimed in Berlin, the Kaiser abdicates and goes into exile in the Netherlands.

November 11. An armistice is signed by the Allies and Germany, temporarily ending the slaughter.

1919

January 18. In Versailles, a peace conference to "negotiate" a settlement between the victorious Allies and the roundly defeated Germany opens; the conference lasts until January 21, 1920.

February 27. LD is seven years old.

April 12. Maurice Kahane, son of the English publisher Jack Kahane, is born in Paris; during the German occupation of France 1940–44 he takes his mother's maiden name, Girodias, to conceal his Jewish heritage.

July 30. LD's sister Margaret ("Margo") Durrell is born in Kurseong.

Early October. The Swedish Academy awards Carl Friedrich Spitteler (Switzerland) the Nobel Prize in Literature.

1920

Yvette Cohen and her family move from Cairo to Alexandria.

February 27. On his eighth birthday LD receives the complete works of Charles Dickens as a present from his parents.

Early October. The Swedish Academy awards Knut Hamsun (Norway) the Nobel Prize in Literature.

1921

February 27. LD is nine years old.

February 28. LD begins at St. Joseph's College at North Point, Darjeeling.

Early October. The Swedish Academy awards Anatole France (France) the Nobel Prize in Literature.

1922

Rainer Maria Rilke's *Die Duineser Elegien* (*The Duino Elegies*), e. e. cummings' *The Enormous Room*, and Virginia Woolf's *Jacob's Room* are published. The first issue of *The Criterion* appears. T. S. Eliot's *The Waste Land* and E. M. Forster's *Alexandria: A History and a Guide* are published in London.

February 2. At her Shakespeare and Company bookshop on the rue de l'Odéon in the VIth arrondissement, Paris, Sylvia Beach publishes James Joyce's *Ulysses.*

February 27. LD is ten years old.

Early October. The Swedish Academy awards Jacinto Benavente (Spain) the Nobel Prize in Literature.

November 1. Marcel Proust dies in Paris at the age of 51 and is buried in the Père Lachaise cemetery in that city.

December. LD finishes at St. Joseph's College.

1923

Sigmund Freud publishes *Das Ich und das Es* (*The Ego and the Id*) and Georg Groddeck publishes *Das Buch vom Es* (mistitled in English as *The Book of the It)*, which eventually exerts a strong influence on LD.

February 27. LD is 11 years old.

March 18. LD unwillingly departs India for school in England accompanied by Lawrence Samuel, Louisa, Leslie and Margo, sailing from Calcutta on the *City of London.*

April 27. The family disembarks at Tilbury, finds lodgings first briefly in a London hotel, then in a rented house in Dulwich, a district in South London.

September. After enrolling LD in a school in Tunbridge Wells and Leslie at another school, the family returns to India, leaving the two boys with "very unsympathetic aunts".[1]

Early October. The Swedish Academy awards W. B. Yeats (Ireland) the Nobel Prize in Literature.

1924

Thomas Mann's *Der Zauberberg* is published in Berlin. Carl Spitteler, Nobel 1919, dies at the age of 79.

Janina Martha Lepska, later Henry Miller's third wife, is born in Poland. Eve McClure, Miller's fourth wife, is born in the USA. At some point during the year Louisa visits England and is shocked at the state of Leslie's health, whereupon she takes him back to India.

---

[1] There is some confusion about the comings and goings of Durrell family members during the years 1923–1924. GB, 20–21, has Lawrence Samuel remaining in India in 1923, his mother leaving India for England to join Louisa and the children, and Louisa and Margo departing for India "early in 1924" leaving Leslie and LD in charge of their grandmother, being schooled partly at home (they were living with the widow of a former colleague of Lawrence Samuel) and "possibly [at] a local day school". This *Log* follows IMN and information from Penelope Durrell Hope in this instance.

February 27. LD is 12 years old.

September. LD lives in Dulwich and is enrolled at St Olave's and St Saviour's Grammar School in Bermondsey across from the Tower of London on the south bank of the river Thames.[2]

Early October. The Swedish Academy awards Władysław Stanisław Reymont (Poland) the Nobel Prize in Literature.

October 12. Anatole France, Nobel 1921, dies at the age of 80 and is buried at the Neuilly-sur-Seine (Ancien) cemetery in Paris.

Christmas. LD receives a typewriter and the complete Shakespeare, but not the elephant he had requested.

1925

Alban Berg's *Wozzek* is first performed. T. S. Eliot's *Poems 1909–1925* and Virginia Woolf's *Mrs Dalloway* are published in London. John Dos Passos' *Manhattan Transfer*, F. Scott Fitzgerald's *The Great Gatsby* and William Carlos Williams' *In the American Grain* are published in the USA.

January 7. Gerald Durrell is born in Jamshedpur, Bihar Province, India.[3]

February 27. LD is 13 years old.

March 10. The British government declares Cyprus a Crown Colony.

March 28. Louisa, Leslie, Margo and GD with his nurse sail from Bombay for England.

c. April 20. The Durrells arrive in England.

April 22. Claude-Marie Vincendon is born in Alexandria, Egypt, to Claire de Menasce, of the well-known wealthy and cultivated Jewish aristocratic family, and Jacques Vincendon, the Christian secretary-general of the

---

[2] GB, 20–21, has Leslie attending the Caldicott school in Hitchen where Malcolm Lowry had been the previous year, and the grandmother returning to India in October.

[3] GB, 24, notes that LD did not see his new brother "for more than a year after he was born", a statement that does not square with the fact that the Durrells, including GD, were in England three months after GD's birth.

Land Bank of Egypt.

Summer. Lawrence Samuel travels to England for a holiday with his family.

June. As a result of a coup d'état in Athens, Theodoros Pangalos becomes prime minister of Greece.

September. Leslie is enrolled at a Dulwich school, but does not do well. The family (except LD and Leslie) returns to India.

Early October. The Swedish Academy awards George Bernard Shaw (Ireland) the Nobel Prize in Literature.

1926

In Paris, André Gide publishes *Les Faux-Monnayeurs* (*The Counterfeiters*).

January 3. In Greece, Prime Minister Theodoros Pangalos proclaims himself dictator.

February 26. In New York, Boni and Liveright publishes Willam Faulkner's *Soldier's Pay.*

February 27. LD is 14 years old.

March 11. Louisa sails for England with her mother-in-law (Dora Durrell), GD and Margo.

Summer. Lawrence Samuel travels to England. Thinking of settling permanently there, he buys a large eight-bedroom house in Dulwich.

June. LD leaves St Saviour's Grammar School.

August 22. The Greek Republican Guard deposes Prime Minister Pangalos.

September. LD is enrolled at St. Edmund's School in Canterbury. The family returns to India taking Leslie with them.[4]

Early October. The Swedish Academy awards Grazia Deledda (Italy) the Nobel Prize in Literature.

---

[4] GB, 31, has Leslie remaining in England.

October 22. In New York, Scribner's and Sons publishes Ernest Hemingway's novel *The Sun Also Rises.*

December 3. At school and to his later chagrin, LD is confirmed in the Church of England.

1927

Virginia Woolf's *To the Lighthouse* is published in London.

February 27. LD is 15 years old.

Early October. The Swedish Academy awards Henri Bergson (France) the Nobel Prize in Literature.

December. LD leaves St Edmund's School at the end of the autumn term.

1928

Kurt Weill and Bertolt Brecht's *Die Dreigroschenoper (The Threepenny Opera)* is performed in Berlin. Seán O'Casey's *The Silver Tassie* and W. B. Yeats' *The Tower* are published in London. D. H. Lawrence's *Lady Chatterley's Lover* is published privately in Italy.

January. LD's father sends him to a military crammer in West Wratting Park in Cambridgeshire to prepare for university entrance exams, which he fails every time.

February 27. LD is 16 years old.

April 16. Lawrence Samuel Durrell dies of a brain haemorrhage in Dalhousie (in Himachal Pradesh State) at age 43 and is buried in the English Cemetery there; shortly thereafter Louisa, Leslie, Margo and GD move to England into the Dulwich house, joining LD in permanent exile from their home in India.

Early October. The Swedish Academy awards Sigrid Undset (Norway) the Nobel Prize in Literature.

1929

Erich Maria Remarque's anti-war novel, *Im Westen nichts Neues* (*All Quiet on the Western Front*), is published in Berlin.

LD discovers the pleasures of the Continent, especially Paris and its sexual delights.

January 31. In New York, Harcourt Brace and Company publishes William Faulkner's novel *Sartoris.*

February 27. LD is 17 years old.

April 14. The Russian poet Vladimir Mayakovsky commits suicide in Moscow after being labelled a Trotskyite.

Autumn. Scribner's and Sons publishes Ernest Hemingway's *A Farewell to Arms* and Thomas Wolfe's *Look Homeward, Angel.*

Early October. The Swedish Academy awards Thomas Mann (Germany) the Nobel Prize in Literature.

October 1. In London, Chatto and Windus publishes Richard Aldington's novel about the First World War, *Death of a Hero*, after the American publication a month earlier.

October 7. In New York, Cape and Smith publishes William Faulkner's progressively modern novel, *The Sound and the Fury.*

December 6. Jacqueline ("Jacquie") Sonia Wolfenden (GD's first wife) is born in Manchester, England.

End of year. Louisa sells the house in Dulwich at a loss and moves to rooms in the annex of the Queen's Hotel in Upper Norwood. She can no longer afford to keep LD at the crammer and he happily leaves to spend more time in the centre of London than at home (he has a limited income from his father's estate).

1930

Sigmund Freud's *Das Unbehagen in der Kultur* (*Civilisation and Its Discontents*), José Ortega y Gasset's *The Revolt of the Masses*, Hart Crane's long poem *The Bridge*, Hermann Hesse's *Narcissus und Goldmund*, John Dos Passos' *The 42nd Parallel*, and Evelyn Waugh's *Vile Bodies* are published. Noël Coward's *Private Lives* has its première. The British government appoints John Masefield as Poet Laureate.

Spending much time in Bohemian London, LD plays piano in nightclubs, writes songs for the British Tin Pan Alley, picks up a fairly mild case of anti-Semitism from association with the music business and his failure to conquer it.

January 23. The poet Derek Walcott is born on the island of Saint Lucia in the West Indies.

February 14. In New York, Alfred A. Knopf publishes Dashiell Hammett's *The Maltese Falcon*.

February 27. LD is 18 years old.

March 2. D. H. Lawrence dies in Vence, France, at the age of 45 and is buried there until his widow Frieda von Richthofen has his remains moved to a shrine in Taos, New Mexico, where she and others can worship in privacy.

July 7. Arthur Conan Doyle dies at the age of 71 and is buried in All Saints Churchyard, Minstead, Hampshire.

Early October. The Swedish Academy awards Sinclair Lewis (USA) the Nobel Prize in Literature.

October 6. In New York, Cape and Smith publishes Faulkner's *As I Lay Dying.*

1931

Eugene O'Neill's *Mourning Becomes Electra*, Samuel Beckett's *Proust*, Anthony Powell's *Afternoon Men*, Dashiell Hammett's *The Glass Key*, Erich Maria Remarque's *Der Weg zurück* (*The Road Back*), George S.

Schuyler's *Black No More* and Virginia Woolf's *The Waves* are published. Robert Frost's *Collected Poems* wins the Pulitzer Prize.

February 9. In New York, Cape and Smith publishes a heavily revised version of William Faulkner's lurid but fascinating *Sanctuary.*

February 27. LD is 19 years old.

c. March. The Durrell family moves to Parkstone near Bournemouth into a large detached house at 6 Spur Hill; Mrs Durrell names it Dixie Lodge after her family. Shortly thereafter LD moves to London, where he publishes his first book of poems, *Quaint Fragment: Poems Written between the Ages of Sixteen and Nineteen* (Cecil Press) in a very limited edition.[5]

March 27. Arnold Bennett dies at the age of 64 and is cremated at Golders Green Cemetery.

April. In London Chatto and Windus publishes Richard Aldington's *The Colonel's Daughter: A Novel.*

April 8. Erik Axel Karlfeldt dies in Stockholm at the age of 67.

Early October. The Swedish Academy posthumously awards Erik Axel Karlfeldt (Sweden) the Nobel Prize in Literature after he refused it in 1918 whilst alive. (See entry for 1918, Early October)

1932

Aldous Huxley's *Brave New World*, Evelyn Waugh's *Black Mischief*, W. H. Auden's *The Orators*, John Dos Passos' *1919*, Isaac Bashevis Singer's *Satan in Goray*, Erskine Caldwell's *Tobacco Road* and Graham Greene's *Stamboul Train* are published. In London, the anthology *New Signatures* publishes W. H. Auden, Stephen Spender and Cecil Day-Lewis. Noël Coward's *Design for Living*, Elias Canetti's *Die Hochzeit* and Marcel Pagnol's *Fanny* are given their première performances.

Early in the year. LD meets Nancy Myers, a student at The Slade School of Fine Art, in one of the Soho public houses; shortly thereafter they meet John Gawsworth (Terence Ian Fytton Armstrong) in the Windmill

---

[5] MH, 32, has Louisa telling LD "You can be as bohemian as you like but not in this house. I think you had better go somewhere where it doesn't show so much."

Café and George Wilkinson.

January 21. Lytton Strachey dies at the age of 52 and is buried in the St Cross Churchyard in Oxford.

February 27. LD is 20 years old.

April 26. At the age of 33, the distraught American poet Hart Crane drowns after jumping off the ship *Orizaba* in the Gulf of Mexico.

Summer. Nancy Myers leaves the Slade and moves in with LD at his Guilford Street bedsitter.

July 6. Kenneth Grahame, author of *The Wind in the Willows*, dies at the age of 73 and is buried in the St Cross Churchyard in Oxford.

Autumn. In London The Caduceus Press publishes LD's *Ten Poems* in a limited edition with cover designed by Nancy. LD and Nancy visit Dixie Lodge in Bournemouth for the first time.

Early October. The Swedish Academy awards John Galsworthy (England) the Nobel Prize in Literature.

October 6. In New York, Smith and Haas publishes Faulkner's novel *Light in August.*

c. October 29. Louisa suffers a nervous breakdown, books first-class tickets for herself and Gerry on the SS *City of Calcutta* sailing from Liverpool to India — tickets which they did not use because they disembarked or failed to board. Possibly LD discovered the plan and at the last moment got them off the ship. Louisa, becoming dependent on alcohol, temporarily enters a nursing home or similar institution.

December. Henry Miller travels by boat from Dieppe to Newhaven, England, where the immigration authorities refuse him entry and send him back to France ostensibly because he has very little money, no bank account in Paris and no visible means of support.[6]

End December. LD obtains reader's ticket to the British Museum North Library. He and Nancy send a Christmas card designed by Nancy with satirical poem by LD ("Ballade of Slow Decay") to friends.

---

[6] For a rather fictionalized but funny account of this event, see Miller's story "Via Dieppe–Newhaven" in his *Nights of Love and Laughter.*

1933

Gertrude Stein's *The Autobiography of Alice B. Toklas*, Claude McKay's *Banana Bottom*, André Malraux's *Man's Fate*, Guy Endore's *Werewolf of Paris*, Erskine Caldwell's *God's Little Acre*, Dashiell Hammett's *The Thin Man*, Nathanael West's *Miss Lonelyhearts* and Zona Gale's *Papa le Fleur* are published.

LD takes Nancy to Paris for a visit where they stay at the Hôtel Royale, room 13, on Boulevard Raspail around the corner from the Café du Dôme. LD often stays in the same room from then on when in Paris. They also meet Alan Thomas working in a Bournemouth bookstore. The Caduceus Press in London publishes the six-page pamphlet satirizing George Bernard Shaw's *The Adventures of a Black Girl in Her Search for God* entitled *Bromo Bombastes: A Fragment from a Laconic Drama* by one Gaffer Peeslake (an LD pseudonym).

Early in the year. LD's friend and first publisher Cecil Jeffries opens a night club called The Blue Peter in a Soho basement; he hires LD to play the piano and sing; a few weeks later it closes when Jeffries runs out of money and the police raid the place.

January 30. The old and senile Field-Marshal Paul von Hindenburg, president of Germany, appoints Adolf Hitler as chancellor to form a new government.

January 31. John Galsworthy, Nobel 1932, dies at the age of 66 and is buried at New College, Oxford.

February 9. The *TLS* prints a short review of LD's *Ten Poems*.

February 27. LD is 21 years old. He pressures his mother into giving him his share of the family estate in cash. In Berlin fire destroys the Reichstag (the German parliament building) giving the new regime an excuse for arresting thousands of opponents and banning the Communist and Social Democratic Parties.

Spring. Knowing nothing about the profession of photography, Nancy and LD set up a photography studio called Witch Photos in Millman Street, between Southampton Row and Gray's Inn Road, financed by a cheque for 300 pounds sterling from Nancy's father (actually her own money from an inheritance, knowledge of which her parents kept from her) — not the last time by any means that Nancy will finance life with LD. Witch Photos does not last long as a business.

March 2. Richard Aldington's *All Men Are Enemies: A Novel* appears in London and New York.

April 29. The great poet C. P. Cavafy dies aged 70 in the Greek hospital in Alexandria, Egypt, and is buried in the Greek Cemetery there.

May 10. In Berlin and elsewhere in Germany, Nazi students organized by the government burn books by Jews, anti-nazis and others the regime fears.

End of May. With Nancy now in possession of her inheritance and freed from the confines of the failed photography business, she and LD move to a cottage in the Sussex village of Loxwood with their friends George Wilkinson and Pamela Black, so that LD can write his novel in peace and quiet.

July 2. Henry Miller meets Anaïs Nin at the Avignon train station during his thwarted bicycle tour of the South of France.[7]

Mid-summer. The cottage lease coming to an end, LD moves with the grand piano, their books and a few sticks of furniture to his family in Bournemouth on Wimborne Road. Nancy remains in Sussex with friends for a while until an illness forces her to join LD and his family.

Early October. The Swedish Academy awards Ivan Bunin (Soviet Union) the Nobel Prize in Literature.

December 6. United States District Judge the Honourable John M. Woolsey lifts the ban on Joyce's *Ulysses* in the United States.

1934

John O'Hara's *Appointment in Samara*, Henry Roth's *Call It Sleep*, Nathanael West's *A Cool Million*, B. Traven's *The Death Ship*, Evelyn Waugh's *A Handful of Dust*, Robert Graves's *I, Claudius*, Samuel Beckett's

---

[7] See Miller's letter to Nin from Avignon, June 29, 1933, in Stuhlmann, *A Literate Passion*, 176–7, for details.

More Pricks than Kicks, James M. Cain's *The Postman Always Rings Twice*, and F. Scott Fitzgerald's *Tender is the Night* are published.

In London, The Caduceus Press publishes LD's *Transition: Poems*.

[1934]

February 27. LD is 22 years old.

May 31. George Wilkinson and Pamela Black marry at Kensington Registry Office.

June. Anaïs Nin arranges to finance the publication of Miller's *Tropic of Cancer* with Jack Kahane at the Obelisk Press in Paris.

c. June 10. The Wilkinsons leave on an extended bicycle trip across Europe intending to end on Corfu where they plan to write books and live cheaply.

Mid-year. LD finishes his first novel, *Pied Piper of Lovers*.

Mid-August. From Corfu George and Pamela begin writing enticing letters to LD and Nancy extolling the good and inexpensive life on the island.

Autumn. The polymath (physician, naturalist, writer, scientist) Theodore Stehpanides meets the Wilkinsons on Corfu. The couple talk about their friends LD and Nancy whom they are trying to lure to the island.

September. The Obelisk Press publishes Miller's *Tropic of Cancer.*

September 9. Roger Fry dies at 68 in London at the Royal Free Hospital and his ashes are placed in the vault of the Chapel of King's College Cambridge.

October. Disgusted with England and strongly attracted by the Wilkinsons' portrayal of life on Corfu, LD convinces Nancy to move to the Greek island; realizing his mother is falling ever more deeply into alcoholism, knowing he cannot leave her essentially alone in England (only Gerry is at home, Leslie and Margo are at school), he also convinces her to move to Corfu with Gerry; the other siblings insist on moving as well, and thus the decision is made.

Early October. The Swedish Academy awards Luigi Pirandello (Italy) the

20

Nobel Prize in Literature.

c. December 1. The American writer, John Dos Passos, writes to Miller from Key West, Florida, asking for a copy of *Tropic of Cancer.*

December 6. The *TLS* prints a critical review of LD's *Transition: Poems.*

CORFU : 1935–1939

1935

W. H. Auden's *The Dog Beneath the Skin*, George Orwell's *Burmese Days*, John O'Hara's *Butterfield 8*, James T. Farrell's *Studs Lonigan Trilogy*, Thomas Wolfe's *Of Time and the River* and B. Traven's *The Treasure of the Sierra Madre* are published. T. S. Eliot's *Murder in the Cathedral*, Clifford Odets' *Waiting for Lefty* and Emlyn Williams' *Night Must Fall* receive their première performances. Penguin publishes its first paperback.

Preparing for the move to Corfu, Louisa Durrell sells the Parkstone house and moves the family into rented quarters in Bournemouth.

Early January. LD sends the poem "Mass for the Old Year" on a card designed by Nancy to friends as a holiday greeting.

January 22. Nancy Myers and LD are married at the Bournemouth Registry Office with Alan Thomas and a book store colleague as witnesses when two dwarves could not be found in time.[1]

February 27. LD is 23 years old.

March 2. LD and Nancy sail on the SS *Oronsay* from Port of London in Tilbury for Naples en route to Corfu.[2]

March 6. From Gibraltar LD mails Alan Thomas two poems and a short-tempered letter. On this day, Louisa and the children sail from Tilbury aboard the SS *Hakone Maru*, a Japanese freighter.

c. March 11. In bad winter weather Nancy and LD are stranded in the Hotel Internazionale in Brindisi where LD writes the first pages of what becomes *Panic Spring*, which won't be published until April 1937, after he completes the manuscript of *The Black Book*. Their passage to Corfu is held up by confusion after an attempted coup d'état led by Eleftherios

---

[1] Joanna Hodgkin, Nancy's daughter with her second husband, Edward Hodgkin, writes in her biography of her mother that LD wanted the dwarves so the Registrar would not think Thomas, a tall thin man, to be the groom, rather than LD himself, some five or six inches shorter than Nancy (JH, 148).

[2] GB, 61, has Margo traveling with them, but this was not the case.

Venizelos in Athens.

[1935]

March 13. Venizelos flees to Rhodes.[3]

March 14. LD finally finds a boat captain willing to take them the 130 miles to Corfu where they land in the old harbour without their baggage, and stay for two weeks at the Pension Suisse, then located in the Ricci Mansion in Moustoxidou Street in Corfu Town (not Kapodistriou Street as is commonly believed).[4]

c. March 28. Louisa, Margo, the two brothers and GD's dog Roger arrive to stay at the Suisse, bringing news that Cassell has accepted *Pied Piper of Lovers* for publication.

Early April. LD and Nancy move to Perama into a small box-like house next to the Villa Agazini, where George and Pamela Wilkinson have been living for a year. The house overlooks Pondikonisi (meaning Mouse Island), a tiny speck of land holding naught but a small whitewashed Byzantine chapel. LD names the house Villa Bumtrinket, but it could hardly be described as a villa, essentially consisting of two tiny rooms and a minuscule kitchen.

Mid-April. The taxicab driver, Spyros Chalikiopoulos (known as Spiro Amerikanos due to his sojourn in the USA, his open Dodge touring car and heavily Brooklyn-accented English) takes Louisa and the children to Perama where he shows them a pinkish building with an outdoor toilet.[5] Enamoured, Louisa signs a six-month lease, and the family moves into the Strawberry Pink Villa (so named by GD twenty years later in *My Family and Other Animals*) one of two built in Perama in 1931 as rental

---

[3] Venizelos died in Paris March 18, 1936. The airport outside Athens built for the Summer Olympic Games in 2004 is named after him.

[4] Personal communication from Richard Pine (January 6, 2011). The building today sits next door to the Serbian Museum, which was the seat of the Serbian government-in-exile, 1915–16.

[5] The importance of this almost mythical figure to the Durrell family has often been misrepresented. MH, 64, offers a more realistic judgement: "Spiro took complete control over the family's affairs", though this does not necessarily apply to LD and Nancy's affairs.

properties by the owner of the Pension Suisse.[6] The house is not far from where LD and Nancy are living.

April. LD and Louisa decide that GD needs some form of schooling and, after rejecting LD's suggestion that the ten-year old read Rabelais, they hire George Wilkinson as a tutor.

May 19. T. E. Lawrence is killed in a motorcycle accident at the age of 47 and is buried in the St. Nicholas Churchyard, Moreton, Dorset.

Early summer. The Durrell family meets the radiologist and natural scientist, Theodore Stephanides, introduced by the Wilkinsons who had met him the previous autumn. LD, Nancy and the Wilkinsons hike across the island for 15 miles to Paleokastritsa above the sea on the west coast.

June 13. In London, Faber and Faber publishes T. S. Eliot's play, *Murder in the Cathedral.*

July 20. LD has pushed the *Panic Spring* manuscript to 40,000 words.

August. One night, LD reads the embalming episode of *Panic Spring* to Nancy and Stephanides at the shore.

Mid-August. The American painter, Barclay Hudson, then living with his wife, Jane, in the northeast of Corfu at Mega Kephali[7] just south of the coastal village of Kalami, lends LD *Tropic of Cancer* to read, after which LD writes a fan letter to Miller in Paris who swiftly responds, thus beginning a friendship and correspondence that continues until Miller's death. Miller's influence is clear in *The Black Book* and helped to break LD out of the residue of his middle-class English mindset.

---

[6] IMN, 112 and 115–17, and JH, 163, incorrectly have the family moving into the Villa Agazini, which was the Wilkinson residence. GB, 62, follows IMN on this point. They were possibly misled by Theodore Stephanides' memoir published as "First Meeting with Lawrence Durrell; and, The House at Kalami", 267, where he confuses the Strawberry Pink Villa with the Villa Agazini. Paipeti, *In the Footsteps of Lawrence Durrell*, 60, and MH, 72, more accurately separate the two buildings.

[7] Earlier publications on LD have contained a somewhat scrambled version of this name: "Mangkephali"; and I am grateful to Hilary Whitton Paipeti, who knows the location, for confirming the correct form of the name. "Mankephali" (pronounced as though spelled "Mangephali" with a hard G) was used locally in the past.

August 17. In Los Angeles, Charlotte Perkins Gilman, author of the much-written about and analysed short story, "The Yellow Wallpaper," and other works, dies at the age of 75.

September. The six-month lease on the Strawberry Pink Villa having expired, Spiro finds a new residence for the family and organizes Louisa and the family's move to the much larger Villa Anemoyanni (Daffodil-Yellow Villa) in Sotiriotissa, four miles north of Corfu Town near Govina Bay, where they live for two years. LD and Nancy move in with them for the winter.[8]

Early October. The Swedish Academy awards the anti-nazi journalist and pacifist Carl von Ossietzky (Germany) the Nobel Peace Prize and awards no prize in literature.

October 17. In London Cassell and Company publishes LD's first novel, *Pied Piper of Lovers*, dedicated to his mother, a fine gesture, with a cover designed by Nancy; the reviews are not particularly good.

November 30. The Portuguese writer Fernando Pessoa, a great utilizer of heteronyms, dies at the age of 47 in Lisbon and is buried at the Jerónimos Monastery there.

December. LD finishes *Panic Spring* (earlier titles include "Music in Limbo" and "Phoenix and Nightingale" as well as Nancy's suggestion: "Panic Spring in Limbo") and sends the last section off to Alan Thomas, having earlier sent sections as they were typed in draft. Thomas edits the manuscript and has it re-typed. It is then submitted to Faber and Faber, who accept it for publication.

1936

The relevant governments form the Berlin–Rome–Tokyo Axis. The German government revokes Thomas Mann's and his family's citizenships. John Dos Passos' *The Big Money*, Arna Bontemps' *Black*

---

[8] IMN, 120, and GB, 64; Paipeti, *In the footsteps of Lawrence Durrell*, 61, has them visiting "occasionally". MH, 94, implies they move into the villa and remain for an indeterminate period of time. TS, 26, simply records, "the Durrell family, including Lawrence and Nancy, all transferred to the much larger Villa Anemoyanni."

Thunder, Margaret Mitchell's *Gone with the Wind*, Walter D. Edmonds' *Drums Along the Mohawk*, and Elizabeth Bowen's *The House in Paris* are published.

January. LD begins writing what becomes *The Black Book*, after thinking about it late the previous year.

January 18. Rudyard Kipling, Nobel 1907, dies at the age of 71 and is cremated at Golders Green Crematorium, London.

February 4. In Davos, the young Yugoslavian Jewish student, David Frankfurter, assassinates Wilhelm Gustloff, the head of the National Socialist (Nazi) organization in Switzerland.

February 27. LD is 24 years old.

March 17. German troops occupy the Rhineland breaking a major provision of the Versailles Treaty; the victorious signatories do nothing.

April. One fine spring day, Spiro drives LD, Nancy and Stephanides to have tea with Madame Gennatas in her Venetian manor house at the port of Kouloura. Sharply attracted by the wild landscape and closeness to the sea at Kouloura, the following day LD and Nancy decide to move to the area to escape the chaotic and loud cacophony of the entire Durrell ménage. Spiro finds two rooms in a smallish house on Kalami Bay on the far northeastern shore owned by Anastasios ("Totsa") and Eleni Athinaios.[9] Ten days after the visit to Madame Gennatas, they move into what becomes known as The White House, ten minutes north of the house in which Jane and Barclay Hudson live. After being shouted at and stoned by irate villagers and priests for swimming and sun bathing naked, they find a nearby cove accessible only by sea with the small shrine to Saint Arsenius where, in season, they can swim in the sea without causing offense.[10] Nancy later wrote, "We were so absolutely mad on taking off

[9] JH, 169–70, dates the trip north to Kouloura and Kalami as April 1936. In a mock dialogue reminiscent of Spiro's portrayal in GD's *My Family and Other Animals*, Stephanides has the driver-factotum finding the house for them. See "First Meeting", 269. See also MH, 112–13.

[10] GB, 69, and IMN, 126, incorrectly have the move being made "around October". On the nude bathing matter, see MH, 114–15. The White House, still owned by the Athinaios family, is run as a tourist business with a good restaurant beside the house, and a plaque on its façade informing the world that LD, whose name is misspelled,

27

our clothes. I just wanted to absolutely drown myself in the sun and the sea."[11] "We used to go and bathe naked together, keeping out of view of the fishermen because we didn't want to shock them too much — at the time the peasants never even took their vests off in summer."[12]

[1936]

c. Mid-April. Nancy undergoes a curettage procedure, illegal in Greece, in a Corfu Town nursing home arranged by Stephanides with a gynaecologist friend.[13]

April 13. The Greek King George II appoints as prime minister Ioannis Metaxas, who turns the country's political structure into a dictatorship banning Pericles' funeral oration and regulating the length of women's skirts among other dictatorial measures.

May. LD decides on "The Black Book" as the title of the new novel, after trying "Lover Anubis" and "Anabasis".

May 8. The German anti-democratic historian Oswald Spengler, author of *The Decline of the West,* which exerted some influence on LD, dies in Munich three weeks before his 56th birthday.

Early summer. Nancy and LD buy a 20-foot sailboat, which, with Miller's approval, they name *Van Norden* after a comic character in *Tropic of Cancer.*

June 18. Maxim Gorki dies at 68 and is buried in the Kremlin wall in Moscow.

End June – early July. In Paris, the Obelisk Press publishes Miller's *Black Spring.*

once lived there. For the decade of its existence, participants in each of the Durrell School of Corfu's seminars enjoyed a well-watered lunch at the restaurant, to which they travelled by caïque.

[11] IMN, 135, quoting from a memoir Nancy wrote much later in her life.

[12] MH, 115, quoting from the same memoir.

[13] DB, 69, has this happening in the summer. JH, 176–8, provides details but no date. IMN, 131, mentions the procedure but gives no date other than quoting LD in a letter to Alan Thomas saying "I'm still 24 but I've aged [...] I must be a very old gentleman in my soul." MH, 113, dates this as soon after the move to Kalami.

July 17. The Spanish Civil War begins with the rightwing attempted coup d'état by fascist military leaders, immediately supported by Germany and Italy. Throughout the war the Western Powers maintain a studied and cowardly "neutrality".

August 2–29. Theodore Stephanides lives in The White House with the Durrells for the month, observing Peltier's Comet.

August 15. Grazia Deledda, Nobel 1926, dies at the age of 65 and is buried in the Cimitero Comunale Monumentale Campo Verano, Rome.

August 19. After completing his drama, *La Casa de Bernarda Alba*, the Spanish poet and playwright, Federico García Lorca travels to Grenada where rightwing Spanish terrorists murder him.

Early October. The Swedish Academy awards Eugene O'Neill (USA) the Nobel Prize in Literature.

October 26. In New York, Random House publishes Faulkner's *Absalom, Absalom.*

Early November. LD writes the first draft of a Hamlet essay for Miller. LD and Nancy move into Corfu Town for the winter, taking a heated hotel room across the square from the Ionian Bank, which they use as their postal address during their Corfu residence.

November–December. LD and Nancy meet Constant (Gostan) Zarian the Armenian poet,[14] Max Nimiec, a Polish poet of means, and others who, with Stephanides, form a rather loose-knit literary club which meets fortnightly for "Ionian Banquets" at The Sign of the Partridge (the Perdika Restaurant in the centre of Corfu Town) throughout the following year.[15]

---

[14] For additional details about Zarian's and LD's friendship, see VM, which alas contains several false statements about LD's life during the early days of the German invasion of Greece and the Durrell's escape to Egypt. See also Hamalian, "Lawrence Durrell and the Armenian Poet" and Hamalian, "Companions in Exile". For LD's appreciation of Zarian, see his "Constant Zarian: Triple Exile", Reprinted in LD, *From the Elephant's Back*, 225–31. LD's letters to Zarian are reprinted in LD, *Endpapers and Inklings.*

[15] The building off Nikiphorou Theotoki Street later became a bakery, parts of which still survive. See also the entry for February 20, 1947 below for LD's apology to

November 27. LD experiences difficulties pushing the draft of the *The Black Book* forward.

December 10. Luigi Pirandello, Nobel 1934, dies in Italy at the age of 69 and is buried at Agrigento, Sicily.

December 19. Despite his problems with the manuscript, LD finishes what is possibly the third draft of *The Black Book.*

End December. He continues to revise the manuscript.

1937

Virginia Woolf's *The Years,* Zora Neale Hurston's *Their Eyes Were Watching God,* John Steinbeck's *Of Mice and Men,* Georges Bernanos' *Diary of a Country Priest* and Karen Blixen's *Out of Africa* are published.

c. January 12. LD sends Miller the text of "Christmas Carol" (Miller suggests the title be changed and LD names it "Asylum in the Snow").

January 14. The *New English Weekly* publishes LD's "The Prince and Hamlet: A Diagnosis", based on the letter he'd sent to Miller in 1936.

February. LD finishes another draft of *The Black Book* and Nancy corrects spelling errors; LD adds handwritten amendments in various coloured inks before it is bound and dispatched to Miller in Paris.

February 27. On his 25th birthday LD makes final revisions and additions to the manuscript of *The Black Book,* adds a dedication to Nancy, and mails the only copy to Miller.[16]

March. LD and Nancy move from Corfu Town to three rented rooms in a peasant's house south of Paleokastritsa on the northwest side of the island for the summer. Stephanides also rents three rooms in the same house for his wife and daughter while he works in town as a radiologist and visits on weekends. Maurice Koster, the American painter, also has a room in the house.[17]

Zarian for the "travesty" of his portrayal in *Prospero's Cell.*
[16] MH, 121. No edition contains the dedication to Nancy.
[17] In an undated letter to Constant Zarian written prior to his and Nancy's trip to

March 8, 13, and 15. Miller responds to *The Black Book* manuscript with wildly enthusiastic letters.[18]

Late March. Nancy and LD travel to Athens to buy a tent for camping excursions stopping on the island of Ithaca, LD's "miracle ground".[19] LD writes to Miller, briefly mentioning his plan for a series of books relating to *agon* (*The Black Book*, then in manuscript), *pathos* (The Book of Miracles) and *anagnorisis* (The Book of the Dead).[20]

March-April. LD is reading Nietzsche, a potentially dangerous undertaking in one so young and volatile.

Early April. The Durrells sail northwest from Corfu to Mathraki Island. After attempting themselves to retype clean copies of *The Black Book*, Anaïs Nin and Miller give it to a professional typist.

April. In London, Faber and Faber publishes LD's *Panic Spring* under the pseudonym Charles Norden.

Mid-May. Louisa, Margo and Gerry visit England to fix Margo's glandular condition that has her gaining weight at a tremendous pace, leaving Leslie in charge of the house.[21]

May 27. Alan Thomas arrives on Corfu for a visit having stopped at the Villa Seurat (a small street in the 14th arrondissement in Paris) to meet Miller who lives in that street with an assortment of artists and writers at

Paris in mid-August 1937, LD writes, "We are here for a little while at Koster's house [...] Came round the island in the boat. She is beautiful, but sailing is a dangerous business" (VM, 83).

18 *DML*, 55–62.

19 The "miracle ground" comes from LD's poem, "On Ithaca Standing", which begins "Tread softly, for here you stand/on miracle ground, boy". See LD's *Collected Poems*, 111. "On Miracle Ground" is also the generic title of the bi-annual conferences organized by the International Lawrence Durrell Society.

20 *DML*, 65. The second and third "books" eventually become *The Alexandria Quartet* and *The Avignon Quintet*. See also the entry for 1945, May 5 (with footnote 4).

21 IMN, DB and GB are silent on whether or not Gerry travelled with Louisa and Margo, but Gerry wrote: "Coming from the calm, slow, sunlit days of Corfu, our arrival in London late in the evening was a shattering experience. So many people were at the station that we did not know, all hurrying to and fro, grey faced and worried" (GD, *The Corfu Trilogy*, 439).

various addresses in the same street. LD, Nancy and Pat Evans,[22] a mutual friend of LD and Thomas and erstwhile tutor for Gerry, meet the visitor at the quay; with Spiro driving the Dodge, they take him to the Daffodil-Yellow Villa near Kontokali to meet Leslie, then to Paleokastritsa where, because the Kalami house cannot accommodate visitors, LD, Nancy, Stephanides and his family rent rooms making Thomas' visit into a holiday.

[1937]

Summer. The New York publisher Covici-Friede accepts *Panic Spring* for American publication.

June 28. Eliot writes to LD that Faber cannot publish *The Black Book* unexpurgated, but does not advise him to change the text.

c. July. The Durrells return to The White House in Kalami where LD saves a village girl from drowning off the beach at Mega Kephali, enhancing his reputation on the island (and giving him a premature model for Clea?).

July 1. LD writes to George Bernard Shaw about helping to get Miller's books into England.

July 13. Shaw's secretary writes that Shaw does not think he can be helpful.

Mid-July. Louisa, Gerry and Margo return to Corfu from England.

Mid-summer. LD and Nancy discuss with Totsa Athinaios, the owner of The White House, the possibility of adding a second storey with large windows so they can stay there during the winter.

July 29. From Paris, Miller writes to LD in Corfu about editing *The Booster: The Monthly Magazine of the American Country Club.*

c. August 10. Nancy and LD board the Corfu–Brindisi ferry to begin the trip to Paris to meet Miller, Anaïs Nin, and other of Miller's friends, before going on to London.

---

[22] Evans, an Oxford graduate, served in Greece during World War II as a member of the Special Operations Executive unit with the partisans. See Evans, *With the SOE in Greece.*

August 11. The American writer Edith Wharton dies in Paris at the age of 75 and is buried in the Cimetière des Gonards, Versailles.

August 12. LD and Nancy arrive at the Gare de Montparnasse[23] to be met on the platform by Miller and Anaïs Nin. They move into the American painter and sculptor Betty Ryan's flat (formerly occupied by Miller's friend, the writer Michael Fraenkel), on the ground floor of No. 18 Villa Seurat across the hall from the artist Chaim Soutine, and thus join the literary circus with Alfred Perlès (with whom a friendship develops that lasts with some interruptions until Perlès' death nine months before LD himself dies), Abraham Rattner and Hans Reichel (American and German painters respectively), and Brassaï (the soon to be famous Hungarian photographer whose real name was Gyula Halász). LD increasingly sidelines and abuses Nancy, who begins to assist Miller and Perlès to edit *The Booster.* They meet André Breton (the Pope of Surrealism), Herbert Read (the influential British art historian), Raymond Queneau (the inventive French writer, author of *Zazie dans le métro* and founding member of OULIPO — Ouvroir de Littérature Potentielle), Eugene Jolas (the French–German–American editor of the journal *transition* — the title is never capitalized — most noted for publishing pieces of James Joyce's *Work in Progress*, which becomes *Finnegans Wake* when published in 1939). The Villa Seurat circus core eats at the Café du Dôme, Le Select, La Coupole, and the Brasserie Zeyer on the Avenue du Maine (how they can afford these places is a mystery given their alleged shortage of funds, except for Anaïs Nin whose husband is a banker), and in Villa Seurat where Nancy (of course) prepares the meals.

August 22. LD and Nancy move on to London where he meets T. S. Eliot (who provides a fine blurb for the flyleaf of *The Black Book*) and Alan Pringle (a senior editor at Faber), the pioneer sexologist Havelock Ellis,[24] Meary James Thurairajah Tambimuttu (the Sinhalese poet and editor), the poet Audrey Beecham, Frank Morley (LD's editor at Faber), and his

---

[23] GB, 93, has them arriving at the Gare du Nord, but trains from the south arrive at the Gare de Montparnasse or the Gare de Lyon.

[24] GD wrote a funny story about owning Ellis' collected works, which he supplied to various employees of a hotel in which he was staying to advise them about their sexual problems. See "The Havoc of Havelock", in GD's *The Picnic and Suchlike Pandemonium*.

33

old friends Mulk Raj Anand the Indian novelist, the poet George Barker, and Alan Thomas.

[1937]

September. Louisa and the family move out of the Daffodil Yellow Villa to the Villa Cressida (the Snow White Villa) near Perama, built in 1824 for the British governor of Corfu. LD's *Panic Spring* appears in the USA.

September 4. *Time and Tide* in London publishes "Ionian Profile" by "Charles Norden" (an LD pseudonym) about the Corfiot priest Father Nicholas (years later the piece is integrated into LD's *Prospero's Cell*).

September 9. George Bernard Shaw writes to LD warning him to watch his step and the company he keeps.

Mid-September. LD and Nancy return to Paris and stay for two weeks with Perlès at 7 Villa Seurat, across the street from No. 18 where Miller lives.

Late September. The Durrells move into an apartment at 21 rue Gazan, on the Parc Montsouris, ten minutes' walk from the Villa Seurat. They meet David Gascoyne (then a young, starving Surrealist poet), Cecily Mackworth (an English poet and scholar of poetry), Buffie Johnson (a painter studying with Francis Picabia), and Conrad Moricand (the astrologer-moocher).[25] LD drafts "The Death of General Uncebunke: A Biography in Little", a long poem about the nature of British colonials, including LD's father and other relatives.

October. *The Booster* issue appears (with a prose poem by GD and LD's "Coda to Nancy" from the end of *The Black Book*) and is severely criticized by George Orwell in the *New English Weekly* for ignoring the horrors of the European situation (Hitler, Stalin, Spain). The Paris American Country Club dissolves its association with the magazine over the Eskimo story "Nukarpiartekak."[26]

Early October. The Swedish Academy awards Roger Martin du Gard

---

[25] Miller has a vivid portrait of this dubious character in *A Devil In Paradise*.

[26] The short piece consists of LD's recasting of the Nordic story of an old man who is so taken by a beautiful young girl that in the course of making love to her he disappears into her vagina. Later she leaves the igloo to have a pee and out falls the old man's skeleton. The text was included by Alfred Perlès in his *My Friend, Henry Miller*, 182.

(France) the Nobel Prize in Literature.

November. The "Trilingual Womb Number" of *The Booster,* edited by LD, appears with the poem "Death" by GD.

December. Miller, LD and Anaïs Nin make plans to create the Villa Seurat Series (financed by Nancy to the tune of £150) to be published by Obelisk Press, the first three volumes to be LD's *The Black Book,* Miller's *Max and the White Phagocytes* and Anaïs Nin's *Winter of Artifice.*

Mid-December. LD travels to London with the painter Buffie Johnson (whom he tells that he and Nancy are washed up, hoping to get Buffie in the buff in the bed) and David Edgar, a mystic, to gather poems for the next issue of *The Booster,* "The Poetry Number". LD meets Dylan Thomas in London and they carouse a bit. He also meets the ballerinas Dorothy Stevenson and Veronica Tester and the latter's boy-actor brother Desmond, Hugh Gordon Porteus (poet and Sinologist), and Anna Wickham (who made the introduction to Dylan Thomas). He takes Buffie to see Alexander Calder's circus performance with wire figures and does his best to seduce her, but she may have resisted until the end.

December 16. Nancy takes the train from Paris to the Austrian Alps to ski (and find some relief from her husband).

c. December 22. LD suddenly leaves London, taking the train to Innsbruck to see Nancy, stopping off in Paris long enough to put Buffie in the hospital, the edgy young woman distraught at LD's erratic treatment of her sensibilities.

December 25. Early in the morning LD finds Nancy in a chalet in the mountains. Ruining the fine time she was having, he insists they return to Innsbruck that day.

December 26. Durrells go to Gris, Austria, to ski for a week and continue the combat.

1938

Graham Greene's *Brighton Rock*, George Orwell's *Homage to Catalonia*, Vladimir Nabokov's *Invitation to a Beheading*, Jean-Paul Sartre's *La Nausée*, John Dos Passos' massive trilogy *USA*, Marjorie Kinnan Rawlings' *The Yearling* and Evelyn Waugh's *Scoop* are published. Emlyn Williams' *The Corn is Green* and Thornton Wilder's *Our Town* are given their première performances.

Early January. In London, Eliot writes to LD turning down "Uncebuncke" for the journal *The Criterion*, which Eliot edits.

January 10. The Durrells leave Innsbruck and return to 21 rue Gazan.

Mid-January. The December–January number of *The Booster* appears, the last under this name, called the "Air Conditioned Womb Number", half the usual length, but containing LD's piece "Down the Styx in an Air-Conditioned Canoe".

Late January – early February. LD writes to Eliot that he has started a novel because Faber would not give him an advance on a book of poems; this is probably what LD referred to over the next several years as "The Book of the Dead", eventually morphing into *The Alexandria Quartet*.

February 15. In New York, Random House publishes Faulkner's *The Unvanquished*.

Late February. Anaïs Nin moves into a houseboat called *La Belle Aurore*[27] on the Quai des Tuileries, the better to conduct sexual dalliances without her husband learning too much about them.

February 27. LD is 26 years old.

March 1. Gabriele D'Annunzio dies at the age of 102 and is buried in Il Vittoriale deli italiani, Gardone Riviera.

Mid-March. Nancy takes an active role in producing the Villa Seurat Series (for which, after all, she is paying) and appreciates Miller and Reichel's

---

[27] Fans of the classic movie, *Casablanca*, will wonder if there is a relationship between the houseboat and the Paris restaurant of that name where, in the film, Rick, Ilse and Sam drink their final champagne cocktails as the Germans are on the point of entering Paris in June 1940.

praise for her paintings.[28]

End March. David Gascoyne, whom Anaïs Nin is paying to type a volume of her diaries, takes the manuscript with him to London on a visit; when Anaïs Nin finds out, their friendship ends. LD was to go with Gascoyne but turns back at the Gare St Lazare, taking a later boat-train to London.

April. The poetry number of *The Booster*, now called *Delta*, at last appears in Paris.

April 8. LD flies back to Paris from London.

April 10. Possibly because of the tumultuous political situation, the Durrells suddenly and abruptly depart Paris for Greece, leaving many possessions behind, some of which are rescued by Miller and Anaïs Nin after they see their friends off at the station.[29] The Austrians welcome

[28] It is difficult today to reach an appreciation of Nancy's paintings since none of them are available to be seen. No one seems to know exactly what happened to them, except they were destroyed or lost during the War. One of the young British girls living on Corfu during the time the Durrells lived there has left a disparaging and terribly condescending memoir of LD and Nancy in which she describes one of Nancy's paintings; it is worth citing at length given the scarcity of knowledge about her paintings: "At the Durrells' I saw a painting by Nancy. It represented Adam and Eve standing in a bathtub. The bathtub was deep but transparent so Adam and Eve were visible in their nakedness, sporting exaggerated pubic hairs that had been painted in hard angry strokes. Their bodies were grotesquely ill-proportioned [...] I was shocked by the ugliness of Nancy's painting. Lawrence talked loudly and drank too much [...] the Durrells were ill-disciplined, with pretentions but without the sensitivity or upbringing to participate in the ancient and settled culture of Corfu. I had heard Mummy's friends talk about degenerates, a term I had not understood, but decided that they must have been referring to people like the Durrells." This snob-priggish reaction is cited in MH, 153. Three of Nancy's drawings are printed in LD, *Endpapers and Inklings*, and JH has her lampoons of two people on board their ship the SS *Oronsay* (149), her cover for *Pied Piper of Lovers* (162), her cartoon "The woods are full of them", her cover illustration for the first issue of the Booster (196), a lithograph (222), a line drawing for LD's story "The Magnetic Island" (242), and an illustration of LD's limerick "There was a fair maid of Corfu" (261). Miller, in his essay, "The Waters Reglitterized" — published in *Sextet* (1977) but originally written in 1973 — opens with the sentence "In this room where I lie I am surrounded with paintings — Nancy's wild Ionian horses" (89). Were these some of Nancy Durrell's works?

[29] GB, 107, lists "a painting by Cézanne" as one of these possessions. One wonders what his source was for this bit of misinformation. It may have been a painting by

German troops and the annexation of Austria to the Greater German Reich, causing an intensely frightening situation.

[1938]

c. April 15. Stephanides and Spiro Amerikanos drive the Durrells from Corfu Town to a spot above Kalami from where they walk down the donkey path to The White House, which now has two storeys but with *small* windows on the seaward side, thus enraging the volatile author who wanted *large* windows out of which he could look at the sea in inclement weather. Later in the winter he realizes the rightness of Athinaios' decision. The new quarters have a calming effect, but the tension between LD and Nancy continues, if temporarily in milder forms.

May. LD writes to Miller he might return to England to study medicine as a return to reality from the turmoil of writing literature. The Durrells spend a week on Ithaca, the "miracle ground".

May 4. Carl von Ossietsky, Nobel Peace Prize 1935, dies at the age of 49 as a result of being tortured in prison by his fellow Germans.

May 5. Miller writes to LD and adds postscript to Nancy: "Don't let Larry browbeat you."

Summer. Nancy's painting reaches new levels of sophistication but LD's selfish demands upon her continue. Veronica Tester and Dorothy Stevenson from London visit, and the Durrells do their best and take them sailing and camping.[30] In Athens Theodore Stephanides introduces the Durrells to George Katsimbalis.[31]

Mid-August. In Paris, Jack Kahane at the Obelisk Press publishes *The Black Book* with serious printers' errors. In March 1937, LD had written to Constant Zarian that the publication "will begin my life as a writer proper".[32]

Reichel, since Betty Ryan had been buying the artist's work on behalf of her friends.

[30] See MH, 143–7, for Tester's reminiscences of their time on Corfu.

[31] IMN, 137, has them introduced "on early trips to the capital". Elsewhere Ian MacNiven notes that the first meeting probably occurred "in 1937 or 38" (personal communication). GB, 111, has the meeting in the summer of 1938. Ergo, this seems to be a reasonable dating.

[32] VM, 81.

September 15. Thomas Wolfe, the American novelist, author of *Look Homeward, Angel* (1929) and other massive fictions, dies at the age of 38 of miliary tuberculosis of the brain and is buried in the Riverside Cemetery in Ashville, North Carolina.

September 25. Miller is in Bordeaux, having fled Paris in a panic at the thought of war over German demands on Czechoslovakia.

c. September 27. The Obelisk Press publishes Miller's *Max and the White Phagocytes* while the author is in Marseille feeling sorry for himself.

September 29. At Munich, Neville Chamberlain and Edouard Daladier capitulate to Hitler and Mussolini over the Czechoslovakia matter.

Early October. Nancy and Veronica Tester travel to Athens for a holiday; LD remains on Corfu ignoring world events. For some arcane reason the Swedish Academy awards Pearl S. Buck (USA) the Nobel Prize in Literature.

October 11. Miller returns to Paris.

Mid-October. Nancy informs LD she wants to have a child, but he resists until September of the following year.

November. The new issue of *Seven* contains two pieces by LD, "Asylum in the Snow" and "Carol on Corfu".

November 19. The Durrells are briefly in Paris on their way to London, where they stay at Hugh Guiler's flat at 140 Campden Hill Road, Notting Hill Gate. Guiler's wife, Anaïs Nin, is with them and LD takes her to see Pringle at Faber.

November 21. *Time* magazine contains an article on the young publisher at New Directions, James Laughlin, and Miller and Durrell.

November 29. The Durrells flee to Paris when rumours of an English general strike circulate. While there LD falls in love with and has a brief but passionate affair with the pretty American journalist, Thérèse "Tessa" Epstein; they continue to see each other sporadically over the next several decades.

Mid-December. When the strike does not materialize the Durrells return to London and Guiler's flat, having convinced Perlès to go with them.

39

December. Anaïs Nin pays the sinister but elegant Conrad Moricand to cast LD and Nancy's horoscope; his description of LD's mind and spirit is close to reality, noting that LD was in a continual state of rebellion and needed all his resources to maintain his mental equipoise. *Delta* publishes its "Special Peace and Dismemberment Number with Jitterbug-Shag Requiem" containing LD's piece about Miller, "Hamlet, Prince of China".[33]

c. December 22. Miller arrives in London on money provided by Nancy and LD, this time Britsh authorities allow him into the country, unlike his 1932 disaster. (See the entry for 1932, December.)

December 29. Eliot comes to dinner to meet Miller; and Dylan Thomas meets Miller at the Campden Hill Road flat. Nancy takes her paintings around to the galleries with Miller's encouragement, while her husband continues to disparage her work.

December 31. Miller, Perlès, the Durrells, the actor Desmond Tester and the poet Audrey Beecham celebrate the coming of the New Year at Gawsworth's flat in St James Street.

1939

Joyce Cary's *Mister Johnson*, John Steinbeck's *The Grapes of Wrath*, Thomas Wolfe's posthumous *The Web and the Rock*, T. S. Eliot's *Old Possum's Book of Practical Cats*, Nathanael West's *Day of the Locust*, Raymond Chandler's *The Big Sleep*, Dalton Trumbo's *Johnny Got His Gun* and Zora Neale Hurston's *Moses, Man of the Mountain* are published. Lillian Hellman's *The Little Foxes* receives its première performance.

The literary magazine *Seven* prints LD's text, "Zero". New Directions brings out *The Cosmological Eye*, the first book of Miller's to be published in the USA.

January. *The Criterion* prints a positive review of *The Black Book* by Desmond Hawkins. LD meets Eliot's secretary Anne Ridler, a poet married to the artist Vivian Ridler, and they form a friendship that lasts

[33] The piece is reprinted in LD, *From the Elephant's Back*, 73–9.

for decades.

January 11. Miller is back in Paris.

January 19. In New York, Random House publishes Faulkner's *The Wild Palms.*

January 28. W. B. Yeats dies at the age of 74 at the Hôtel Idéal Séjour in Menton in the south of France and is buried in Roquebrune. (In 1948 his remains are exhumed and shipped to Ireland where he is buried at Drumcliff in Sligo with lines from one of his final poems on the grave stone: "Cast a cold Eye/On Life, on Death./Horseman, pass by!")

End January. Lack of funds forces Eliot to shut down *The Criterion* — a sad day for mainstream Western culture. LD never appeared in the magazine.

January–April. In London, LD carouses and talks with Dylan Thomas. Miller is planning a trip to Greece. None of them seems concerned with the political situation in Europe.[34]

February. LD meets the psychologist Graham Howe, author of *Time and the Child.* In London and New York, Faber and Viking Press publish Joyce's epic joke, *Finnegans Wake.*

End February. Tambimuttu launches his magazine *Poetry London*, the issue includes LD's "Epitaph" and "Island Fugue".

February 27. LD is 27 years old.

March. Geographical Magazine prints LD's "Corfu: Isle of Legends" with Nancy's photographs.[35]

March 15. The Germans invade Czechoslovakia, putting paid to LD's

---

[34] In his 1988 preface to *DML* (x), Perlès wrote, "There was a war in the offing — we laughed it off." It is only fair to note that IMN writes, "I don't think Perlès's [comment] can be taken at face value [...] Absurdist laughter? Perlès was a WWI vet., was nearly shot for not giving an order to fire on French troops; was sent to an insane asylum instead only because of family connections. No, he knew war [was] not a laughing matter" (personal communication). Nonetheless, there is no context for the comment that might lead one to think it was anything less than meant as it stands.

[35] Reprinted, alas without the photographs, in LD, *From the Elephant's Back,* 287–93.

idea of barging down the Rhine with the last of Nancy's inheritance.

[1939]

March 21. The Durrells attend the opening of Eliot's play, *The Family Reunion.*

March 25. Eliot lunches with LD and recommends he write a novel before publishing a book of poetry.

March 26. LD receives a letter Eliot wrote the previous day reinforcing his suggestion that LD should write prose rather than "the by-products of a prose writer".[36]

April. The Durrells travel to Stratford-upon-Avon to review *Othello* and *A Comedy of Errors* for the *International Post,* which folds after the first number, and thus did not print LD's reviews, though it did print his article "Theatre: Sense and Sensibility" in its one and only issue.[37] Stephanides' wife Mary and their daughter Alexia have left Corfu for England where they stay with Mary's relatives until they join Louisa Durrell and family (still in Corfu at this point) in Bournemouth.

April 7. The Italian Army invades and conquers Albania a little more than two miles across the sea from Corfu.

May. The Durrells take Hugh Guiler and Anaïs Nin through Kipling's Sussex.

May 10. In Paris, the Obelisk Press publishes Miller's *Tropic of Capricorn.*

May 22. The Durrells leave London to return to Greece, stopping briefly in Paris, where Miller gives them an inscribed copy of *Tropic of Capricorn* dated May 26. Ernst Toller, German playwright, poet and anti-Fascist, hangs himself in despair at the age of 46 in his room at the Mayflower Hotel in New York and is buried at the Ferncliff Cemetery and Mausoleam, Hartsdale, New York.

May 27. Joseph Roth, Austrian Jew, novelist and journalist, dies in a Paris pauper's hospital from exile and alcoholism at the age of 45 and is buried

[36] IMN, 211.

[37] This brief text contains LD's review of Eliot's *The Family Reunion* and the play *Heaven and Charing Cross* by A. Danvers-Walker. It is reprinted in LD, *From the Elephant's Back,* 183–5.

in the Cimetière de Thiais, Département du Val-de-Marne.

Summer. LD and Nancy travel to Athens so they can better assess the political situation, now an inescapable presence in their lives; they meet their friend from Corfu, Max Nimiec, and a new friend, Robin Fedden, poet, cultural attaché at the British Legation and author of *The Land of Egypt* (1939), a country he had lived in since 1934. In Athens at some point they meet the then unemployed Paul and Billie Gotch on a bicycle tour through Italy, Yugoslavia, Albania and Greece. Paul Gotch eventually goes to work for the British Council and they become LD's lifelong friends. The quarrels with Nancy increase in level of intensity. Eliot's critique of his poems continues to depress LD.

June. To escape the coming war and the possibility of being marooned in Greece without access to funds in England, Louisa, Leslie, Gerry, and Margo leave Corfu returning to Bournemouth. Miller is in Nice fearing Hitler will interfere with his vacation.

June 26. The prolific English writer and publisher Ford Madox Ford dies in Deauville at the age of 66 and is buried there.

July 8. Havelock Ellis dies at the age of 80 and is buried at Golders Green Cemetery, London.

July 10. Miller sails from Marseille for Greece on the *Théophile Gautier.*

July 19. Miller lands at Piraeus.

July 22. Miller lands on Corfu and is met by LD and Nancy; Spiro Amerikanos drives them to Kalami. The American is disappointed that the Durrells are still fighting with such vehemence, but becomes completely absorbed in Corfiot life, food and drink. He offends LD's sense of the holy by committing sexual intercourse with an English girl at the St Arsenius shrine.

August. Margo suddenly reappears on Corfu and stays with the Kondos family in Perama.

Early August. The delayed, slender Easter poetry number of *Delta* appears, the final one, with three of Anne Ridler's poems and LD's "A Soliloquy of Hamlet" dedicated to Ridler.

August 8. On Corfu, Greek authorities issue a passport to Maria Kondos who has been working as a maid in Louisa's household.

[1939]

August 15. Maria Kondos, arrives in England where she continues to work for the family.[38]

September 1–3. Germany invades Poland and war is declared in Europe. With Miller the Durrells leave Corfu for Athens, stopping at the Hotel Cecil in Patras, where Nancy and LD quarrel with vehemence. From his home in Kanoni, Spiro sends a note to Margo, "War has been declared. Don't tell a soul."

September 2. Katsimbalis and his wife Aspasia invite Stephanides, Miller and the Durrells to tea at their house in Maroussi; George Seferis (pseudonym of Seferiades), Cultural Attaché Robin Fedden's opposite number in the Greek government, arrives later in the evening, meeting them for the first time. Miller is bowled over, especially by Katsimbalis who becomes his "Colossus of Maroussi". Jack Kahane dies in Paris at the age of 52 and is thus spared the fate of a Jew in German-occupied Europe.

September 3. Olivia Manning and her husband Reggie Smith arrive in Bucharest where he has a contract to teach English at the British Council. Their lives in part follow the developments portrayed in Manning's later novels, *The Balkan Trilogy* and *The Levant Trilogy*, in some ways briefly paralleling the Durrells' lives.[39]

c. September 12. Regretting the interruption of his island holiday, Miller

[38] This is the date on her alien registration and naturalization documents. I am grateful for this information to Anthony Hirst, who, in the summer of 2012, corresponded with Maria's son by Leslie Durrell, Tony Kondos (born September 19, 1945). It is not entirely clear how Maria travelled or with whom to England; she spoke scant English. GB, 71, is mistaken when he writes that Maria travelled to England with the Durrells in June. Alexia Stephanides-Mercouri, the daughter of Theodore and Mary Stephanides, also confirmed Maria did not travel with her and nor, according to Alexia, did she travel there with Alexia and her mother when they left Corfu for England by April 1939 (personal communication from Anthony Hirst).

[39] The BBC made a fine television series based on the two trilogies called *Fortunes of War*, introducing the actors Emma Thompson and Kenneth Branagh, both of whom made careers in the movies, although their marriage to each other did not last.

returns to Corfu to stay at The White House. He "saw no reason why I should not return and make the most of the remaining days of summer."[40] He is disgusted with what, in a wild generalization, he considered to be LD's circle of pompous homosexual English literati (except Xan Fielding whom he liked possibly because he was heterosexual) but enthralled by the Greeks he met.[41] Margo prepares meals for him.

Mid-September. Through Robin Fedden's recommendation LD, Nancy and Stephanides work as temporary staff in the British Embassy's Information Services section. Nancy becomes pregnant. Katsimbalis also introduces LD to Emmanuel Royidis' novel, *Pope Joan.*

September 23. Suffering excruciating pain from incurable cancer, Sigmund Freud dies in London at the age of 83 by a physician-administered overdose of morphine; his ashes are interred at the Golders Green Cemetery.

September 28. The *New English Weekly* prints Stephanides' and LD's partial translation of Cavafy's poem "Waiting for The Barbarians", with the title "Waiting for Them".

Early October. The Swedish Academy awards F. E. Sillanpää (Finland) the Nobel Prize in Literature.

Mid-October. The Foreign Office sends non-Greek speaking staff from London to take over Information Services in Athens. The FO of course dismisses the temporary staff, all of whom who read and speak Greek.

Early November. Nancy travels to Corfu to retrieve some household goods and Miller returns to Athens with her. Miller, Katsimbalis and Seferis travel to Hydra to visit the painter Nikos Ghika (Nikos Hadjikyriakos-Ghikas),[42] after which Katsimbalis takes Miller to Nafplion, Epidavros, Mycenae, Knossos, Phestos, and Spetses, providing the material for the

---

[40] Miller, *The Colossus of Maroussi*, 40.

[41] There is a certain sense of exaggeration in this sentence, which is something of a riff on the statement made about Miller's relations with Englishmen in Greece by IMN, 219, but Ian MacNiven also notes that the "flaming" homosexuals LD knew probably numbered no more than two or three (personal communication).

[42] Ghika's home and studio have been converted into a permanent gallery to exhibit his work as part of the Benaki Museum's chain of exhibition spaces.

core of *The Colossus of Maroussi.*

[1939]

November. In Athens, LD teaches English for the British Council's Institute of English Studies, where he meets the poet Bernard Spencer,[43] the novelist Robert Liddell (later author of the first, unfortunately unsatisfactory, Cavafy biography), David Abercrombie, and the young diplomat Bernard Burrows. LD introduces all of them to Seferis.

December 24. The Durrells drive with Miller from Athens on a brief tour of the Peloponnese in Max Nimiec's tiny car, first to Corinth where they spend an unhappy Christmas Eve, then through the rain to Mycenae, Sparta and Tripolis.

December 26. In Tripolis they part from Miller, who takes the train to Athens, then they drive through the Argos Plain, Nafplion, Epidavros,[44] Mycenae, Tiryns and the Valley of Nemea before returning to Athens.[45]

c. December 26. A young British flight engineer at Imperial Airways, Jack Breeze, whom she would later marry, convinces Margo to leave and packs her aboard one of the last British aircraft to fly out of Corfu on the way to England.

December 28. Miller sails on the *Exochorda* for New York, after having given his notebook of the Greece sojourn to Seferis in a fit of pure generosity, which does not seem to hinder his ability to write *The Colossus of Maroussi.*

---

[43] GB, 132, has LD meeting Spencer and his wife Nora in February 1940 when they arrived to work for the British Council in Thessaloniki.

[44] LD wrote in *The Listener* (September 1947) a text entitled "Can Dreams Live on When Dreamers Die" in which he claims to have visited Epidaurus "one hot August day in 1939", but this is unlikely because he and Nancy had Henry Miller with them on Corfu at this time. Reprinted in LD, *From the Elephant's Back*, 311–15.

[45] IMN, 222–4. GB, 130–31, has the Durrells dropping Miller off in Tripolis on December 24, then driving on to visit Mystras, Delphi, and Argos. GB also notes that this trip "heralded one of the finest bursts of lyrical landscape poetry by any English poet in this century" and that here LD "found his finest poetic voice" (ibid.).

MAINLAND GREECE
AND EGYPT : 1940–1944

1940

Richard Wright's controversial *Native Son*, Thomas Wolfe's *You Can't Go Home Again*, Arthur Koestler's *Darkness at Noon*, Mikhail Sholokov's *The Don Flows Home to the Sea*, Raymond Chandler's *Farewell, My Lovely*, Carson McCullers' *The Heart is a Lonely Hunter*, and Walter van Tilberg Clark's *The Oxbow Incident* are published.

January 27. Secret police agents murder the Russian writer Isaac Babel in the Lubyanka prison in Moscow.

Early February. Nancy Durrell flies to London to await the birth of the baby.

February 27. LD is 28 years old.

March. New Directions in Prose and Poetry 1939, published by James Laughlin's New Directions, appears in New York containing extracts from *The Black Book* but not LD's poetry. The taxi driver and Louise Durrell's factotum, Spiro Amerikanos, dies on Corfu at his home in Kanoni.

April. Germany invades Norway and Denmark.

April 1. In New York, Random House publishes Faulkner's *The Hamlet*.

May. Germany invades the Netherlands, Belgium, Luxembourg and France. The British Council School closes for the season and Miller cables the Durrells escape money from New York.

Mid-May. Nancy flies back to Athens at LD's request.[1]

May 27 – June 4. The British evacuate 338,226 soldiers, 148,000 of them

---

[1] IMN, 225, has her arriving on the Orient Express, but that railroad company suspended operations after the War started in September 1939. GB, 133, has Nancy flying back to Athens in early June, which is not correct either.

French, from the beaches at Dunkirk, Belgium.

[1940]

Summer. In New York, Miller completes his Greek memoir *The Colossus of Maroussi* and writes *The World of Sex.*

June 4. In Athens, Nancy gives birth to a daughter, Penelope Berengaria Durrell.[2]

c. June 9. Wallace Southam (a Shell Oil executive in Athens) and his wife Anna take the Durrells in for several weeks while Nancy recuperates;[3] their daughter is baptized according to the Greek Orthodox rite in Seferis' presence.

June 12. Italy declares war on Britain.

June 14. German troops enter Paris.

End June – early July. Robin Fedden resigns from the British Embassy and moves back to Cairo.

July. The Durrells are living with Hugh Gordon Porteus in a house just outside Athens. LD writes enthusiastically to Miller that he is "in the middle of Moby Dick, the strangest book ever written in America I think. Metaphysics side by side with frantic action: like a cowboy film with a running commentary prepared from the deeper parts of Augustine's confessions. Really something quite new. Have you read it? It's all about the great white whale."[4]

August. LD, Bernard Spencer (who was about to join Fedden in Cairo and whose wife Nora was not allowed to return to Greece from London, where she had gone for a visit) and Nanos Valaoritis spend a brief holiday on Mykonos in the Cyclades; LD is inspired to write the lengthy "Fangbrand: A Biography".[5]

August 10. LD writes the letter to Miller that the latter publishes verbatim

---

[2] GB, 133, has Penelope born on June 18.

[3] See entries for Early Spring 1962 and January–February 1970 for LD's collaboration with Southam on musical recordings projects.

[4] *DML*, 142.

[5] IMN, 226. GB, 134, has LD and Spencer making the trip with Nancy in July.

at the end of *The Colossus of Maroussi*.

August 20. A killer hired by the Soviet government murders Leon Trotsky at his home in Coyoacán, Mexico City.

End August. LD is posted to Kalamata in the southern Peloponnese to teach English for the British Council and direct the Institute of English Studies. While in Kalamata he begins to write what would eventually become *Prospero's Cell*.[6]

September 13. Italian troops invade Egypt from Libya and move forward 60 miles before the British contain the advance.

September 27. Walter Benjamin, German writer and Jew, attempting to escape the Nazis commits suicide in Port Bou on the French-Spanish border at the age of 48, believing the Gestapo is about to arrest him; he is buried somewhere in the Port Bou cemetery.

October. The Swedish Academy awards no Nobel Prize in Literature this year.

October 21. In New York, Scribner's & Sons publishes Ernest Hemingway's novel about the Spanish Civil War, *For Whom the Bell Tolls*.

October 28. The Greek prime minister and dictator, General Ioannis Metaxas, allegedly in a one-word telegram to Mussolini, using the Greek word *Ochi* (No!), refuses the Italian demand to occupy the country without resistance, and Italian troops invade Greece from Albania. Theodore Stephanides joins the British Royal Army Medical Corps.

Early November. The Royal Air Force bombs Brindisi and Bari. The Greeks mount a strong counter-attack, aiming to force the Italians back across the border into Albania.

November 22. The outnumbered and outgunned Greeks cross the border into Albania and occupy the town of Koritsa (Korçë in Albanian), pushing the Italians out of Greece and stabilizing the front.

December 21. F. Scott Fitzgerald dies of a heart attack in Hollywood at the

---

[6] Communication from Richard Pine who has it from a letter LD wrote to the Benaki librarian in the winter 1940–41. Thus the dating of LD's beginning to write the book in Alexandria in 1943 is not accurate.

age of 44 and is buried in Rockville, Maryland.

December 22. The American writer Nathanael West and his bride Eileen die in a motorcar accident in California; he is 36 years old and is buried in the Mount Zion Cemetery in Maspeth, New York.

End of the year. LD's friend Max Nimiec dies in Athens whilst attending a performance at the Argentine Cabaret.[7]

1941

Let Us Now Praise Famous Men with James Agee's text and Walker Evan's photographs,[8] Franz Werfel's *The Song of Bernadette*, Rebecca West's *Black Lamb and Grey Falcon*, Vladimir Nabokov's *The Real Life of Sebastian Knight*, Joyce Cary's *Herself Surprised*, Eudora Welty's *A Curtain of Green* are published. *New Directions in Prose and Poetry 1940* appears in New York with four LD poems.

January 4. Henri Bergson, Nobel 1927, dies at the age of 82 and is buried in the Garches cemetery, Île de France.

January 13. In Zurich, James Joyce dies at the age of 59 and is buried in the Fluntern Cemetery in the hills above the city where he remains to this day.

January 29. In Greece, Metaxas dies and is succeeded by Alexandros Koryzis as prime minister.

February. The British Council closes its schools, putting LD out of a job.[9]

---

[7] LD wrote to Miller (*c.* February 12, 1941) about Niemic's death "on the field of battle. To die in a Balkan cabaret surrounded by blondes! Max is a great loss: goodness and innocence were so deeply fused in him that from the surface he seemed vapid" (*DML*, 145).

[8] The book went unrecognized at the time as one of the great Shakespearean works of the 20th century. Houghton Mifflin republished it in 1960 after which it gained the reputation it deserves.

[9] IMN, 227. Michael Haag, who is currently writing a biography of LD for Yale University Press, has written "I do not think the schools were closed, and certainly Durrell was not out of a job; in fact BC employees were specifically asked to remain at their posts" (personal communication).

February 12. General Erwin Rommel arrives in North Africa to take command of the German Afrikakorps.

February 13. LD writes to Miller that on the previous afternoon "the cloud lifted and I saw the WHOLE BOOK OF THE DEAD lying below me like a forbidden superb city."[10] Two years later LD writes to Seferis hinting that he has begun work on a book about Alexandria (which eventually becomes *Justine* (see the entry for October 1943).

February 27. LD is 29 years old.

March 1. Bulgaria joins the Axis Powers.

March 5. The influential poet and essayist, Kenneth Rexroth, writes to his publisher, James Laughlin, about the current poetry scene: "I think the realm beyond the wall DH Lawrence [*sic*] battered for so long was a world far more like Catullus than like Mr. [Lawrence] Durrell."[11] (See also entries for September 2, 1955 and May 18, 1957.)

Mid-March. The Durrells are still in Kalamata.

March 28. At 56, Virginia Woolf commits suicide by drowning herself in the River Ouse near her home in Rodmell, England; her ashes are buried under an elm tree in the Rodmell garden.

April 6. German forces invade Greece from Bulgaria and Yugoslavia.

April 9. Thessaloniki falls to the German onslaught.

c. April 10. Nancy cables London for the last £50 of her capital.

April 17. The Germans occupy Yugoslavia.

April 18. Greek Prime Minister Koryzis commits suicide.

April 19. Larissa falls to the Germans.

April 20. Ioannina falls to the Germans.

April 22. During the night the Durrells and Alexis Ladas leave the village port of Pylos for Crete on an overloaded, battered caïque.

April 23. At dawn LD's caïque puts in to a small inlet near Cape Matapan

---

[10] *DML*, 146.
[11] Bartlett, *Kenneth Rexroth and James Laughlin*, 7.

(site of a major naval battle some three weeks earlier) to prepare for the voyage to Crete and to hide from German aircraft; in the afternoon the villagers from Yerolimenas prepare two lambs for a final feast for the refugees, who leave the cove by night. The Greek king and government (including Seferis) depart Athens for Crete. Stephanides leaves the Piraeus harbour with his military unit on the ancient Greek collier, *Julia*.

[1941]

April 24. During the day the caïque hides in a small bay on Kythera.

April 25. The caïque arrives at Chania, Crete.[12]

April 27. German forces enter Athens.

April 30. At dusk an Australian transport ship takes the Durrells and others to Egypt.

May 1. At 4.00 a.m. the Australian ship arrives in the Western Harbour of Alexandria. The Field Security sergeant and poet, John Cromer Braun, recognizges LD; the Durrells are separated; Nancy and Penelope are sent to the women's transit centre, LD is placed in the men's, where Braun visits him that evening to talk about literature and Paris.[13]

May 2. Early in the morning the Durrells proceed to Cairo by truck on a dusty ride south.[14] In Cairo they are put up in the Luna Park Hotel, which the ever inventive LD immediately renames the Lunatic Park Hotel.

Summer. The Durrells meet friends from Greece: Robin Fedden (under suspicion as a convinced pacifist, now teaching at Fuad I University in Cairo), Alexis Ladas, David Abercrombie (now with the British Council), Bernard Burrows (now Second Secretary at the British Embassy), Xan Fielding (in hush-hush "intelligence" work), Bernard Spencer (working for the British Council), and Hugh Gordon Porteus; in Cairo LD meets

[12] GB, 137, has them remaining for six weeks, yet arriving in Alexandria "around April 25" which would have been something of a time-bending miracle had it happened. In an editorial note to *DML*, 151, MacNiven has the Durrells leaving Greece on the 25th, but corrects this to April 30 in his LD biography (IMN, 231).

[13] Haag, *Alexandria*, 191–4. Haag interviewed Braun at length about the Durrells' arrival in Alexandria.

[14] GB, 140, has LD remaining in the camp for several days while Nancy and Penelope are taken to the Luna Park Hotel in Cairo with the other women and children.

Freya Stark (the great travel writer), Terence Tiller (poet and Fuad I University lecturer in literature and history since September 1939), the poet Gwyn Williams (head of the English Department at Fuad I University), Betsy and John Uldall, John and Ruth Speirs, the Greek marxist poet Elie Papadimitriou, Robert Liddell (British Council employee now teaching at Fuad I University), and the poet G. S. Fraser,[15] all of whom play a lesser or greater role in LD's future life.

June 1. Stephanides finally arrives in Alexandria from Crete at 2.00 a.m.

c. June 2. Stephanides visits the Durrells at the Luna Park Hotel as they are about to move into the Gezira Guest House in the Zamalek neighbourhood of Cairo on the island of Gezira.

June 6. LD begins to write editorials and several comic short pieces, under the heading "Yorick's Column", for the *Egyptian Gazette* to make some money.[16]

June 22. Germany invades the Soviet Union, making the same mistake Napoleon made in 1812.

July 27. The last "Yorick" column appears.

Early August. Sir Walter Smart, the oriental counsellor at the British Embassy and a living link to Cavafy, hires LD as junior press officer;[17] LD briefly meets George Seferis, who was working at the Greek exile government's Embassy in Cairo before he was transferred to South Africa.

August 7. Rabindranath Tagore, Nobel 1913, dies at the age of 80 in Calcutta and his ashes are scattered in the River Ganges.

Late summer. In the garden of the Anglo-Egyptian Union LD, Robin Fedden and Bernard Spencer form the idea of publishing a poetry journal to be called *Personal Landscape*, for which they receive support from Smart

---

[15] Fraser published the first book-length study of LD: *Lawrence Durrell: A Critical Study*. His memoirs, *A Stranger and Afraid*, contain a pungent and evocative portrait of Cairo during the War (120–70).

[16] GB, 141, calls the publication the *Egyptian Times*. LD's pieces were republished as LD, "'Yorick's Column': Lawrence Durrell's Unsigned Humor Sketches".

[17] IMN, 240; GB, 141. Michael Haag writes, "I very much doubt that Smart was involved in the hiring or had even met Durrell yet" (personal communication).

and Terence Tiller; LD persuades Panayiotis Kannellopoulos, a minister in the Greek government in exile, to finance it, and Fedden arranges with the French Institute of Oriental Archeology to print it.[18]

Late August. Now with a steady income the Durrells move into a three bedroom flat at 14 Saleh Ayoub in Zamalek.

September. George A. Reisner, a Harvard University Egyptologist, invites Stephanides and LD to tour the recently excavated tomb of a queen in Giza.

October. The Swedish Academy awards no Nobel Prize in Literature.

December. The Colt Press in San Francisco publishes Miller's *The Colossus of Maroussi.* Later it is published by New Directions and other presses with wide distribution and remains in print today.

December 7. The Japanese launch a surprise attack on Pearl Harbor, in Hawaii.

December 11. Germany and Italy declare war on the USA.

End of the year. Alfred Perlès is in Scotland, having joined the British Pioneer Corps.

1942

Albert Camus' *L'Étranger,* T. S. Eliot's *Little Gidding,* Marjorie Kinnan Rawlings' *Cross Creek,* C. S. Lewis' *The Screwtape Letters,* and Raymond Queneau's *Pierrot mon ami* are published.

The Durrells meet the lovely Elizabeth Gwynne (soon to be the lovely Elizabeth David), Olivia Manning and her husband Reggie Smith, and Patrick Leigh Fermor (the latter in the Smarts' garden to which the Olivia and Reggie would only rarely be invited).[19] *Poetry in Wartime,* edited by

[18] For an appreciation and analysis of the journal and other English poetry publications in Egypt during the war, see Roger Bowen's excellent *Many Histories Deep.*

[19] Olivia Manning wrote at the time, "We are not part of their inner sanctum. They do not think us grand enough" (Neville and June Braybrooke, *Olivia Manning,* 123). The Braybrookes (deliberately?) misspell Lawrence (as in Durrell) as "Laurence" in

54

Tambimuttu and published by Faber in London, contains LD poems, as does an issue of *Poetry London* also edited by the "crazy Tamil".

January. The first issue of *Personal Landscape* appears with poems LD had written in Greece ("Je est un Autre", "To Ping-Kû, Asleep", "Argos"), a short essay, "Ideas about Poetry", and Seferis' "Letter from a Greek Poet". The British Institute in Cairo begins publication of the literary journal *Citadel*, edited first by Reggie Smith, and then by David Hicks, an Oxford economist and pupil of G. D. H. Cole.

February. The Durrells' marriage is increasingly shaky; Stephanides' account of his visit to LD this month makes no mention of Nancy. LD is making notes about Egyptian life which will eventually be used for *The Alexandria Quartet*.

February 4. British Ambassador Sir Miles Lampson forces King Farouk to appoint a pro-British prime minister, watering the roots of the already flourishing nationalist fanaticism that will affect Middle East history for the rest of the century and beyond.

February 22. The Austrian Jewish writer in exile, Stefan Zweig, and his wife Charlotte Altmann commit suicide in Petrópolis, Brazil.

February 27. LD is 30 years old.

March. The second *Personal Landscape* number appears; it includes "Anatolia" by Elie Papadimitriou and the second part of LD's "Ideas about Poetry". The first issue of G. S. Fraser's *Orientations*, in Cairo, publishes "A Landmark Gone" by "Charles Norden" (LD) about life in The White House at Kalami on Corfu.[20]

May. The Durrells have dinner with George Seferis and his wife Maro (Marika). The British Army sends Stephanides to the front. Anaïs Nin publishes a limited edition (500 copies) of her *Winter of Artifice* on a handpress at her publishing company Gemor Press in Greenwich Village, New York.

May 25. The British make a stand on the Egyptian border at Sidi Barani

two of the book's four references to LD. On the other hand, Manning and Smith were very good to Nancy and Penelope in Jerusalem after they left LD. See JH, 286f.
20 Reprinted in LD, *Spirit of Place*, 187–90.

as Rommel's troops threaten Alexandria.

[1942]

June. George A. Reisner is carried from a Cairo hospital to Giza to die. The third number of *Personal Landscape* appears, including LD's "Conon in Exile" and Robert Liddell's "Note on Cavafy", his first attempt at what later becomes a book-length biography.[21]

June 24. A run on the banks in Cairo begins.

June 29. Alexandria is heavily bombed; Rommel's troops take Mersa Matruh.

July 1. Rommel reaches El Alamein, 80 miles from Alexandria, causing "The Flap" during which Embassy officials in a panic burn their files, filling the air with debris so the day became known as Ash Wednesday. LD is sent briefly to Alexandria to inspect Information Services offices and burn sensitive documents. There is panic amongst the British and Allied civilian public.

c. July 3. Nancy and Penelope, and many other "non-essential personnel", are evacuated from Cairo to Jerusalem on a refugee train with Nancy's friend Mary Bentley.[22] Paul Gotch (a friend of the Durrells from Athens, working for the British Council), his wife Billie and their infant daughter Linnet are also on the train and stay at the same pension in Jerusalem as Nancy and Penelope.

July 4. After more than a year of silence LD writes to Miller, noting his wife and daughter have gone to Palestine. Rommel admits his troops cannot move forward.

July 9. The military situation is stabilized and The Flap is over.

c. July 10. Mary Bentley returns to Cairo; Nancy and Penelope do not.

[21] Liddell, *Cavafy: A Biography.*

[22] GB, 147, has Nancy and Penelope leaving "sometime in July" with "a free French unit", and cites Cooper, *Cairo in the War*, 201, as the source. Cooper in fact writes, "In the general evacuation of wives and children in July, Adam Watson arranged for Nancy Durrell and her daughter to travel to Jerusalem in a Free French vehicle." But is Cooper to be relied upon? On the same page she has LD moving out of the flat before Nancy was evacuated and moving to Alexandria on the day of The Flap. Neither is true.

Unable to find work in Jerusalem, Nancy takes Penelope to Beirut where they stay for several months with the Wallace Southams.

Early August. Churchill arrives in Cairo to oversee a change of command: Sir Harold Alexander becomes Commander-in-Chief in the Middle East and Bernard Montgomery takes over command of the 8th Army.

August 14. Stephanides arrives in Cairo on a weekend leave to find LD cheerful.

Third week in August. Churchill is back in Cairo after meeting Stalin in Moscow.

August 25. Nancy and Penelope are still in Beirut.

August 30. Rommel again takes the offensive in the Battle of Alam Halfa.

Autumn. In Alexandria, Egyptian and British officials inaugurate Farouk University; Gwyn Williams, Harold Edwards and Robert Liddell are seconded by the British Council in Cairo to teach there; Williams is appointed head of the English Department.

September 3. The British 8th Army halts the German offensive, resulting in a stalemate.

Early September. LD receives a letter from Nancy, now back in Jerusalem, telling him she will not return and that the marriage is over; several days later Dudley Honor organizes a light bomber and flies LD to Jerusalem for a brief meeting with Nancy who remains firm in her intentions.

September 15. LD meets Nancy in Beirut and they travel on the overnight train to Jerusalem; Nancy does not change her mind about the separation.

October. The Swedish Academy awards no Nobel Prize in Literature. LD moves in with Bernard Spencer at 27 Sharia Malika Farida, across the street from the *Personal Landscape* editorial office in the Mohammed Ali Club, in a flat locally known as "the Orgy Flat" due to the social proclivities of LD and Spencer. Robin Fedden marries Renée Catzeflis.

October 23. The Second Battle of El Alamein commences with the British on the offensive.

November 2. The Germans begin the long retreat west into the desert.

November 7. The Allies land at Casablanca, Oran and Algiers, and the Germans respond by occupying the up to now "free zone" in the South of France.

November 11. A grand party is held at the Orgy Flat to celebrate the new issue of *Personal Landscape* (which includes LD's "The Heraldic Universe" and "For a Nursery Mirror"), in addition to Fedden's marriage and LD's appointment as the press attaché in Alexandria, the summer seat of the government and various embassies.

Mid-November. LD moves to Alexandria, staying briefly at the Cecil Hotel, then moves into a flat with Gwyn Williams, where he socializes with Harold Edwards[23] and Robert Liddell.

Late November. LD moves from Williams' villa to the seafront at Anfushi along the Corniche toward Fort Kait Bey at the end of the Eastern Harbour.[24]

1943

Naguib Mahfouz' *Radopis of Nubia*, Jean-Paul Sartre's *L'Être et le néant*, T. S. Eliot's *Four Quartets*, Ayn Rand's *The Fountainhead*, Antoine de Saint-Exupéry's *Le petit prince*, Robert Graves' *Claudius the God*, Robert Musil's unfinished *Der Mann ohne Eigenschaften* and Raymond Chandler's *The Lady in the Lake* are published. David Gascoyne publishes *Poems 1937–1942* in London.

Nancy Durrell visits a Greek refugee camp at Nuseirat, near Gaza in Palestine where she meets Raymond Mills, the physician who later serves with LD on Rhodes. LD spends some weekends in Cairo with friends throughout the year.

January. Nancy and Penelope return to Jerusalem where Nancy works

---

[23] GB, 150, calls him Evans.

[24] Haag, *Alexandria*, 347, n. 121. IMN, 264, has LD moving into a flat at 11bis, rue des Pharaons, several blocks from Cavafy's apartment at 10, rue Lepsius. Haag, ibid., shows that this was not the case. LD may have moved directly from Williams' to 40, rue Fuad. It is also possible that LD gave out the Rue des Pharaons as a contact address even before he moved to Alexandria (Haag, personal communication).

briefly in the censorship office before Olivia Manning helps her find a sub-editor job with the *Palestine Post* and introduces her to Aidan Philip, the director of the (British) Near East Arab Broadcasting Station in Haifa, who offers her a job at the radio station, and to Edward Hodgkin, who succeeds Philip in that position in 1945 after the office moves to Jerusalem.[25]

January 17. On a picnic in the desert, Walter and Amy Smart's eleven-year old son Mickey picks up a stick bomb that explodes in his hand; he dies several hours later.

February 27. LD is 31 years old.

February 28. At the funeral of the great Greek poet, Kostis Palamas (b. 1859) in Athens, Katsimbalis shouts abuse at the German Embassy representative laying a wreath, then begins to loudly sing the Greek national anthem — banned on the threat of death. By the end of the second line a few friends tentatively join him, but from the third the entire crowd roars out the hymn to its finale. Katsimbalis goes into hiding. LD hears the story from Seferis, whose sister stood next to the "Colossus" during the event.[26]

March. Anaïs Nin's Gemor Press in New York publishes Paul Éluard's *Misfortunes of the Immortals* with illustrations by Max Ernst.

Late March – Early April. LD moves to a room in a large apartment rented by acquaintances at 40 rue Fuad, a ten-minute walk from Pastroudis' and Baudrot's cafés, the Atelier and the Mohammed Ali Club.[27]

April. The darkly lovely Yvette Cohen meets LD at a party at Baudrot's café. Eliot writes to LD, saying that because they had been unable to contact him, Anne Ridler and he had put together a selection of LD's poems for publication.

---

[25] IMN, 260. Braybrooke, *Olivia Manning*, 113, omits mention of Philip, simply noting the introduction to Hodgkin. Cooper, 201, notes that Olivia Manning "lent her [Nancy] a room, and Nancy found work in the Censorship Department".

[26] Haag, *Alexandria*, 253. Curiously, in his splendid biography of Seferis (*George Seferis: Waiting for the Angel*), Roderick Beaton does not mention this highly emotional and dangerous episode, nor does GB, but IMN, 322, notes it in passing.

[27] Haag notes that LD may have moved in much earlier (personal communication).

[1943]

April 19. Working in the Sandoz laboratory in Switzerland, Albert Hoffmann experiments on himself with the compound drug lysergic acid diethylamide and opens the doors of perception, taking the first LSD trip.[28]

May. Eve (LD's name for Yvette Cohen) becomes mildly unbalanced because of troubles with two boyfriends and her parents and seeks LD's help; he takes her to Gwyn Williams' villa for several days, then sends her to the Gotches in Tanta, southeast of Alexandria, where Gotch was employed by the British Council, for ten days to rest, after which she moves into the Rue Fuad apartment with LD, while ostensibly living at the Greek Cozzika Hospital where she is a trainee nurse.[29]

May 13. The Axis forces in North Africa surrender to the Allies.

May 15. Under British pressure, the French fleet sails out of Alexandria for Algiers to join the Free French.

June. LD writes to Stephanides that he has had no word from Nancy since she left Egypt, forgetting (deliberately?) he had seen her the previous September when they met in Jerusalem, then in Beirut and took the train together back to Jerusalem. This month's *Personal Landscape* issue contains two LD poems ("Mythology" and "On First Looking into Loeb's Horace") along with a poem by Keith Douglas, the poet-soldier. After the other tenants move out, LD and Eve invite the Gotches, who were being transferred to Alexandria, to share the large rue Fuad apartment.

June 4. Penelope celebrates her third birthday.

June 28. Paul and Billie Gotch and their daughter Linnet, with a nanny, the dog Sappho, and Billie's friend Jean Hill move in (recreating perhaps the Durrell family situation on Corfu).

c. Early July. LD proposes to Eliot and Dimitris Lambros (at the Greek

[28] Hoffmann called the later indiscriminate distribution of the drug by those like Timothy Leary "a crime" and said the drug should never be taken except under controlled conditions.

[29] IMN, 283, incorrectly has LD moving Eve from the Williams' villa to the rue des Pharaons address.

exile government's Department of Information) that he write a short book on the chaotic and bloody Greek War of Independence against the Turks to be published by Lambros' office in Cairo and Faber in England.

July 10. Operation Husky, the liberating invasion of Sicily by American and British troops, begins.

August 22. LD interviews Noël Coward.

Autumn. LD meets Patrick Balfour, Lord Kinross, the RAF press officer in Cairo.

September. G. S. Fraser in *Orientations* begins a polemic with LD and other *Personal Landscape* poets by calling their magazine "isolationist".

September 3. The Italians surrender to the Allies and the German army takes over northern Italy.

September 10. The Germans occupy Corfu after strafing and bombing the island, killing Stephanides' parents, GD's tutor Krajewsky and Krajewsky's mother.

September 21. Eliot writes to LD, rejecting the notion of publishing an expurgated version of *The Black Book*, noting that LD should establish his reputation as a writer first, then publish it *in toto*.

October. The Swedish Academy awards no Nobel Prize in Literature. LD writes to Seferis in Cairo that he has started working on "a novel about Alexandria", but soon puts it aside to return to recreating the paradise of Corfu in what will become *Prospero's Cell*.[30]

October 1. LD and Eve and the Gotches' menagerie move into a house with a tall tower offering a grand view of the city and Lake Mareotis at 17 (later 19), rue Maamoun in Moharrem Bey, owned by the Ambron family, friends of Sir Walter and Amy Smart; soon Harold and Epy Edwards and Alexis Ladas join the group house.[31] Through the Italian-

---

[30] There is some debate about the dating of the letter to Seferis, who himself dates the undated letter as "around October 1943". Haag, *Alexandria*, 293, notes that internal evidence shows it to have been written later.

[31] Haag, *Alexandria*, 261, based on Paul Gotch's captioned photograph album wherein he noted the exact date of the move. IMN, 283, writes that the move was made "by December 1943" based on a comment by LD to Miller in a letter dated

Jewish Ambrons, whom the fascists had forced to leave Italy, LD advances into the centre of high Jewish society in Alexandria. About this time LD also meets the painter Clea Badaro.

[1943]

October 2. Eliot responds to LD's proposal to write a book about Greece, saying he wants something by Durrell — not Byron — but does not reject the proposal.

Mid-October. Stephanides is invalided to Alexandria with dysentery and helps LD with research into the proposed Greek history book.

October 21. Anne Ridler writes to LD supporting Eliot's stand on the Greek book.

November. Nancy Durrell begins teaching English to Polish officers at the Anglo-Polish Institute in Jerusalem. Later on she runs a Teachers' Course there for the British Council.

c. November. LD takes the night train from Cairo to Aswan for a brief holiday and stays at the Old Cataract Hotel.

c. November 1. LD lectures to the troops on Eliot's poetry.

November 13. LD takes the duty train to Beirut for a ten days' holiday where he meets Barclay Hudson, who first gave him a copy of *Tropic of Cancer* on Corfu in 1935.[32]

November 22. Cecil Day-Lewis reads LD's poems "In Arcadia" and "At Corinth" on the BBC Home Service.

November 23 – December 6. Churchill hosts the American president, Franklin Delano Roosevelt, at a meeting of the Combined Chiefs of Staff in the Mena House near the Pyramids just outside Cairo.

by the editor as *c.* 25 December 1943 (*DML*, 159).

[32] There is some confusion in the sources about this trip. In reference to it, IMN, 280, notes that LD apparently made no attempt to see Nancy and Penelope; Haag, *Alexandria*, 280, notes that "it seems [Nancy] refused to meet with him face to face". At the time Nancy and Penelope were living in Jerusalem, not Beirut. Apparently misled by LD's February 8 letter to Miller where he says of the Beirut visit "lately I had a short holiday in Beirut", GB, 157, dates the trip to "shortly after the new year", i.e. January 1944. Caution is advised whenever LD dates anything.

December. Faber publishes LD's *A Private Country*, his first major collection of poetry from a mainstream publisher, which receives mainly good, if few, reviews. It is dedicated to "Nancy and Ping-Kû for her second birthday out of Greece" ("Ping-Kû" is Penelope, daughter of LD and Nancy).

Late December. LD is working on what becomes *Prospero's Cell*, rather than the "history" book.

December 31. LD sends Eliot a copy of the poem "Cities, Plains and People".

1944

New Directions publishes Henry Miller's, *Sunday After the War*. Two stage productions, Jean Anouilh's *Antigone* and Jean-Paul Sartre's *No Exit* are produced in occupied Paris. Romain Gary's *L'Education européene*, John Hersey's *A Bell for Adano*, Jorge Luis Borges' *The Book of Imaginary Beings* and *Ficciones*, Saul Bellow's *Dangling Man*, Joyce Cary's *The Horse's Mouth*, Gunnar Myrdal's *An American Dilemma*, Paul Éluard's *Au rendez-vous allemand* and W. Somerset Maugham's *The Razor's Edge* are published.

January–February. A mock combat in verse takes place between the poets in Alexandria (LD, Harold Edwards, Robert Liddell and Gwyn Williams) and those in Cairo (Bernard Spencer, G. S. Fraser, Robin Fedden, Terence Tiller, and Bryn Davies).[33]

January 31. Jean Giraudoux dies at 62 and is buried in the Passy cemetery in Paris.

February. In New York, the Gemor Press publishes Anaïs Nin's *Under a Glass Bell* in an edition of 300 copies.

February 6. In Cairo, Robin Fedden meets the dancer Diana Gould and gives her a letter of introduction to LD whom she meets when her travelling troupe performs *The Merry Widow* in Alexandria.

February 8. What is to become *Prospero's Cell* has reached 20,000 words. LD has given up on the "history" book because the Greeks are not

---

[33] See Gwyn Williams, *Flyting in Egypt*, 278–9, and IMN, 282–5.

cooperating: the political problems caused by the Communist-led resistance in Greece and the exile government's efforts to reduce Communist influence, combined with Britiain's blind support of the Greek king-in-exile, makes the time unpropitious for a book symbolically talking about heroic anti-Nazi resistance; silence was the discrete resolution.

[1944]

February 25. *The Merry Widow,* with Diana Gould as Frou Frou, opens for a week at the Alhambra Theatre in Alexandria. LD squires her around the city and environs. Enraptured by her beauty and tallness, during a jaunt to Lake Mareotis he asks her to marry him, but for the moment she is Fedden's lover, and in any case departs after a week or ten days with the troupe for Italy. Nonetheless, she (and her future husband, the great violinist Yehudi Menuhin) and LD remain good friends for the remainder of his life.

February 27. LD is 32 years old.

Spring–Summer. LD regularly makes short visits to Cairo for official business at the Embassy and to discuss the anthology of poems from *Personal Landscape* that Fedden is editing for publication in London.[34]

March. *Personal Landscape* issue number six contains a mock review of LD's *A Private Country* by LD himself.

March 29. The formation of the Greek Political Committee of National Liberation by the communist-dominated EAM (the National Liberation Front) in the liberated mountain regions of Greece intensifies the left/right political conflict as the exile government refuses the Committee's demand to create a government of national unity with representatives from all parties and resistance groups.

April 1. Eliot accepts another book of poems for 1945 publication but wishes LD would write a prose book. He likes the idea of a book on Corfu, which in fact LD is already writing, though he has not yet given it the title *Prospero's Cell.*

April 6. Greek military units support the EAM mutiny at a camp near Burg al-Arab to the west of Alexandria; the British surround the camp

---

[34] Fedden et al., *Personal Landscape: An Anthology of Exile.*

to starve those units into surrender.

April 17. LD and the Gotches attend a dinner in the Ambrons' garden for thirty of the city's exemplars, including Enrico Terni who knew E. M. Forster during the First World War when the writer lived in Alexandria.[35]

April 23. The British encourage Greek soldiers loyal to the royal government-in-exile to board three rebellious Greek ships in the Western Harbour at 2.00 a.m. By 8.00 o'clock that evening the struggle is over and the exile government controls the ships. Royalist officer Alexis Ladas, sharing the house with LD, Eve and the Gotches, returns to the residence in the rue Maamoun after the battle and explodes at LD's jocular reference to the event.[36]

May. Eve and LD with the Gotches tour the battlefields of the Western Desert and Burg al-Arab to Aboukir where they swim nude in the silky satiny blue waters of the Mediterranean and LD feels he has returned to Greece.[37]

June 6. The Allies begin the invasion of the Continent (Operation Overlord) on the French coast, opening the second front in the war against Germany.

June 9. Keith Douglas, soldier-poet published in *Personal Landscape*, dies at the age of 24 during the invasion of France.

July 11–25. Stephanides stays with LD to discuss Corfiot folkways for the Corfu book.

Late summer. Eve is working as a nurse in the UNRRA refugee camp at Aboukir, east of Alexandria, but she returns to the Ambron villa on weekends.

July 31. Antoine de Saint-Exupéry, at the age of 44, disappears while on a flying mission over the Mediterranean Sea off the French coast and is presumed dead.

---

[35] See Haag, *Alexandria*, 11–118 and passim, for a smoothly written account of Forster's years in Alexandria, as well as the relevant pages of Furbank, *E. M. Forster* and Beauman, *Morgan*.

[36] Haag, *Alexandria*, 292, but he cites IMN, 288, who gives the date as April 24.

[37] *DML*, 172–3.

[1944]

August. LD secures a tentative posting to a Greek island after the War. He writes to Miller that he has an idea for a novel about English people caught in a Cretan labyrinth (which he originally called *The Dark Labyrinth* but changed the title before its original publication to *Cefalû*). Nancy Durrell moves to Tel Aviv to work with Major McClelland, a colleague from the British Council in Jerusalem, teaching in the Greek Camp at Nuseirat.

August 22. After sending *Prospero's Cell* off to Faber in London, LD writes to Miller that he has a wonderful idea for a novel about Alexandria.

August 24. French and American troops begin the liberation of Paris.

Autumn. LD begins writing *The Dark Labyrinth.* The seventh issue of *Personal Landscape* appears with "Byron" by LD and "Three Clerigrams" by Diana Gould and an essay on "Ideas about Poetry" by "Mathios Pascal" (George Seferis) and Seferis' poem "The King of Asine" translated by LD, Nanos Valaoritis and Spencer. On their way to a British Council event Eve, LD and friends meet her father, Moise Cohen (a pathologically possessive type),[38] on the street and invite him to go along; shortly thereafter LD and the Gotches invite Eve's parents to dinner so the Gotches can explain what a wonderful fellow LD is. Apparently Eve is not informed of the dinner.[39]

September. LD writes to Miller apologizing for the errors in his essay on him ("The Happy Rock")[40] and noting he is reading deeply in Groddeck's *The Book of the It.* Stephanides again visits the Ambron villa.

September 10. Diana Gould writes to LD gently refusing his renewed proposal of marriage.[41]

---

[38] This is Eve's characterization and may in fact be one of those occasions when caution is advised in crediting her opinion.

[39] Haag, *Alexandria*, 304, who has the story from the Gotches. IMN and GB do not mention the event.

[40] The essay originally appeared in Anon, *The Happy Rock*, and was reprinted in LD, *From the Elephant's Back*, 187–94, presumably with the errors corrected.

[41] GB, 161, citing her letter in the Durrell Collection at the Morris Library, Southern Illinois University at Carbondale, IL.

October. This month's issue of *Horizon*, edited by Cyril Connolly in London, prints Olivia Manning's dyspeptic article, "Poets in Exile", about the British poets in Egypt.

Early October. The Swedish Academy awards Johannes Vilhelm Jensen (Denmark) the Nobel Prize in Literature. LD meets the Egyptian writer Albert Cossery.

October 7. The Pan Arab conference members sign the Alexandria Protocol establishing the fundaments of the Arab League with its seat in Cairo.

October 13. Anne Ridler writes that she thinks LD's new poems brilliant and is arranging them for publication as *Cities, Plains and People.*

October 14. British troops land in Greece.

November 6. As part of the terrorist campaign to drive the British out of Palestine, having twice failed to assassinate the British High Commissioner there, members of the Stern Gang murder Lord Moyne, Britain's senior representative in Egypt, severely damaging the Zionist cause in Britain.

December 1. LD writes to Eliot that the "pot-boiler" (still called *The Dark Labyrinth*) would be ready soon.

December 18. Henry Miller marries Janina Martha Lepska in Boulder, Colorado.

December 16. German forces begin a counter-attack known as the Ardennes Offensive and, more popularly, the Battle of the Bulge, the last major German military action on the Western Front.

December 30. The French pacifist writer Romain Rolland, Nobel 1915, dies at the age of 78 in Vézelay and is buried at the Cimetière de Brèves.

RHODES : 1945–1947

1945

George Orwell's *Animal Farm*, Richard Wright's *Black Boy*, Evelyn Waugh's *Brideshead Revisited*, John Steinbeck's *Cannery Row*, Ivo Andrić's *The Bosnian Trilogy*, Arthur Koestler's *The Yogi and the Commissar and Other Essays* and Henry Green's *Loving* are published. In Alexandria, Whitehead Morris publishes Paul Gotch's account of his trip to various points in the Middle East, *Three Caravan Cities: Petra, Jerash and Baalbek and Saint Catherine's Monastery Sinai* with a one page introduction by LD.[1]

February. LD receives orders appointing him director of public relations for the Overseas Information Service on the island of Rhodes in the Dodecanese as soon as the islands are liberated; he takes off for a month with Eve to finish writing *Cefalû*.

February 4–11. Churchill, Roosevelt and Stalin meet at Yalta to discuss borders in liberated Eastern Europe; the two Western leaders then travel to Egypt for a brief visit.

February 27. LD is 33 years old.

End February. An extreme nationalist lawyer, member of the Egyptian Wafd movement, assassinates Egyptian Prime Minister, Achmed Maher, for "selling out" to the British.

March. LD begins making notes for a play called "Black Honey" about Baudelaire's mulatto mistress.

March 23. An Egyptian court having sentenced Lord Moyne's assassins to be executed, they are hanged on this date (see the entry for November 6, 1944).

April 5. In an aerogramme received in Alexandria on April 12, Eliot tells LD Faber would not publish *Cefalû* (later LD sends it to Tambimuttu in London after major rewriting while on Rhodes) and that several of the new poems had already been published so could not appear in a new

---

[1] The introduction is reprinted in LD, *Endpapers and Inklings*.

book, postponing publication until LD can replace them. Eliot asks LD if he wants to be primarily a poet or a prose writer; LD does not respond. [1945]

April 12. Franklin D. Roosevelt dies in Warm Springs, Georgia, and the unprepared but quick-learning Vice President Harry S Truman assumes the office of president.[2]

April 29. American troops liberate Dachau concentration camp as the war in Europe draws to a close.

April 30. Hitler commits suicide in his Berlin bunker where his newly married wife Eva Braun follows him into the netherworld while Goebbels and his wife murder their children, then take their own lives.

May. The last issue of *Personal Landscape* appears in Cairo; it includes LD's "Conon in Alexandria" and "The Poetry of Cavafy" by Amy Nimr (Smart). Paul Gotch is transferred to the British Council office in Thessaloniki leaving the Ambron villa much quieter and a little lonely.

May 1. An Anglo-Greek military force liberates Rhodes.

May 5. LD writes to Eliot outlining his plans for a series of books following the elements of the scheme of a Greek drama about which he wrote to Miller in March 1937:[3] *agon* — the dislocation (*The Black Book*), *pathos* — the uniting (The Book of the Dead [which became *The Alexandria Quartet*]), and *anagnorisis* — the acceptance and death (The Book of Time [which became *The Avignon Quintet*]).[4]

---

[2] The S initial in Truman's name stands for nothing, thus does not require a full stop after it, though Truman himself often used that punctuation.

[3] See the entry for Late March, 1937.

[4] Pine, *Lawrence Durrell: The Mindscape*, 53, points out that this scheme leaves out "the fourth element in Greek drama, the *sparagmos* or tearing to pieces of the hero", but when he (Pine) pointed this out to LD, the latter agreed that *The Revolt of Aphrodite* "did represent this stage". (*The Mindscape* is available on the Durrell Library of Corfu web site.) LD has some rather strange ideas about the meaning of the Greek terms, especially *pathos*, which in this context means "calamity" or "downfall [of the hero]", and it is *anagnorisis* (properly "recognition") rather than *pathos* which is sometimes referred to as "the uniting" (in the sense of things coming together and leading to the dénouement). However, what matters here is what the terms meant to LD as

May 7. VE Day (Victory in Europe): in Rheims, France, the German military leaders sign a surrender document. In Paris with the British forces, Alfred Perlès celebrates at the Café du Dôme.

May 9. The German military signs a second surrender document with the Soviet generals in Berlin.

May 30. LD departs Alexandria by military boat for ten days on Rhodes to reconnoitre the war-torn island.

June. Tambimuttu's Editions Poetry London publishes the *Personal Landscape* anthology edited by Robin Fedden and others. The British Council closes the Greek Camp at Nuseirat and Nancy Durrell returns to Jerusalem in July to work as a sub-editor at the Palestine Radio Station with Reggie Smith, who had given her parts in radio dramatizations in 1943–44.

June 9/10. LD returns to Alexandria to wrap up his business affairs and disentangle the bureaucratic morass of Eve's stateless status so she can go with him as his administrative-cum-secretarial assistant. This turned into a complicated process involving Egyptian authorities, the chief rabbi in Cairo, a letter from Eve's father, Moise Cohen, and the intervention of Bernard Burrows, LD's friend and First Secretary at the British Embassy in Cairo.[5] LD is angered and embittered against the Egyptians, whom he blames for almost losing Eve.

Mid-July. LD and Eve depart Alexandria and storms keep them away from Rhodes for several days, which they spend on Karpathos.

July 19. Once on Rhodes they take two rooms at the Albergo della Rosa, a formerly grand hotel on the sea shore adjacent to the Turkish cemetery. LD takes up his job as chief information officer, editing the daily newspaper *Techni* (*Art*) and information bulletins distributed throughout the Dodecanese islands.

July 20. Paul Valéry dies in Paris at the age of 74 and is buried in the Sète

descriptions of his own accomplished or projected writings.

[5] Haag, *Alexandria*, 313, who has the story from Eve Durrell. None of the other biographers mentions this particular matter, though IMN, 308, briefly discusses LD's "feints and dodges" on Eve's behalf.

cemetery on the Mediterranean coast.

[1945]

August. LD writes to Eliot about a book on Rhodes in a style similar to *Prospero's Cell.* (The new book becomes *Reflections on a Marine Venus.*) He gives up trying to revise *The Dark Labyrinth* (now called *Cefalû*) for Faber and sells it to Tambimuttu, for whom he nonetheless extensively revises it over the next several months.

August 6 and 9. The Americans drop atomic bombs on the non-military targets of Hiroshima and Nagasaki with terrible consequences for the civilian populations of those two Japanese cities.

Autumn. LD meets Raymond Mills the Scottish physician (who had met Nancy two years earlier at Nuseirat in Gaza and knew LD's poetry) and his Alexandria-born Greek wife, Georgina, both of whom became life-long friends, and the consular official John S. Hoyland (Hoyle in *Reflections on a Marine Venus*).[6]

Early October. The Swedish Academy awards Gabriela Mistral, nom de plume of Lucila Godoy Alcayaga (Chile) the Nobel Prize in Literature, the first woman poet and the first Latin American to be so honoured.

October 24. The United Nations Organisation (UNO) charter comes into force.

November. In London, Faber publishes *Prospero's Cell: A Guide to the Landscape and Manners of the Island of Corcyra,* dedicated to Theodore Stephanides, Zarian, Count D and Max Nimiec, to good reviews.[7] LD provides a new ending for *Cefalû.*[8]

November 19. In California, Janina gives birth to her daughter with Miller, Valentine.

c. December. LD writes to Miller, "Now I am racing through the Cretan novel at top speed for another 50 pounds for the divorce people.

---

[6] IMN, 315. GB, 176, has the name as Edward Hoyland.

[7] IMN, 318. GB, 170, has it published in October.

[8] When the book was republished after the success of the first three volumes of *The Alexandria Quartet,* it regained its original title, *The Dark Labyrinth.*

CEFALU it is called."[9]

December. Poetry London contains LD's "Airgraph on Refugee Poets in Africa", mainly about Seferis and Elie Papadimitriou. He continues hastily revising *Cefalû*, the "divorce novel", the royalties from which he intends to use to pay for the divorce from Nancy, and signs contracts with Tambimuttu and an American publisher Reynal and Hitchcock (in the end the latter does not publish the book).

Christmas. LD and Eve spend Christmas as the guests of Father Porphyrios, Orthodox Abbot of the Monastery of St John on Patmos. Eve's fluent Greek eases their stay. LD at least enjoyed the violent thunderstorm that accompanied their lunch.[10]

1946

Eudora Welty's *Delta Wedding*, Ivo Andrič's *Bridge on the Drina*, Jean Genet's *Miracle de la rose*, Thomas Heggen's *Mister Roberts*, Ann Petry's *The Street*, Miguel Angel Asturias' *Mr. President* and Robert Penn Warren's *All the King's Men* are published. Eugene O'Neill's *The Iceman Cometh*, Terence Rattigan's *The Winslow Boy* and Eduardo De Filippo's *Filumena Marturano* receive their première performances.

January. LD arranges the limited printing on the government press of his *Zero and Asylum in the Snow* and *Six Poems from the Greek of Sikelianos and Seferis.*

January 26. In Alexandria, Claude-Marie Vincendon, age 20, plays the role of Praxinoë in Theocritos' *Fifteenth Idyll* at the Royal Archaeological Society's dinner at Baudrot's restaurant, where LD and his friends often met during the war.

Early February. LD travels to Athens for the first time since 1941, where it snows and he meets Seferis, Katsimbalis, Patrick Reilly (First Secretary at the British Embassy, later Ambassador in Moscow and Paris), Steven Runciman, Maurice Cardiff, Rex Warner, Wallace Southam, Patrick

[9] IMN, 317.
[10] For further details of the visit see IMN, 320; and LD's letter to Miller of January 1, 1946 (*DML*, 191).

Leigh Fermor, John Waller and Osbert Lancaster. He tries without success to find a position in the country for after the transfer of the sovereignty of the Dodecanese Islands to Greece and the British withdrawal.

[1946]

February 27. LD is 34 years old.

February 28 – March 2. LD writes his racially prejudiced opinion of Egyptians to Miller: "I feel like a crusader when I think of Egypt. I'd gladly put an army corps into the country and slaughter the lot of those bigoted, filthy, leprous bastards!"[11]

Spring. London authorities inform LD that he will not get the British Council job in Athens and must wait for another opening somewhere else. King Farouk visits Rhodes and causes havoc by demanding luxury on an island devastated by war.

March 30. While sporadic fighting between Greek government forces (supported by Great Britain and the United States) and parts of the Greek Communist Party's military arm (supported by Yugoslavia, Bulgaria and Albania) began in December 1943, the Greek Civil War now begins in earnest in Macedonia.

Early April. Mary Mollo, photographer for the British Forces magazine *Parade*, visits Rhodes and begins a life-long friendship with LD; he and Eve take her and another journalist on a tour of the Dodecanese islands in a caïque.

April. In London, Faber publishes LD's *Cities, Plains and People* (poems) to generally fine reviews. LD writes to Eliot that "the only big subject left in England is sex really" and that he wants to do a novel about sex in the near-Levant.

Mid-April. LD returns to Athens for a short visit, where he finds two trunks of manuscripts (including the "Book of the Dead") and other materials he'd left with friends in 1941.

April 29. In New York, Viking publishes *The Portable Faulkner*, resus-

---

[11] *DML*, 196.

74

citating that author's sagging reputation.

May. Claude-Marie Vincendon, working in Alexandria as a secretary to Tim Forde, a married Irishman employed by the Quartermaster Corps of the Royal Navy at the Western Harbour, finds herself pregnant by her boss.

Summer. Claude's mother, Claire de Menasce, sends her to London to work as a press attaché for the French Embassy while Claire, wishing to give her grandchild a legal father, goes about arranging for Forde's divorce.

June. LD is writing furiously at "Black Honey"[12] and planning a play about Sappho; mid-month sends proofs of *Cefalù* to London; also begins translating Emmanuel Royidis' *Papissa Joanna* (*Pope Joan*).[13] Mary Mollo and her husband, Henry Hadkinson, move to Athens for two years and host LD and Eve several times.

June 6. Gerhard Hauptmann, Nobel 1912, dies at the age of 84 and is buried in the cemetery in Kloster auf Hiddensee near Rügen

June 28. The Greek Prime Minister announces in parliament that the British will turn over the Dodecanese Islands to Greek sovereignty in the following year.

July 22. In Jerusalem, members of the radical Jewish terrorist group Irgun blow up part of the King David Hotel, killing 90 people, in the campaign to force the British out of Palestine.

July 31. LD moves into Villa Cleobolus, a tiny house on the edge of the Turkish cemetery on one of the main town thoroughfares, at a time when there is very little traffic. Eve maintains her room at the Albergo della Rosa for the sake of propriety, but is very often seen in LD's company at the minuscule "villa".[14]

August. Mary Mollo Hadkinson returns to Rhodes to finish up her photo-

---

[12] Copies of the typescript in various versions are in the Durrell Library of Corfu and the British Library in London. While there have been readings of the play, it has to my knowledge never been produced. A version of it is reprinted in LD, *Endpapers and Inklings.*

[13] IMN, 327. GB, 180, has this happening in the autumn.

[14] IMN, 328. GB, 176, has the move in early September.

journalism assignment.

[1946]

Summer's end. Patrick Leigh Fermor, his future wife Joan Eyres-Monsell and Xan Fielding visit for a week of talk and touring. The photograph of this visit includes a box of Kellogg's Corn Flakes on the table, reminiscent of the image taken of Robert Desnos and friends at the Café du Dôme in the mid-1920s with a box of Quaker Oats on the table, a conjuncture LD would have appreciated.[15]

September. Stephanides' book about his early wartime experiences, *Climax in Crete*, is published with a preface by LD, who is briefly in Cairo mid-month.

End September. With misguided British support, the hidebound conservative Greek king, George II, returns to Athens.

October. LD is halfway through the manuscript of *Reflections on a Marine Venus* but is overwhelmed by the material.

Early October. The Swedish Academy awards Hermann Hesse (Switzerland) the Nobel Prize in Literature.

October 20. LD tells Eliot he has a new collection of poems for Faber.

End October. LD and Eve fly to Athens to look for a position and to meet his friends Katsimbalis, Seferis, Henry Hadkinson, Patrick Reilly, Patrick Leigh Fermor, Steven Runciman, Rex Warner, and the poet Angelos Sikelianos.

November.[16] Claude Vincendon gives birth to a daughter, Diana, fathered by Tim Forde, whose divorce becomes final, whereupon they marry, and trundle off to Cork, Ireland, to operate a pub.

---

[15] The Villa Cleobolus photograph is in IMN, and the Desnos image is in Klüver and Martin, *Kiki's Paris*, 169.

[16] GB, 179, inaccurately has LD taking Eve to Corfu in November 1946 for a brief visit to discover that the wife of the owner of the house in Kalami, Eleni, had died of starvation in 1940 and that Athinaios had shortly thereafter married a girl named Kerkyra, with whom he now has a five-year old daughter. IMN, 539–40, correctly has LD's first visit since the war taking place in May 1964. Michael Haag notes that Eve never went to Corfu with LD (personal communication).

November 15. LD is granted a provisional divorce from Nancy.

December 5. The ship *Rafiah*, carrying 785 Jewish Holocaust survivors on their way illegally to Palestine, is wrecked on Syrina Island in bad weather. Mills, LD and Eve sail there on a Greek destroyer to attend the sick and injured, who are transported to Rhodes for hospital treatment, while the British navy ships their fellow passengers to detention camps in Cyprus. Two British destroyers eventually take the women and children to Palestine.

End December. LD finishes the lyric drama *Sappho.*[17]

1947

Thomas Mann's *Doctor Faustus*, Mickey Spillane's *I, the Jury*, Willard Motley's *Knock on Any Door*,[18] James A. Michener's *Tales of the South Pacific*, Malcolm Lowry's *Under the Volcano*, Albert Camus' *La Peste (The Plague)*, Yasunari Kawabata's *Snow Country* and Italo Calvino's *The Path to the Nest of Spiders* are published. In America, Robert Lowell's *Lord Weary's Castle* wins the Pulitzer Prize for Poetry.

January 13. LD is granted an absolute divorce from Nancy.

February 17. Yvette Cohen and LD are married at military headquarters on Rhodes to ensure Eve receives British papers relieving her of her stateless condition.[19]

February 20 (postmark on the envelope). LD writes to Constant Zarian responding to the latter's letter after many years, "…one of the reasons

---

[17] GB, 180.

[18] It contains the memorable words describing the life-goal of the young men in the Denver underworld: "Live fast, die young and have a good looking corpse."

[19] IMN, 334, has the marriage taking place on February 26. GB, 173, has LD deciding to marry Eve after his 34th birthday and notes, 182, that "his divorce papers indicate he married on the 17th" of February. Presumably he means the papers for the divorce from Nancy, which of course would not contain this information. Cooper, *Cairo in the War*, 257–8, has LD and Eve returning to Alexandria to marry, conflating the story of her departure for Rhodes with the marriage. Cooper gives no source for this but elsewhere indicated she interviewed both Eve and LD in 1987. One must wonder who told Cooper what stories.

for using your name in Prospero was that I hoped you would somehow come across the book and get in touch with me again. I apologize for the travesty, but the historical material had to [be] permeated by as much humour as possible to convey anything like the real atmosphere of those lazy halcyon days in Corfu." He also writes that "I have got married again — I think for the better this time."[20]

[1947]

February 27. LD is 35 years old.

March 15. The newlyweds travel to Athens to see about obtaining a British passport for Eve.[21] They meet LD's friends, Katsimbalis, the painter Ghika, Seferis and Rex Warner, for whom LD plays a recording Miller made of himself reading from *Tropic of Cancer.* He leaves the record with Seferis when he and Eve leave the city.[22]

March 31. The British formally hand over the Dodecanese Islands to Greek sovereignty, officially ending LD's employment.

---

[20] VM, 84. At the end of November 1948, LD writes to Zarian, "But I long to wring your hand again, my dear friend. No doubt you long to wring my *neck* after my nonsense portrait in 'Prospero'!" (ibid., 88).

[21] GB, 183, citing Cooper, *Cairo in the War,* 258, who apparently got it from Eve, tells the incoherent story about the Durrells flying from Athens to Cairo to attempt to placate Eve's parents with an Orthodox Jewish wedding. While LD remains in Cairo, she visits the parents in Alexandria where they have the Chief Rabbi try to commit her to an asylum; at this point LD tells her to go into hiding at Gwyn Williams' flat. Then with the Chief Rabbi's help (in what would have been a curious turn-around) the parents are somehow mollified and the Orthodox Jewish wedding takes place in Cairo. This conflation of fabrication and confused chronology should have warned GB about the story's authenticity and Cooper's reliability. But then LD was a novelist whose job was fiction so why should those who write about him not join in the genre? Michael Haag insists, quite correctly I believe, that Eve was a "straightforward, sensible, and chronologically well-founded [and] entirely reliable witness", adding that only with regard to intimately psychological subjects in her relations with loved ones is caution advised (personal communication). Cooper clearly did a sloppy research job, or simply made up the story; we shall perhaps never know which. As noted above in the entry for February 17, 1947, LD and Eve were actually married on Rhodes.

[22] George Thaniel, "Dwellers in the Greek Eye: George Seferis and Lawrence Durrell" in his *Seferis and Friends.*

Early April. The Durrells travel to London via Alexandria; Eve does not tell her parents they are coming through the city and does not see them.[23]

Mid-April. LD and Eve stay provisionally with Louisa Durrell at 52 St Alban's Avenue, Bournemouth. (Margo, her husband and two-year old son, as well as Gerald and Leslie, are also living there.)

Spring–Summer. LD continues work on the book about Rhodes and meets the rightwing poet Roy Campbell while recording a programme for the BBC.

June. LD interviews for and is offered a two-year job as lecturer at the British Council Institute in Córdoba, Argentina, which he accepts. His lengthy article on Groddeck is published in *Horizon.*[24]

June 27. LD and Eve travel to Scotland by train for a week to visit Perlès.

July 9. LD and Eve are back in Bournemouth, 52 St Alban's Avenue.

Mid-July. The Durrells travel to Paris for three weeks, staying in a cheap hotel on the rue Notre Dame des Champs.

Summer–Autumn. LD lectures on the BBC. He finishes the *Pope Joan* translation and sends it to the publisher, Rodney Philips and Green, and sends Eliot the manuscript of *Sappho.*

August 27. Nancy Myers Durrell marries Edward Hodgkin in Jerusalem as their jobs in broadcasting end; they and Penelope return to England to live a quiet, retiring life.

September. The Durrells move into Ines and Bernard Burrows' London flat until they depart for South America. Eve makes lunch for Eliot and Gwyn Williams. Penelope is enrolled in a school west of Bournemouth.

September 9. LD talks on the BBC Home Service on the subject of "Greek Peasant Superstitions".

---

[23] IMN, 334–5, who also states here that LD never met his Cohen in-laws, contrary to the Gotches' story noted above. IMN's information comes from a letter to him from Eve Durrell, 14 September 1991.

[24] "Studies in Genius VI: Groddeck", *Horizon* (June, 1947). Curiously, on March 19, 1947, W. H. Auden discovered someone had stolen his copy of Groddeck and was trying to sell it (Ansen, *The Table Talk of W. H. Auden*, 41).

[1947]

September 17. LD talks on BBC Home Service about his dreams in Greece, the text of which is later published in *The Listener.*[25]

Early October. The Swedish Academy awards André Gide (France) the Nobel Prize in Literature.

October 28. The Durrells sail on the *Brazil Star* for Argentina via Lisbon, where they meet Bernard Spencer who works for the British Council there,[26] then move on to Rio de Janeiro and Buenos Aires via Montevideo.

Early December. The Durrells briefly visit Córdoba, where they meet the Argentine writer, Enrique "Quique" Revol, who introduces them to the aristocrat Jorge "Monono" Ferreyra and his wife "Bebita", with whom they become friends.

Winter. In London, Tambimuttu's Editions Poetry London publishes *Cefalû.*

[25] "Can Dreams Live on when Dreamers Die?", *The Listener* (September 25, 1947). The text is reprinted in LD, *From the Elephant's Back*, 311–15.

[26] GB, 187–8; IMN does not mention this stop.

ARGENTINA
AND BELGRADE : 1948–1952

1948

Aldous Huxley's *Ape and Essence*, Henry Green's *Concluding*, Graham Greene's *The Heart of the Matter*, Thomas Mann's *Joseph and His Brothers* (English translation), William Gardner Smith's *Last of the Conquerors*, Norman Mailer's *The Naked and the Dead*, Ross Lockridge Jr.'s *Raintree County*, Zora Neale Hurston's *Seraph On the Sewanee* and Irwin Shaw's *The Young Lions* are published. In America W. H. Auden's *The Age of Anxiety*, James A. Michener's *Tales of the South Pacific* and Tennessee Williams' *A Streetcar Named Desire* win the Pulitzer Prizes for poetry, fiction and drama respectively.

January. LD types the final version of *On Seeming to Presume* and sends it to Eliot.[1]

January 10. A Hindu radical assassinates Mohandas Karamchand Gandhi (better known as "Mahatma" Gandhi); his ashes are scattered in the Holy Triveni Sangam at Allahabad.

February. In a coup, the Communist Party takes power in Czechoslovakia.

February 27. LD is 36 years old.

End February. From Buenos Aires the Durrells leave to visit the Ferreyra summer home in Cruz Chica, in the hills near Córdoba. LD writes to Constant Zarian, "Here the feeling of utter blankness and hopelessness is extraordinary. One simply cannot combat it at all; and though I have been in worse climates and uglier places, I have never felt absolutely weighed down by the blank hopeless depression of these immense and meaningless spaces . . . the pampas. Ugh!"[2]

Early March. At the end of the summer school holiday the Durrells leave

---

[1] IMN, 345; GB, 185, has the poems sent to Eliot in the summer–autumn of the previous year.
[2] VM, 86.

the Ferreyras for LD to take up his post in Córdoba.

[1948]

March 6. The one-book writer, author of the great American novel *Raintree County*, Ross Lockridge Jr., commits suicide at the age of 34, apparently unable to handle the immediate success of his book.

March 10. Zelda Sayre Fitzgerald dies by fire in Asheville, North Carolina at the age of 48 and is eventually buried with her husband in a Rockville, Maryland churchyard.

End March. LD is taking the herbal drug Valerian to calm his nerves under the stress of hating (with certain exceptions, of course) Argentina, its people and its culture.

April. The current director of the British Council Institute, between whom and LD no love is lost, resigns. LD lectures on the road in Cruz Chica, La Plata and other towns. Faber publishes LD's *On Seeming to Presume.*[3]

End April. LD writes to Zarian, "Don't come here. It's an awful dead country and the people are half asleep. No passion, no alertness, simply the cow-like trance of the Argentine. And such awful weather! We are counting the days to the end of the year when we shall be free."[4]

May. LD admits that taking the Argentine job was a serious error.

May 14. In Tel-Aviv, David Ben-Gurion proclaims the existence of the State of Israel. The surrounding Arab nations immediately attack the new state in an attempt to drive the Jews into the sea.

May 19. P. G. Wodehouse writes a long letter to LD in reply to his enquiry about the characters of Jeeves and Wooster; this precipitates

---

[3] IMN, 354; GB, 193, has both the poems and *Pope Joan* published in October, but as IMN (ibid.) notes the translation though scheduled for publication in October by Rodney Phillips and Green in London, did not appear because the firm went bankrupt before printing began.

[4] VM, 86. This about the land of the tango and the gauchos? In the same letter he writes, "I am sick of being pushed out of places I want to live in and being sent to places I hate. When will we ever be satisfied with what we have? That's what I ask myself. In Greece. That's what I answer. In Greece!!!!!"

LD's essay "The Minor Mythologies".[5]

Summer. LD intensely dislikes Córdoba despite making several good friends there; he works on selecting texts for an anthology of Miller's writings for which he has a contract from New Directions, Miller's main American publisher.

June 18. Soviet troops stop most land traffic into Berlin from the Western-occupied zones in Germany.

June 24. Soviet troops stop barge traffic from the Western zones entering Berlin, in effect enforcing a somewhat porous but troublesome blockade of the Western sectors of the city.

July 5. Georges Bernanos dies in the Paris suburb of Neuilly-sur-Seine at the age of 68 and is buried in the Pellevoisin Cemetery, Département de l'Indre.

Mid-July. At Faber, Eliot accepts LD's *Sappho* for publication after revisions.

August. LD is fed up with Córdoba, resigns his position giving a medical condition as the ostensible reason.

August 28. In California, Janina gives birth to Tony, Miller's first and only son.

September–October. The Durrells flee Córdoba for Buenos Aires where they stay in the Ferreyras' apartment until they leave South America. LD meets Jorge Luis Borges at a party.[6]

September 27. In New York, Random House publishes Faulkner's *Intruder in the Dust.*

Early October. The Swedish Academy awards T. S. Eliot (UK) the Nobel Prize in Literature.

December 4. The Durrells depart Argentina on the SS *Andes* for London.

Mid-December. On arrival in London, the British Council informs LD that his services are no longer required. He and Eve move into his mother

---

[5] The essay was published for the first time in *Deus Loci* NS 7 (1999–2000) and reprinted in LD, *Endpapers and Inklings.*

[6] IMN, 358; GB, 187–8, has LD meeting Borges in November of the previous year.

Louisa's Bournemouth house, ever a safe-haven.[7]

1949

Jorge Luis Borges' *The Aleph*, John Hawkes' *The Cannibal*, Paul Bowles' *The Sheltering Sky*, Nelson Algren's *The Man with the Golden Arm*, Elizabeth Bowen's *The Heat of the Day*, Nancy Mitford's *Love in a Cold Climate*, Simone de Beauvoir's *The Second Sex* and John O'Hara's *A Rage to Live* are published. Arthur Miller's *Death of a Salesman*, T. S. Eliot's *The Cocktail Party*, Christopher Fry's *The Lady's Not for Burning* and Jean Genet's *Haute surveillance* receive their première performances.

Winter-spring. LD sees nine-year-old Penelope for the first time since 1942. He writes an essay on Miller for *Horizon*.

January. In London, Allan Wingate publishes *The Complete Poems of Richard Aldington*.

February. Perlès visits Bournemouth for a weekend.

February 27. LD is 37 years old.

April. The Foreign Office appoints LD as press attaché at the British Embassy in Belgrade on a three-year contract with rank of First Secretary on the FO list and a commensurate salary. He has his horoscope cast again, this time by Arthur Gauntlett, who forecasts with some accuracy the rest of LD's life, not as optimistic as Moricand's earlier prognostication.

May. The Durrells travel by train to Belgrade via Paris, Switzerland and Trieste.

May 11–12. Traffic resumes between West Berlin and the western zones of Germany as the Soviets lift the blockade.

May 13. The *TLS* prints LD's "Hellene and Philhellene".[8]

---

[7] The Argentine sojourn was not a total waste, of course, because LD's lectures formed the basis of his book *Key to Modern Poetry* (*A Key to Modern British Poetry* is the more accurate American title).

[8] Reprinted in LD, *From the Elephant's Back*, 107–18.

May 20. The Durrells cross into Yugoslavia at Trieste. Life in the communist nation turns LD sharply to the political right (as he becomes a self-described, to some extent humourously, as a "monarcho-fascist").

June. In London, Secker and Warburg publishes George Orwell's *1984*; LD writes a letter of praise to the author.

June 10. The Norwegian novelist Sigrid Undset, Nobel 1928, dies at the age of 67 and is buried in the Lillehammer churchyard.

June 28. The Moscow-dominated Communist Information Bureau (Cominform), successor to the Moscow-dominated Communist International (Comintern), expels Yugoslavia; the Soviets move armoured divisions to the border.

July. LD writes to Stephanides for vitamins (mainly for his staff), sedatives (Valerian) and drugs for illnesses. And notes what becomes a familiar refrain in an early letter from Belgrade: "Conditions are rather gloomy here — almost mid-war conditions, overcrowding, poverty. As for Communism — my dear Theodore a short visit here is enough to make one decide that Capitalism is worth fighting for. Black as it might be, with all its bloodstains, it is less gloomy and arid and hopeless than this inert and ghastly police state." And a bit later, "There is little news except that what I have seen here has turned me firmly reactionary and Tory: the blank dead end which labour [*sic*] leads towards seems to be this machine state, with its censored press, its long marching columns of political prisoners guarded by tommy guns. Philistinism, puritanism and cruelty. Luckily the whole edifice is beginning to crumble, and one has the pleasurable job of aiding and abetting this blockheaded people to demolish their own ideological Palace of Pleasures."[9]

July 20. Horizon publishes LD's essay "Studies in Genius — Henry Miller".[10]

End July. The Durrells move into their own house at 3 Puskinova Street, in Belgrade.

---

[9] LD, *Spirit of Place*, 100–01. See also his letters to Zarian from Yugoslavia printed in LD, *Endpapers and Inklings*, and those to Anne Ridler from the same period in *Spirit of Place*, 101–6.

[10] Reprinted in LD, *Endpapers and Inklings*.

[1949]

August 16. Margaret Mitchell, author of *Gone with the Wind,* is killed by a taxicab in Atlanta, Georgia, at the age of 48 and is buried in the Oakland Cemetery, Atlanta.

Early September. The Yugoslav–Soviet naval and air pacts are dissolved.

Early September. Maurice Girodias in Paris, whose Olympia Press succeeded his father's Obelisk Press after the liberation of France, sends LD a copy of Miller's book, *Sexus,* which LD has promised to review.

September 5. Halfway through the volume, LD writes a letter to Miller expressing his bitter disappointment in the book. Lee McGeorge, who will become GD's second wife, is born in Memphis, Tennessee.

September 10. After finishing the book, LD sends a cable to Miller asking that *Sexus* be withdrawn before the latter's reputation is fatally damaged; he also writes to Girodias about his embarrassment having promised to review the book for several journals, thinking it would be the old Miller. Miller and Perlès receive copies of the letter.

September 28. Miller responds with a calm letter, which LD doesn't receive until weeks later.

September 29. LD cables Miller with apologies for his intemperate response (although he was of course correct in his analysis of the book, if not about the damage it would do to Miller's reputation).

End September. LD goes by train to Zagreb with other members of the diplomatic corps on a Yugoslav-government-sponsored public relations trip, at which point his blatant caricature, Antrobus, begins his service.[11] LD meets Malcolm Muggeridge in Belgrade.

October 3. In a letter Miller responds graciously to LD's cable.

Early October. Having corresponded with Perlès, who chastized him about his opinion, LD writes to Miller reaffirming his admiration and friendship; he writes to Girodias along the same lines. He takes Eve on a trip to Sarajevo. The Swedish Academy awards William Faulkner (USA)

---

[11] LD's collected Antrobus stories, detailing the colourful and satirical foibles of diplomatic life behind the Iron Curtain, and elsewhere, published piecemeal in magazines and short volumes over the years, appear in *Antrobus Complete* (1985).

the Nobel Prize in Literature.

October 12. LD writes again to Miller about *Sexus.*

End October. The Durrells visit Thessaloniki and the Macedonian hills on a duty trip, the nature of which is not completely clear, but probably to gather various kinds of information for MI6, the British intelligence agency.

November. Back in Yugoslavia the Durrells make yet another ten-day duty trip driving to Sarajevo, Dubrovnik, Split and Zagreb, absorbing geography and other information to be used later in his thriller *White Eagles over Serbia,* and, not coincidentally, passing the information on to the MI6 representative at the Embassy.[12]

December. LD is thinking about reinvigorating an old project: a study of Elizabethan writers. He appears as a dwarf in the Embassy's holiday production of *Snow White and the Seven Dwarfs.*

1950

Ernest Hemingway's *Across the River and into the Trees,* Jack Kerouac's *The Town and the City,* John Hersey's *The Wall,* A. E. van Vogt's *The Voyage of the Space Beagle* and Ford Madox Ford's *Parade's End* (a sequence of four novels from the 1920s in a single volume) are published. Eugène Ionseco's *La Cantatrice chauve* receives its première performance in Paris.

First week in January. LD and Eve travel to Trieste for a week to get away from the gray cold dullness of Belgrade.[13]

January 21. George Orwell dies of tuberculosis complications in Uni-

---

[12] This is speculative, but in keeping with the duties of an Embassy official stationed in a hostile country. MI6 is the British equivalent of the American Central Intelligence Agency. The tour is recorded in an official report by LD and the Information Officer in Zagreb, John Gibbs. It was printed in the *TLS,* August 7, 2009, as " 'No Bugs or Fleas': A Road Trip through Tito's Yugoslavia" by Lawrence Durrell and John Gibbs. The article is reprinted in LD, *Endpapers and Inklings.*

[13] "What a miracle after this country to see the shops full and the people warmly clad. However, things are slowly improving here" (letter to Zarian in LD, *Endpapers and Inklings*).

versity College Hospital in London at the age of 46 and, as Eric Blair, is buried in the Anglican churchyard in the village of Sutton Courtenay in the Thames Valley.

[1950]

February. Constant Zarian, his old friend from Corfu, writes to LD about the pleasures of Ischia, the island off Naples, where the sun shines all day, where the wine flows liberally and where people laugh freely with gusto.

February 27. LD is 38 years old.

March. In New York, Duell, Sloan and Pearce publish Richard Aldington's biography of his one-time close friend, *D. H. Lawrence: Portrait of a Genius, But . . .*

April. Faber publishes LD's *Sappho: A Play in Verse.* British voters re-elect Atlee and the Labour Government, angering LD, who hoped for the election of the strongly anti-communist Churchill and the Conservative Party.

June 1. The Durrells leave Belgrade to take the Simplon-Orient-Express for a month-long holiday on Ischia at the northern end of the Gulf of Naples.

June 3. The Durrells arrive in Naples and move on to Ischia where they reunite with Zarian and his wife, the American painter Frances Brooks, and Xan Fielding; they meet Auden for dinner, and Norman Douglas. LD writes and privately prints the long poem "Deus Loci".

June 25. The North Korean army invades the South, beginning the Korean War.

June 27. The UN passes a resolution for member nations to aid South Korea militarily, and United Nations military units commanded by the United States begin landing in Korea to throw back the North's army, confirming LD in his belief that only the USA understands what communism is and how it must be fought.

July 10. The Durrells leave Ischia to return to Belgrade via Rome, where they stay for two nights to visit with Zarian's son Hovan, and Venice where they attend the twenty-fifth Venice Biennale (June 8 to October

15, 1950), the second held since World War II.[14]

August 23. The actress Margaret Rawlings writes from London requesting a year's option on *Sappho.*

End of August. The Durrells go to a dinner at the home of Toder Obradović, a Serbian journalist for Agence France Presse, whose wife Miller knew during the Villa Seurat days in 1937; Miller had asked LD to locate her.

September. Kingsley Amis publishes LD's poems "Epitaph" and "Water Colour of Venice" in the *New Statesman.*[15]

Early October. The Swedish Academy awards Bertrand Russell (UK) the Nobel Prize in Literature.

November. LD pays John Gawsworth to edit and index the manuscript of *A Key to Modern Poetry* for publication.

November 2. George Bernard Shaw, Nobel 1925, dies at the age of 94 and his ashes are scattered in the garden of his home, Shaws Corner in Ayot Saint Lawrence, Hertfordshire, England.

End November. Eve discovers she is pregnant.

December. The *New Statesman* publishes LD's poem "Education of a Cloud". LD begins a short affair with the Yugoslav ballerina, Smilja (prototype of Mountolive's ballerina mistress in *The Alexandria Quartet*).

1951

Norman Mailer's *Barbary Shore*, Herman Wouk's *The Caine Mutiny*, J. D. Salinger's *The Catcher in the Rye*, Nicholas Monsarrat's *The Cruel Sea*, William Styron's *Lie Down in Darkness*, Josephine Tey's *The Daughter of Time*, Marguerite Yourcenar's *Mémoires d'Hadrien* and James Jones' *From Here to Eternity* are published. Jean-Paul Sartre's *Le diable et le bon dieu* and

---

[14] "The English pavilion rather dull but the French and Italian astonishingly full of life" (LD to Zarian, July 1950, in VM, 98).

[15] Interestingly, Amis published at least one nativist criticism of British writers like LD who lived outside the UK, noting that, "no one wants any more poems about [...] foreign cities" (cited in Roger Bowen, *Many Histories Deep*, 187).

Tennessee Williams' *The Rose Tattoo* receive their première performances.

[1951]

Winter. LD is bogged down in revisions of *Reflections on a Marine Venus* and also works on a play that becomes *Acte.*

Henry Miller and Janina separate; she takes the children to Los Angeles.

January. For the first time the *TLS* publishes an LD poem ("Sarajevo"). LD gives three lectures on literature at Belgrade University.

January 10. Sinclair Lewis, Nobel 1930, dies in Rome of alcoholism and disappointment at the age of 66 and is buried in the Greenwood Cemetery, Sauk Centre, Minnesota.

Early February. Visiting Trieste, LD discovers an armour-plated Horch once owned by Hermann Göring which he buys cheaply and drives back to Belgrade, its ostentatious grandeur annoying his colleagues in the diplomatic corps.[16]

February 19. André Gide, Nobel 1947, dies in Paris at the age of 82 and is buried in the Cimetière de Cuberville, Basse-Normandie, France.

February 26. GD marries Jacquie Wolfenden in Bournemouth.

February 27. LD is 39 years old.

March 15. BBC Third Programme broadcasts a selection of LD's poems produced by an old Cairo friend, Terence Tiller.

April 6. Eve travels to England to look for a suitable house in which to live while she gives birth; LD's mother Louisa and Mary Mollo Hadkinson help find a house at 84 Old Road in Headington near the Churchill Hospital in Oxford.

May 22. LD arrives in Oxford from Belgrade.

May 30. Eve gives birth to Sappho Jane with Louisa on hand, as are Alfred Perlès and his new wife Anne, Anne Ridler and her husband Vivian, and Mary Mollo Hadkinson, herself in mid-pregnancy with her first child.[17]

---

[16] How the vehicle made its way to Trieste is as yet an unanswered question.

[17] When Eve left for Oxford on April 6, she and LD apparently agreed that if the

June. The *TLS* publishes "The Sirens", indicating LD's increasingly strong desire to return to live in Greece.

Early June. LD meets Francis John Mott, an American eccentric with theories to explain everything.[18] Before departing for Belgrade, LD records his "Iron Curtain Blues" on a 78 rpm disk and gives it to Alan Thomas.[19]

June 11. LD returns to work in Yugoslavia while Eve and Sappho remain in England until September 1.

July 31. The BBC Third Programme broadcasts a reading of "Deus Loci" on a show produced by John Lehmann, in the series *New Soundings*, No. 6.

August 9. LD returns to Oxford and the family, where he stays with the Motts.

Mid-August. LD meets Alfred and Anne Perlès, and Seferis, now counsellor at the Greek Embassy in London, and lunches with Eliot at the Garrick.

September 1. LD and family return by train to Belgrade where he continues to work on *Reflections on a Marine Venus* in his spare time.

September 27. In New York, Random House publishes William Faulkner's *Requiem for a Nun.*

Early October. The Swedish Academy awards Pär Lagerkvist (Sweden) the Nobel Prize in Literature.

---

child was a boy his name would be Oliver. "Eve is going to get herself a house in Oxford for 3 months and produce Oliver June 1st–15th and after a month or so's rest proposes to take Oliver on his first European journey!" (LD to Zarian, April 7, 1950, in VM, 100).

[18] Francis J. Mott's *Universal Design of the Oedipus Complex* (1950) and *Universal Design of Birth* were both read and marked up by LD.

[19] Sections of it are printed in IMN, 374–5. The disk is in the Alan Thomas collection at the British Library in London. In 2012, the BBC and British Library released a CD containing extracts from a radio interview with Malcolm Muggeridge from 1965, LD reading several of his poems (1963), an interview with D. G. Bridson (1963) and rare recordings of his piano playing and singing two songs from 1935. "Iron Curtain Blues" is not on this CD.

October 26. Churchill and the Conservatives return to power in England.

December. LD writes a "Little Red Riding Hood" sketch for the Embassy Christmas performance.[20] The Foreign Office drastically reduces wages and perks for contract staff: LD's income plummets from £5,000 to £1,500 per annum.

1952

Ralph Ellison's *Invisible Man*, John Steinbeck's *East of Eden*, Italo Calvino's *La Formica Argentina*, Ernest Hemingway's *The Old Man and the Sea*, and Robert Heinlein's *The Rolling Stones* are published. Jean-Paul Sartre's *Les jeux sont faits* receives its première performance. Robert Liddell's claustrophobic novel *Unreal City*, about homosexuals in Alexandria (called Caesarea in the book) during the War, is published in London, its main character supposedly based on Cavafy.[21]

Between January and March. Henry Miller and Janina are divorced.

January. LD finishes *Reflections on a Marine Venus* and publishes an appreciation of his friend Constant Zarian in *The Poetry Review*.[22]

January 21. In London, Margaret Rawlings organizes a reading of a shortened version of *Sappho*.

February 19. Knut Hamsun, Nobel 1920, supporter of the Nazis and admired by Miller, dies at the age of 93, not quite comprehending why his reputation has suffered since 1945; his ashes are buried at his farm, Nordhom, near Grimstad, Norway.

February 27. LD is 40 years old.

March. Leslie Durrell marries Doris Hall.

April. In London, Peter Neville publishes LD's *Key to Modern Poetry* based

---

[20] The timing of this event is unclear; it could have taken place the previous year.

[21] Peter Owen Publishers, London, reissued the book, along with several other Liddell novels, in 1993. Curiously, there is no mention of Liddell's Cavafy biography anywhere on the jacket or the listing of books "by the same author".

[22] "Constant Zarian: Triple Exile" *The Poetry Review* 1 (1952). Reprinted in LD, *From the Elephant's Back*, 225–31.

on the Argentine lectures, and in the USA the University of Oklahoma Press publishes the book as *A Key to Modern British Poetry*, a title more reflective of the contents.

April 1. Eve McClure moves to Big Sur to care for Miller's two young children, who are temporarily living with him following his divorce from Janina earlier in the year.

May. LD takes his family on a six-week camping trip, through the People's Republic of Macedonia (the southernmost constituent republic of the Yugoslav Federation) and into the larger Greek region of Macedonia.

c. June 8. The Durrells are camping on the Chalkidiki peninsula.

July 8. The Durrells return to Belgrade.

End July. They make another duty camping trip to the lakeside at Bled, the summer home of the Yugoslav government.

August 17. LD writes to Anne Ridler that he's thinking of moving the family to Cyprus when his contract in Yugoslavia is up. He believes, with reason, that there is no chance he could be posted to Athens because he is fluent in Greek!

September 18. British Foreign Secretary Anthony Eden arrives in Belgrade for a five-day visit in support of Tito against Stalin.

September 23. Eden departs, having publicly praised LD's information team. LD drives to Trieste on "errands".

September 24. The Foreign Office releases LD from service by not renewing his contract.[23]

October. Repeating his request to George Wilkinson in 1935 to find him a house on Corfu, LD now asks him to find one on Cyprus where he thinks his family could live for a year on savings and he could turn to the notes he has made for the Egyptian novel.

Early October. The Swedish Academy awards François Mauriac (France) the Nobel Prize in Literature.

---

[23] GB, 208.

[1952]

October 15. LD writes to Alan Thomas that he is quitting the Foreign Office in December, noting that, "Looks as if I am getting the push for a year or two from the F.O."[24]

Late autumn. Eve shows signs of manic depression syndrome, believing LD does not care about her any more.

November 1. The Americans explode the first hydrogen bomb over an atoll in the South Pacific.

Late November. Eve falls into deep depressions and suffers schizophrenic hallucinations similar to those from the period in Alexandria prior to meeting LD.

December 4. Accompanied by LD, Eve is admitted to the Psychiatric Division of the British military hospital in Hanover, Germany (the closest British psychiatric facility) for treatment, delaying their departure from Belgrade for Cyprus.

Mid-December. LD returns to Belgrade and decides to write a series of thrillers to make additional cash.

December 31. Miller arrives in Europe with Eve McClure (soon to be his fourth wife), her sister Louise and the latter's husband, the painter Bezalel Schatz.

---

[24] IMN, 380, interprets this to mean "his departure may not have been entirely voluntary".

CYPRUS : 1953–1956

1953

James Baldwin's *Go Tell It on the Mountain*, Saul Bellow's *The Adventures of Augie March*, Françoise Sagan's *Bonjour Tristesse*, Ray Bradbury's *Fahrenheit 451*, Raymond Chandler's *The Long Goodbye*, Davis Grubb's *The Night of the Hunter*, Leon Uris' *Battle Cry*, Ivy Compton-Burnett's *The Present and the Past* and Marjorie Kinnan Rawlings' *The Sojourner* are published. Samuel Beckett's *En attendant Godot* receives its première performance in Paris.

January 5. In the Hanover hospital, Eve is diagnosed as schizophrenic, but released and enters an observation ward in Trieste.

January 14. LD and Sappho visit Eve in Trieste. Eve asks for a year alone in England to continue therapy.

January 19. LD and Sappho depart Belgrade for Venice, where they take a boat to Limassol, on the southern coast of Cyprus.

January 26. Disembarking at Limassol port, they travel to Kyrenia, a fair-sized harbour town on the north coast, and stay briefly with George and Iris Wilkinson at their Villa Christina until they move into two rooms in a house on the town's main street.[1]

End January. Eve voluntarily returns to Hanover for further treatment.

February 27. LD is 41 years old.

March 3. With the help of a clever Turkish real estate agent, Sabri Tahir, LD buys a dilapidated Turkish house in the hamlet of Bellapaix a few miles east of Kyrenia and four miles from the sea, and begins the process

---

[1] Haag, *Alexandria*, 318. Kyrenia did not have a sea connection to Italy. George Wilkinson divorced Pamela in 1947 and a year later married Iris Flavia Antoinette Mantura, who had been Nancy Durrell's boss at the Near East Arab Broadcasting Station in Jerusalem and Haifa. As IMN, 383, notes, "Larry had known Iris before she met George, when Larry had visited Jerusalem during and just after the war."

of restoring it.[2]

[1953]

April. John Lehmann visits LD for several days.[3]

April 9. Eve is discharged from the military hospital and flies from Hanover to England by military air transport.

Mid-May. Miller and Eve McClure meet Perlès and his wife Anne in Barcelona for two days of wine and laughter, reminding Miller of the days in Paris before the War.[4]

End May. Louisa Durrell arrives in Bellapaix to help care for Sappho. The novelist Rose Macaulay celebrates Sappho's second birthday with the Durrells.

Early June. The Durrells move into the Bellapaix house, still crowded with workers and their equipment and plaster dust and noise.[5]

June. LD meets the architect Austen Harrison in Lapithos, where a circle of friends forms, including Pearce Hubbard, another architect, and by the end of this year the very lovely and extraordinarily intelligent blonde Marie Millington-Drake.

July. Miller and Eve McClure decide to return to the USA without visiting Cyprus.

Mid-summer. Constant Zarian visits with his wife, the American painter, Frances Brooks.

July 26. In Egypt, Nasser and other military officers overthrow King Farouk and seize power.

July 31. In London, Faber publishes GD's *The Overloaded Ark*, which is

---

[2] See *Bitter Lemons*, 47ff., for LD's version of the purchase negotiations. He got the house for £300; according to GB, 213, it sold for £160,000 in 1995.

[3] IMN, 393; GB, 216, has the visit in November.

[4] The meeting is commemorated in Miller's idiosyncratic "Reunion in Barcelona", written a year later and available in Miller, *The Intimate Henry Miller.*

[5] IMN, 396. GB, 216, has the move in October, possibly misled by LD's letter to Miller (postmarked October 24) saying, "We should be all set in another ten days" (*DML*, 27).

an immediate bestseller.

Early August. Faber publishes *Reflections on a Marine Venus*, dedicated to Walter and Amy Smart, to excellent notices.

End August. An early version of the "Book of the Dead" has reached 100 pages.

Autumn. LD begins teaching at the Pancyprian Gymnasium in Nicosia, 30 miles away, rising at 4:30 to write for an hour before leaving for work.

September. Eve takes a permanent position as matron at Bedales boarding school in Petersfield, Hampshire.

End September. The "Book of the Dead," now called "Justine in Alexandria", has reached 25,000 words.

Early October. The Swedish Academy awards Winston Churchill (UK) the Nobel Prize in Literature.

November 6. Seferis arrives at Nicosia airport; he spends more time with Maurice Cardiff than with LD, whose loyalty to the Greek cause (*Enosis*, meaning "Union", i.e. of Cyprus with Greece) he correctly suspects is not unconditional.

c. November 8. Seferis visits LD at Bellapaix, they discuss the Cypriot variations on the effect of Aphrodite, the goddess of sexual love, and the many incidences of hermaphrodites on Cyprus.

November 8. Ivan Bunin, Nobel 1933, in exile in France since 1918, dies in Paris at the age of 83 and is buried in the Cimetière de Sainte-Geneviève-des-Bois, Île-de-France.

November 9. The mellifluous poet Dylan Thomas dies in New York at the age of 39 and is buried in the over-spill graveyard of St Martin's Church, Laugharne, Dyfed, Wales.

Mid-November. Patrick Leigh Fermor visits the Durrells for a week.[6]

November 27. Eugene O'Neill, Nobel 1936, dies in a Boston hotel room at the age of 65 and is buried at Forest Hills Cemetery and Crematory, Jamaica Plain, Suffolk County, Massachusetts.

---

[6] IMN, 402; GB, 216, has the visit at the end of October.

November 30. Seferis reads his poems to LD's class at the Pancyprian Gymnasium, increasing LD's prestige among the students.

December. Miller and Eve McClure marry in Carmel Highlands, California.

December 6. LD, Seferis, Maurice Cardiff, the painter Adamantios Diamantis, his wife Antoinette Diamanti and Cardiff's young son visit the Acheiropoietos monastery.

December 25. Austen Harrison, Diane Newall (flying in from Beirut for the holidays), Sappho, Louisa, the cook Mrs Cooke, and LD enjoy a holiday feast.

1954

Mordecai Richler's *The Acrobats*, Pierre Boulle's *Le Pont de la rivière Kwai*, William Golding's *Lord of the Flies*, Pauline Réage's *L'Histoire d'O*, Simone de Beauvoir's *Les mandarins*, Kingsley Amis' *Lucky Jim*, Kamala Markandaya's *Nectar in a Sieve*, John Steinbeck's *Sweet Thursday* and Iris Murdoch's *Under the Net* are published. Brendan Behan's *The Quare Fellow*, Terence Rattigan's *Separate Tables* and Dylan Thomas' *Under Milk Wood* receive their première performances.

Pope Joan by Emmanuel Royidis in LD's translation, dedicated to George Katsimbalis, is published by Derek Verschoyle in London.[7]

February. Eve, who is staying with the Burrows, decides she is ready to return to LD and Sappho, but asks Alan and Ella Thomas to find her and Sappho a place to stay if she returns to England.

February 18. "Justine in Alexandria" remains in neutral at 25,000 words.

February–March. LD writes the Balkan thriller *White Eagles over Serbia*.

February 27. LD is 42 years old.

Spring. Rupert Hart-Davis publishes GD's *Three Singles to Adventure* in London.

---

[7] The revised 1960 American edition published by Overlook Press in Woodstock, New York, lists LD as the author of the book with the notation "translated and adapted from the Greek of Emmanuel Royidis".

Mid-March. Freya Stark and Sir Harry Luke visit Bellapaix.

April. Daphne and Xan Fielding (whose war memoir *Hide and Seek* has just been published), and Katsimbalis visit.

April 1. Eve flies to Nicosia to rejoin her family, but shortly thereafter becomes convinced that nothing has changed.[8]

May 17. The U.S. Supreme Court declares racial segregation in public schools to be unconstitutional.

June. Ines Burrows and her children come for a week, during which time she talks to LD honestly about the marriage and his behaviour, which annoys him.

June 10. LD is invited to become a Fellow of the Royal Society of Literature, and accepts.

Summer. Tension increases among LD, Eve and Louisa.

July. Louisa leaves to return to Bournemouth. LD accepts an appointment as the Director of Information Services for the Cyprus (British) government. Maurice Cardiff presciently tells him if he takes the job he'll lose all his Greek friends. The job includes responsibility for the monthly magazine *Cyprus Review*, the Cyprus Tourist Office and the Cyprus Broadcasting Station.

July 30. Eve knows the marriage is not going to work any longer but remains *pro tem* on Cyprus.

August. LD moves into a small villa in Nicosia to be near his job, but keeps the Bellapaix house where Eve and Sappho continue to live. The *TLS* prints his poem "On Mirrors".

August 2. In New York, Random House publishes Faulkner's *A Fable.*

August 8. LD gives Eve a copy of William James' *Varieties of Religious Experience* for her birthday.

August 22. Adamantios Diamantis writes to Seferis that LD is in a "dangerous" position doing "delicate" work.

---

[8] Haag, *Alexandria*, 320–21. IMN, 408, agrees that Eve returned in April, but GB, 218, has it in March after LD sends her a cable asking her to return.

[1954]

September. The first issue of the *Cyprus Review* under LD's editorship appears. LD tries to raise the intellectual level of the magazine but it remains a venue for British policy support, in which almost no Cypriot Greek authors are published during LD's tenure. George Wilkinson is the magazine's deputy editor. *London Magazine* prints LD's poem "Letters in Darkness".

October. *London Magazine* prints translations of four Cypriot poets by LD and Maurice Cardiff.

October 8. Cardiff and a drunken LD with Eve in tow show up at a reception for Seferis; this is the only time Seferis sees LD on the island during his visits in 1954–55.[9]

October 15. Rupert Hart-Davis publishes GD's *The Bafut Beagles* in London.

October 26. In Alexandria, a near-sighted Muslim Brotherhood assassin attempts to shoot Egyptian President Gamal Abdul Nasser; the six shots miss their target but shatter several light bulbs and bring down the wrath of security forces on the Brotherhood membership.

October 28. The Swedish Academy awards Ernest Hemingway (USA) the Nobel Prize in Literature.

November. Alfred Perlès arrives in California to write *My Friend Henry Miller*.[10]

November 3. Henri Matisse dies in Nice at the age of 84 and is buried at the Cimetière du Monastère de Cimiez above Nice.

December. In Limassol British troops open fire on demonstrating students, wounding three of them.

December 18. The United Nations resolves to shelve the Greek demand for Cypriot self-determination.

---

[9] Seferis wrote in his diary on October 8, 1954, "Larry was there (drunk) with his wife" (Beaton, *George Seferis*, 316–17 and 475, n63). IMN, 413, writes "Whatever the reason, [Seferis] stayed clear of Larry during his trips to Cyprus in 1954 and 1955."
[10] Published in 1956 by John Day in New York.

Mid-December. The "Justine in Alexandria" manuscript, now entitled simply "Justine" has reached 200 typescript pages.

Late in the year. Eve travels to Egypt to see her mother, who is dying.[11]

1955

Norman Mailer's *The Deer Park*, James Baldwin's *Notes of a Native Son*, J. P. Donleavy's *The Ginger Man*, Flannery O'Connor's *A Good Man is Hard to Find*, Herbert Marcuse's *Eros and Civilization*, Vladimir Nabokov's *Lolita*, Graham Greene's *The Quiet American*, Patricia Highsmith's *The Talented Mr. Ripley* and D. J. Enright's *Academic Year* are published. Tennessee Williams' *Cat on a Hot Tin Roof* receives its première performance.

LD's *Private Drafts* (poems) is privately printed in a limited edition.

In London, Collins publishes GD's *The New Noah.*

Early in the year. Curtis Brown (LD's literary agent) rejects the *White Eagles* manuscript, refusing to submit it to Faber.

January. This month's edition of the *Cyprus Review* lists the contributors for the year: Gerald Durrell, Freya Stark, Lord Kinross, Osbert Lancaster, Sir Harry Luke, Patrick Leigh Fermor, John LeMillerann, John Pudney and Vernon Bartlett (not a Greek among them). LD writes to Miller that he's never worked so hard and is tired all the time.

February 20. In London, Collins publishes Richard Aldington's controversial *Lawrence of Arabia: A Biographical Enquiry*; Aldington's book had been published in French the previous October, thus thwarting British attempts to prevent its appearance.

February 23. The French diplomat, poet and playwright Paul Claudel, younger brother of the great sculptress, Camille Claudel, dies at the age of 86.

---

[11] IMN, 417, notes that she went to visit her parents. Neither GB nor Haag mentions this trip in their books, though the latter has kindly confirmed that she made the trip to see her mother, her father having previously died; he also notes that the trip may have been made early the following year (personal communication).

[1955]

February 27. LD is 43 years old.

March. On Cyprus, Archbishop Makarios instructs Yeoryios Grivas, a Cyprus-born former general in the Greek Army, leader of EOKA (*Ethniki Organosis Kyprion Agoniston* — the paramilitary National Organization of Cypriot Fighters) to begin insurrection against the British.

March 31. GD and Jacquie arrive in Nicosia to make a nature film; that night explosions destroy the radio station and other buildings; shortly thereafter GD and Jacquie move into the Bellapaix house.

April 1. The EOKA campaign of violence is inaugurated with bomb explosions in the main Cypriot towns.

May. In London, Faber publishes LD's *The Tree of Idleness and Other Poems.*[12]

May 24. Empire Day, school children rout a Cypriot police detachment with stones; a bomb explodes in the Nicosia cinema.

End May. Patrick Leigh Fermor visits to lecture at the British Institute and meets GD and Jacquie before they depart at the end of the month.

Mid-year. LD becomes interested in Zen Buddhism.

July 3. LD flies to London for a secret conference at the Colonial Office; he travels via Athens where he meets Katsimbalis and they celebrate without reference to Cyprus; shortly thereafter LD accompanies a high official delegation to Nicosia for a conference with Cypriot and British authorities.

July 12. LD flies to London to continue official meetings and also meets Juliet O'Hea, his new agent at Curtis Brown. As a result of the official meetings LD's job is changed to director of public relations concentrating on "the care and feeding" of foreign correspondents.

c. July 20. Upon LD's return to Cyprus, Eve tells him she is taking Sappho

---

[12] GB, 220. Oddly, IMN does not mention this book in the index or in the chapter on Cyprus in the main text.

to England and will not come back.[13]

August 12. Thomas Mann, Nobel 1929, dies in Zurich at the age of 80 and is buried in the Kilchberg village cemetery above the city.

Mid-August. LD accompanies Eve and Sappho to Athens whence they fly to London and go on to Bournemouth to stay with Alan and Ella Thomas. LD stays for a week in Athens after their departure.

August 29. Tripartite Conference (Britain, Greece and Turkey) opens in London but produces no agreement on self-government for Cyprus.

Autumn. LD gives a room in the Nicosia house to Richard Lumley for six months. The blonde Alexandrian Claude-Marie Vincendon Forde, having lived in Australia and Israel with her family (daughter Diana, son Barry and spouse), is now in Cyprus. She refuses to go with her peripatetic husband to Bombay and applies for a job at the public relations department. LD hires her to run the French section of the Cyprus Broadcasting Station.

September 2. From San Francisco, the poet and essayist Kenneth Rexroth writes to James Laughlin about the local Poetry Center regarding who should be invited to speak in the following years: "if possible a furriner — first choice Larry Durrell, 2nd René Char, 3rd (or 1st, except that it is most unlikely he could come) [Hugh] MacDiarmid, 4th Edwin Muir."[14]

September 15. The British outlaw EOKA.

September 17–18. During the night, schoolboys burn to the ground the British Institute Library in Nicosia, containing the best English literature collection in the Middle East.

September 25. Field Marshal Allan Francis Harding replaces a civilian, Sir Robert Percival Armitage, as British governor of Cyprus, combining the position with that of Commander-in-Chief.

Early October. The Swedish Academy awards Halldor Laxness (Iceland)

---

[13] In his memoir of LD on Cyprus, in *Friends Abroad*, 30, Maurice Cardiff writes that LD's and Eve's relationship occasionally degenerated into physical violence and that he felt no surprise at Eve's departure.

[14] Bartlett, *Kenneth Rexroth and James Laughlin*, 207. See also entries for March 5, 1941 and May 18, 1957.

the Nobel Prize in Literature.

October 7. The American poet, Allen Ginsberg, performs his controversial poem, "Howl", at the Six Gallery in San Francisco at a well-watered reading hosted by the distracted Kenneth Rexroth, at which Gary Snyder, Michael McClure, Philip Lamantia, and Phil Whalen also perform their poems. When City Lights Books publishes *Howl and Other Poems* a year later, the police arrest the publisher, the poet Lawrence Ferlinghetti, for selling an obscene book.

October 18. José Ortega y Gasset dies at the age of 72 and is buried in the Cementerio Sacramental de San Isidro, Madrid.

November. LD locks up the Bellapaix house and does not live there any more, except for some weekend visits.

December 9 and 16. In the *Spectator*, Patrick Leigh Fermor publishes a passionate political polemic arguing that supporting *Enosis* would strongly benefit British policy in the eastern Mediterranean.

Mid-December. LD is infected by a flu-like germ and remains in bed for several days.

December 24. LD is on duty at the Information Office.

1956

Allen Ginsberg's *Howl and Other Poems*, Romain Gary's *Les Racines du ciel*, James Baldwin's *Giovanni's Room*, Naguib Mahfouz' *Cairo Trilogy*, Albert Camus' *La chute*, Mary Renault's *The Last of the Wine*, Saul Bellow's *Seize the Day* and Norman Mailer's *The White Negro: Superficial Reflections on the Hipster* are published. John Osborne's *Look Back in Anger* and Jean Genet's *Le Balcon* receive their première performances.

Rupert Hart-Davis in London publishes GD's *The Drunken Forest*.

Winter. LD begins a story with the title "A Village of Turtle-Doves", which eventually becomes *Tunc*, but leaves it after 17 typescript pages.[15]

---

[15] Copies are deposited in the Durrell Library of Corfu and the Durrell collection at Southern Illinois University. In 2018, in London, Colenso Books for the Durrell Library of Corfu published *The Placebo* edited and extensively introduced by Richard

LD and Claude begin living together. LD is writing short comic pieces about diplomatic life in Belgrade.

January. Diana Gould, now Yehudi Menuhin's wife, and her husband come to visit for the first time in a decade; the violinist inspires LD to take up yoga.

February 27. LD is 44 years old.

February 28. The Colonial Secretary and his entourage arrive in Nicosia for a meeting with Makarios.

Spring. Maurice Cardiff introduces LD to the poet Penelope Tremayne, who works for the International Committee of the Red Cross on Cyprus.

March 9. The British take Makarios to the Seychelles under house arrest for a year, leaving the more violent Grivas in charge of the Enosis movement's political as well as military activities on the island.

March 10. The *New Statesman* prints LD's poem "Bitter Lemons".

April. EOKA begins the targeted killing of British civilians, hoping this will force the British to leave the island which would then be united with Greece.

c. April 2. Freya Stark and Sir Harry Luke visit LD and tour the island, but many of LD's British friends are leaving.

May 10. British authorities hang Michael Karaolidis for murdering a police constable; riots ensue. LD visits the Bellapaix house for the last time to retrieve books and papers.

Late Spring or early Summer. LD sends the "Justine" manuscript to Faber in London and it is accepted for publication in February of the following year.

Summer. Makarios' secretary pointedly suggests to LD that it is time for him to leave Cyprus. LD writes to Sir Patrick Reilly, then British minister in Paris, about an official British cultural position in France.

Early June. An incendiary bomb is put in LD's garage in Nicosia and on a second occasion three youths bomb the house across the street,

Pine and David Roessel. It contains three early drafts of what eventually became *Tunc*: "A Village of Turtle-Doves", "The Placebo: An Attic Comedy" and "Dactyl".

possibly mistaking it for LD's.[16]

[1956]

June. LD gives Joan Pepper the manuscript of *White Eagles over Serbia* to "improve" for publication under both their names or a pseudonym, which she does on the ship out of Cyprus, when she and her husband, Dennis Wetherell-Pepper, leave for England. Faber reads this and LD's first version and asks him to revise the latter manuscript for younger people.

June 29. The playwright Arthur Miller marries the actress Marilyn Monroe.

July 19. LD proposes to share the advance on *White Eagles over Serbia* with Joan Pepper.

July 24. Alan Pringle, an editor at Faber, receives a letter from LD noting that further volumes will follow *Justine.* This is the first time LD mentions a possible multi-volume series.[17]

July 25. Laurence Olivier rejects *Sappho* for production at the National Theatre.

July 26. Nasser gives a lengthy speech in Alexandria announcing the military occupation of the Canal Zone and the nationalization of the Suez Canal Company.

End July. Penelope Tremayne takes over the Bellapaix house for the International Committee of the Red Cross. Claude takes her children to London where she places them in a boarding school.

August 26. LD departs Cyprus for London, leaving his library behind.[18]

Early September. After several days in London LD and Claude move in

---

[16] The bombing is described in Penelope Tremayne's *Below the Tide*, for which LD writes a preface, 13ff; but the notion that the terrorists might have mistaken the house is in GB, 41.

[17] Haag, *Alexandria*, 326.

[18] IMN, 442, has LD and Claude leaving together and does not mention her children. GB does not give a departure date. Haag, *Alexandria*, 326, has their departures as presented here.

with Louisa in Bornemouth.

September 6. LD has a reunion with Sappho, who remains for several months with her father and Claude because Eve cannot have her at her job at Bedales. LD and Claude's plans for a place near Paris fall through.

September 12. Freya Stark writes from Asolo, Italy, inviting the Durrells to live in her house, a good place to write; in January LD turns down the offer.

October. Faber in London and Grove Press in USA publish LD's *Selected Poems* and Heinemann publishes Richard Aldington's *Introduction to Mistral* in London.

Early October. The Swedish Academy awards Juan Ramón Jiménez (Spain) the Nobel Prize in Literature. Claude, LD and Sappho move to Diana Hambros Ladas' isolated cottage at Donhead St Andrews near Shaftesbury in Dorset while he finishes his memoir about his experiences in Cyprus, *Bitter Lemons*, published in 1957. Claude submits her book, *Mrs. O'* to Faber. Eve files a petition for a divorce.

October 4. LD reviews Nikos Kazantzakis' *Freedom and Death* on the BBC Third Programme.

October 11. Rupert Hart-Davis in London publishes GD's partly fictional memoir *My Family and Other Animals*, an immediate and continuing bestseller, which formed the basis for a TV series (1987), a movie (2005), and a recent multiple TV series (2017–19) known as *The Durrells* in the UK and *The Durrells in Corfu* in the USA, in which in my opinion the fiction quotient increases with each episode, so the later series are almost purely fictional. The lack of veracity to the historic past does, for fans, in no way diminish the pleasure of watching all the episodes.

October 16. LD meets Miller's friends James and Tania Stern through Diana Ladas; the Sterns know the south of France well and offer advice on living there.

October 29. Israeli forces begin to march through the Sinai, followed by the landing of French and British paratroopers in Port Said (November 5), all intending to overthrow Nasser and re-internationalize the canal.

October 30. LD and Claude invite the Sterns to tea to further discuss the possibility of living in Provence.

[1956]

November 4. Soviet military forces intervene in Hungary, repressing a nationalist revolt.

November 6. *Bitter Lemons* has reached 40,000 words. The Soviet Union threatens to intervene in the war in Egypt.

November 7. Bending to pressure from the United Nations, the USA and other sources, the British and the French accept a ceasefire in Egypt, after which the Egyptians begin forcing the country's non-Arab population, including a third of the country's Jews, to leave, effectively putting an end to the perception of Alexandria as a cosmopolitan, culturally European urban centre.

November 21. The British hand over control of the Suez Canal to the United Nations.

Winter. At the completion of *Bitter Lemons*, LD, Claude and Sappho move to Bournemouth to stay with the very accommodating Alan and Ella Thomas at their house.

End December. LD finishes revising *White Eagles over Serbia*, which Faber will publish for the "younger" reader, and begins "Justine II".

FRANCE
WITH CLAUDE : 1957–1967

1957

The Viking Press, eventually to become LD's American publisher, brings out Jack Kerouac's novel *On the Road*, introducing the so-called "Beat Generation" to a wide public. Bernard Malamud's *The Assistant*, Ayn Rand's *Atlas Shrugged*, Boris Pasternak's *Doctor Zhivago*, Nevil Shute's *On the Beach*, James Jones' *Some Came Running*, Naguib Mahfouz' *Sugar Street* and John Cheever's *The Wapshot Chronicle* are published. Samuel Beckett's *Endgame*, Eugene O'Neill's *Long Day's Journey into Night* and John Osborne's *The Entertainer* receive their première performances.

Claude writes *The Rum Go*, based on her work in Alexandria for the British navy and begins a third novel based on her experience living in Israel.

January. The *New Statesman* publishes LD's "Moulder of Minds". LD and Claude are in Paris staying with her father at his apartment on the Boulevard des Invalides, and Sappho is back with her mother. Missing Aldington by minutes in Paris, LD writes to his address in Provence asking advice about affordable housing.

January 10. Gabriela Mistral, Chilean Nobel 1945, dies of pancreatic cancer in Hempstead, Long Island, New York, at the age of 68 and her remains are buried in Chile.[1]

February 1. LD and Claude return to London for the publication of *Justine*, dedicated to Eve, which receives ambiguous reviews. Aldington responds to LD's letter about moving to Provence, offering advice and to be of help.

February. Faber accepts Claude's *Mrs. O'* for publication later in the year.

February 7. Claude and LD travel to Paris, where they again briefly stay

---

[1] The author of this *Log* lived in Hempstead from 1947 to 1959 and had no idea Mistral also resided there.

with her father, on their way to the Mediterranean coast. Girodias cannot pay royalties on *The Black Book* because of court actions prohibiting his list in France.

[1957]

c. February 12. LD and Claude meet Aldington and his daughter Catherine (Catha) in Montpellier. Shortly thereafter they locate the primitive Villa Louis outside Sommières, 100 metres from the railroad station on the Vidourle River in the Gard, and rent it for six months.

February 27. LD is 45 years old.

Late February. The publisher E. P. Dutton in New York promises a substantial advance for *Justine*.

Spring. Sappho is enrolled in Bedales School where Eve is a matron. LD and Claude plant a *potager* (vegetable garden) at the Villa Louis.

March 8. The (perhaps) Canadian writer, painter and Vorticist Wyndham Lewis dies at the age of 72 and is interred at Golders Green Crematorium, London.

March 16. Time and Tide publishes LD's "Enigma Variations", a mainly negative review of Ezra Pound's *Cantos*.

March 25. Terence Tiller's BBC Third Programme radio production of LD's *Sappho* evokes less than rave reviews.

March 26. LD is seriously working on "Justine II", hoping to finish by June.

March 29. The Irish novelist Joyce Cary (*Mister Johnson, The Horse's Mouth*, etc.) dies in Oxford at the age of 69.

April. Jean Fanchette buys a copy of *Justine* in Blackwell's shop in Oxford.

April 19. Penelope Tremayne writes that she'll ship LD's paintings from his Bellapaix home, which she's rented to Peter Storrs for the summer.[2]

April 23. Christopher Middleton broadcasts on the BBC Third Programme a perceptive programme called "The Heraldic Universe" on

---

[2] The extant records do not indicate what happened to the paintings, nor whether they were done by LD or others.

Justine. The South African poet and Franco-supporter Roy Campbell is killed in car crash near Setúbal in Portugal at the age of 55.

End April. "Justine II" (*Balthazar*) is almost finished. Rowohlt-Verlag in Hamburg, Miller's German publisher, offers a generous contract for *Justine* and, at Miller's urging, for the subsequent volumes as well.

May 1–6. LD is within a few pages of finishing "Justine II".

May 1. In New York, Random House publishes Faulkner's *The Town.*

May 4. LD's review of Aldington's book *Introduction to Mistral* appears in the *New Statesman.*

May 18. In the USA, the San Francisco poet, essayist and translator Kenneth Rexroth positively reviews the British editions of *Justine* and LD's *Selected Poems* in *The Nation.*[3]

May 24. In London, Faber publishes *White Eagles over Serbia.*

May 25. Claude is typing a clean copy of "Justine II".

End May. Amy and Sir Walter Smart visit Sommières.

June. In New York, Dutton pays a large advance for *Bitter Lemons.*

June 20. Gerald Sykes, Buffie Johnson's husband, writes to LD that he will review the American edition of *Justine* for *The New York Times Book Review.*

June 27. The unlucky writer Malcolm Lowry dies at the age of 48 in Ripe, Sussex, and is buried in the St John the Baptist churchyard there.

July. Faber publishes the British edition of *Bitter Lemons*, dedicated to the architect Austen Harrison, to generally positive reviews, but not in Greece where it greatly angers Seferis and Diamantis. At a farewell party for Aldington, Claude and LD meet the poet and broadcasting executive Frédéric-Jacques Temple at Aldington's pension in Montpellier. Temple becomes a good friend and ally. Faber offers LD a £500 advance for each of the final two volumes of what comes to be known as *The*

---

[3] This review and the two following by Rexroth on the *Quartet* and other LD works are reprinted in Rexroth, *Assays*, 11–30. See also the entries for March 5, 1941, September 2, 1955, and June 4, 1960.

Alexandria Quartet.

[1957]

Early July. Claude travels to London for ten days to discuss her second novel, *The Rum Go*, with Faber (who agree to publish it) and buy two chemical toilets for the Villa Louis. The wily LD writes the obscurantist nonsense that constitutes the introductory Note to *Balthazar* intended to buffalo the critics and intrigue the reader, dating it "Ascona 1957".[4]

Mid-July. Aldington moves to the hamlet of Maison Sallé, Sury-en-Vaux, two hours south of Paris.

Early August. Claude's children (Diana, 11, and Barry, 8), Sappho, 6, and Margo and her son Nicholas, 12, visit the Villa Louis. Dutton publishes *Justine* in the USA.

August 25. Sykes' rave review of *Justine* appears in *The New York Times Book Review.*

August 26. Time magazine prints a positive review of *Justine.*

September. The Atlantic Monthly also prints a positive review of *Justine.* David Gascoyne, now living in Aix-en-Provence, visits the Villa Louis.

Autumn. In London, Faber publishes Claude's first novel, *Mrs. O'*.

October. LD begins a correspondence with Arthur Guirdham, a psychiatrist.

Early October. The Swedish Academy awards Albert Camus (France) the Nobel Prize in Literature.

October 10. "Justine III" stands at approximately 100 typescript pages.

November. LD is invited to become an honorary member of the annual Class of 1936 reunion by the regulars at a local café.[5] Eve is granted a divorce decree absolute.

November 22. In London *The Evening Standard* publishes LD's "Letter in

---

[4] GB, 246, calls this "a fictional place, to imply spacelessness and to put people off the scent of where he was really living".

[5] IMN, 450; GB, 252, has it the class of 1930–32 and describes the group as made up of "soldiers and resistance fighters".

the Sofa", a story set on Rhodes of the finding of a letter from a Jewish woman to a German Officer.

December. Buchet-Chastel publishes a French translation of *Justine* by Roger Giroux.

Early December. LD and Claude travel by stuffy sleeping car to London so LD can accept the Duff Cooper Memorial Award for *Bitter Lemons* from the Queen Mother (£200 and a copy of *Old Men Forget* by Sir Alfred Duff Cooper, Lord Norwich).

December 9. LD takes Penelope, now 17, to the ceremony, which passes splendidly despite LD's misgivings. Faber publishes LD's *Esprit de Corps: Sketches from Diplomatic Life.*

Mid-December. Claude and LD spend several emotionally high days in Paris on the trip back to Sommières.

1958

Truman Capote's *Breakfast at Tiffany's*, Thomas Berger's *Crazy in Berlin*, Maxwell Kenton's *Candy*, Giuseppe di Lampedusa's *The Leopard*, Graham Greene's *Our Man in Havana*, Jack Kerouac's *The Dharma Bums*, Chinua Achebe's *Things Fall Apart* and Kingsley Amis' *I Like It Here* are published. Samuel Beckett's *Krapp's Last Tape*, Max Frisch's *Biedermann und die Brandstifter* and Tennessee Williams' *Suddenly, Last Summer* receive their première performances.

Justine is short-listed for the French annual Prix du Meilleur Livre Étranger, but does not win.

Rupert Hart-Davis in London publishes GD's *Encounters with Animals.*

LD begins a correspondence with Perlès about Miller's work and status, eventually published as *Art and Outrage* (1959).

January. Curtis Brown sells some of LD's Antrobus stories to *Harper's* and *The Atlantic Monthly* in America; the London *Sunday Times* contracts for six stories annually. LD works quickly on *Mountolive* ("Justine III"), about 5,000 words a day. Claude sells *Mrs. O'* to Rinehart in New York. Miller has horoscopes cast for LD and Claude, predicting they would move in October and that they fit well together.

[1958]

January 10. LD finishes the first draft of *Mountolive*.

February – March. The French reviews of *Justine* are generally good.

February 27. LD is 46 years old.

End February. In the USA, Dutton publishes *Bitter Lemons* to mixed critical reaction.

Spring. The landlord of the Villa Louis notifies LD he needs the place for his family, but Frédéric-Jacques Temple finds a local lawyer who arranges for LD and Claude to remain until the end of the summer school holidays, so the children can spend the time there.

Before March 4. The medical student, Jean Fanchette, sends LD his piece on *Justine* published in the literary section (*Lettres Suivent*) of a medical students' monthly magazine in Paris.

March 4. LD responds to Fanchette, beginning a long-term exchange of letters and friendship.

March 6. Miller writes to LD that he should stop wasting his time on the Antrobus "stuff" and concentrate on the real thing.

April 1–2. Miller writes an eight-page letter to LD and Perlès about their letters on his literary career, later published in *Art and Outrage.*

April 11. Faber publishes *Balthazar*, dedicated to the author's mother, to positive reviews.[6]

April 18. Judge Bolitha Laws dismisses the indictment of Ezra Pound for treason on grounds of insanity thus allowing the release of the incorrigibly foolish poet from St. Elizabeths mental hospital in Washington DC where he has been incarcerated since 1945.

May. Faber accepts Claude's third novel, *A Chair for the Prophet*. The American publisher, New Directions, agrees to publish LD's anthology of Miller's writings which he has been working on since Argentina.

---

[6] IMN, 472; GB, 256, has the publication date as April 15.

May 7. The St. Elizabeths authorities formally release Ezra Pound into the custody of his wife Dorothy Shakespear and several weeks later they sail to Italy where the addled poet spends the rest of his life.

May 11. LD picks up Anaïs Nin at Nîmes railroad station.[7]

May 19. Ignoring the festering Algerian crisis, LD and Claude drive to Paris in an old Peugeot 203 to attend a party organized by his publisher Corréa. They meet Fanchette (who tells them of plans to publish an Anglo-French literary magazine *Two Cities*), Anaïs Nin (who agrees to finance the magazine) and Guiler, as well as the Israeli painter Zvi Milshtein (from whom LD buys a painting).

May 23. LD and Claude visit Amy and Sir Walter Smart in Pacy-sur-Eure.

May 28. Back in Paris, Claude picks up Sappho, Penelope and Penelope's ballet-school friend, Jill Dawkins, at the railway station and takes them directly to the Corréa reception where they meet Diana and Yehudi Menuhin; following the party they go to the Café du Dôme to meet Fanchette and his wife Martine.

May 30. The Fanchettes have the Durrell crew and the Smarts for drinks at their efficiency apartment in the rue Scipion, after which they all go to a Chinese restaurant in the rue Claude-Bernard.

May 31. The Durrell ménage leaves Paris for the south, stopping for the night in Lyon.

June 1. They continue on, stopping at Orange and Avignon, and cross over the Pont-du-Gard and on to Sommières, some 65km beyond. Prime minister, Charles de Gaulle, forms a new government with the aim of resolving the Algerian crisis.

June 2. French parliament gives de Gaulle permission to draft a new constitution (for the Fifth Republic), which he does, shifting power from the prime minister's government to the president's office.

June 4. The Durrell group properly celebrates Penelope's 18th birthday.

June 6. Sappho and Claude are felled by chicken pox.

---

[7] IMN, 475; GB, 257, has Nin and her husband Hugh Guiler visiting Sommières in late April.

[1958]

June 11. Miller writes to insist on LD receiving half the royalties for the anthology of his writings that LD is editing for New Directions.[8]

Summer. LD and Claude take the children on excursions to Aigues Mortes, Avignon, Les Saintes-Maries-de-la-Mer, Arles, Les Baux, Saint-Rémy, Le Grau du Roi; they swim in the sea, in the river at the Pont du Gard and in the Vidourle River in Sommières. Life is primitive and adventurous at the tiny Villa Louis with so many people. Alfred and Anne Perlès with Frédéric-Jacques Temple visit there for a day.

June 21. Penelope and Jill Dawkins return to Paris and on to London.

July. Claude's children spend time at the Villa Louis, along with Heinz Ledig Rowohlt, LD's German publisher.

Mid-summer. Claude and LD visit an isolated ruined farmhouse (the Mazet Michel) with 22 acres of garrigue and olive groves with a small out-building for guests, off the chemin d'Engances near Uzès on the Avignon-Nîmes road, about 15 miles from Sommières, which they rent for five years with an option to buy.

July 21. Gerald Sykes sends LD a copy of his review of *Balthazar* written for *The New York Times Book Review*, which appears on August 24.

Late July. Anaïs Nin and Rupert Pole (her California "husband") visit, staying at a Nîmes hotel.[9]

Early August. In the USA, Dutton publishes *Balthazar.*

August 22. In Sérigny, Orne, Roger Martin du Gard, Nobel 1937, dies at the age of 77 and is buried in the Cimetière du Monastère de Cimiez above Nice, where Henri Matisse is also buried.

August 27. The Fanchettes visit for several days and they discuss Fanchette's idea of the magazine, *Two Cities: La Revue Bilingue de Paris*, in the first issue of which will be an *hommage* to LD.

---

[8] In the works since 1948, the book is published in New York the following year as *The Henry Miller Reader* and in England as *The Best of Henry Miller.*

[9] Nin lived in what appears to be two-marriage life: her New York, and legal, husband was Hugh Guiler.

September 6. The last of the LD–Claude children depart the Villa Louis for home.

c. September 9. LD finishes editing the Miller anthology.

c. September 12. With Claude, LD travels to Grenoble to research a well-paid article for *Holiday* magazine, pleased to be in Stendhal's home town. They will use the money to install a toilet and waterpump at the Mazet Michel.

September 15. Claude and LD move into the Mazet.

Early October. The Swedish Academy awards Boris Pasternak (USSR) the Nobel Prize in Literature, but the Soviet government forces him to refuse it.

October 10. Faber publishes *Mountolive*, dedicated to Claude, to positive early reviews (somewhat later Dutton publishes an American edition). The Hollywood movie studio 20th Century Fox cables an offer for LD to write the screenplay for a movie about Cleopatra.

October 17. GD signs the lease for Les Augrès Manor on Jersey, which he intends to make his home and a zoo.

c. October 25. LD sends Miller his preface to the Miller anthology, which delights the older man.

November 3. LD flies to London alone for the publication of *Stiff Upper Lip* and publisher meetings, with a six-hour layover in Paris where he eats a late dinner at the Café du Dôme, probably with Fanchette. *Mountolive* has sold 10,000 copies.

November 10. Juliet O'Hea at Curtis Brown telegraphs LD that the Book of the Month Club in the USA has taken *Mountolive* for circulation to its members, for a fee of at least $20,000 — a large amount of money in those days.

Mid-November. Anaïs Nin asks for an immediate preface to the British publication of *Children of the Albatross*; LD acquiesces, but she finds the result inadequate and edits it to her own satisfaction.

December 15. LD is discomforted by the lack of attention he's paying to the completion of *Clea* ("Justine IV").

December 21. The French elect Charles de Gaulle president of France under the new constitution; he takes office on January 8, 1959.

December 25. LD settles into an early morning routine to write *Clea* at a rate of 2,000 words each day, breaking occasionally to work on the dry-stone walls outside the house.

1959

Norman Mailer's *Advertisements for Myself,* Naguib Mahfouz' *The Children of Gebelaawi,* Philip Roth's *Goodbye, Columbus,* Mordecai Richler's *The Apprenticeship of Duddy Kravitz,* Saul Bellow's *Henderson the Rain King,* Terry Southern's *The Magic Christian,* Richard Condon's *The Manchurian Candidate,* Günter Grass' *Die Blechtrommel* and Kurt Vonnegut's *The Sirens of Titan* are published. Tennessee Williams' *Sweet Bird of Youth* receives its première performance.

In London, Faber publishes Claude's novel set in Israel, *A Chair for the Prophet.*

January. Aldington and Temple visit the Mazet Michel. Anaïs Nin sends Fanchette $400 for the first issue of *Two Cities,* the "hommage to LD" issue.

End January. The typescript of *Clea* has reached 40 pages.

February. Roger Giroux has almost finished translating *Balthazar* into French.

February 1. Dominique Arban interviews LD for the French radio programme "Étranger mon ami".

February 27. LD is 47 years old.

Mid-March. The *Clea* typescript has reached 130 pages.

March 26. GD and Jacquie's zoo on Jersey opens to the public. Raymond Chandler dies in Los Angeles at the age of 71 and is buried in the Mount Hope Cemetery at San Diego, California.

April. LD wins the Prix du Meilleur Livre Étranger for *Balthazar.* The Cyprus crisis prevents the broadcast of a radio dramatization of *Bitter*

Lemons prepared by Xan Fielding for the BBC.

c. April 7. The first draft of *Clea* is finished.

April 8. The Smarts visit the Mazet Michel for lunch.

Mid-April. Buffie Johnson and Gerald Sykes visit.

April 14. Miller, Eve and his children leave for Europe and rent a Paris apartment for two months in the rue Campagne-Première.

April 23. Julian Mitchell and Gene Andrewski interview LD in Sommières for the *The Paris Review.*[10]

May 5. Amidst violence against Algerians in Paris, Fanchette arranges a launch party for the French edition of *Balthazar.* Henry and Eve Miller, with Henry's children in attendance, spend several days with LD and Claude; the Sykeses are also there along with several others.

May 7. LD has drinks with Mary Mollo Hadkinson at Les Deux Magots.

May 18. Temple and Catha Aldington visit the Mazet Michel.

End May. The Swedish film actress and director, Mai Zetterling, and her English writer husband, David Hughes, visit.[11]

c. June 19. The four Millers and Perlès (who stays only a week) arrive in Sommières where the Millers rent an apartment for two months and tour parts of Provence with LD; Girodias visits.

c. June 25. LD sends the revised *Clea* manuscript to Faber in London.

End June. Claude's and LD's children arrive for the summer holidays; Eve brings Sappho, then departs.

Mid-summer. LD and Claude jointly buy the Mazet Michel on the strength of *Justine* being taken up by the Club Française du Livre.[12] They hire a

---

[10] *The Paris Review* 22 (Autumn–Winter 1959–1960); also published in Plimpton, *Writers at Work.*

[11] For an account of this and other visits, including one with Miller, see Hughes, *Himself and Other Animals.* Zetterling wrote briefly about the visits in her memoir, *All Those Tomorrows.* Hughes died in May 2005 at the age of 74; Zetterling on March 17, 1994 in London.

[12] GB, 277, has this as "helped by a huge advance for *Clea* from Buchet", that is, Éditions Buchet-Chastel.

sharecropper/caretaker, Alphonse Tritignac, to live in the small cottage at the edge of the property and develop a *potager* (vegetable garden).

[1959]

Late July. Richard Aldington comes south, where he meets Miller, Temple, Claude and LD in Sommières for a lively dinner and drinks, during which much hearty mutual appreciationing takes place.

c. August 23. The Millers depart Europe for Big Sur, their marriage in trouble.

September 2. Claude and LD drive to London to return Sappho and do a publicity round for *Clea* at Faber's request, although *Clea* would not appear until the following February. They stay in Leigh Fermor's apartment. LD appears on television and discovers he's a natural for the medium. Surgeons operate on Claude to remove a cyst, she recuperates in Bournemouth at the Thomases', where LD packs his books and papers from the attic to take back to France. LD then spends several days alone in Paris doing publicity events.

September 15. LD appears on the BBC television programme *Tonight.*

October. Sappho is planned to open in Hamburg, but is postponed for a month. LD and Claude return from England to the Mazet Michel to find it flooded and the waterpump damaged by a mason working on the house (he also drank all their wine).

Early October. The Swedish Academy awards Salvatore Quasimodo (Italy) the Nobel Prize in Literature.

November 7. Aldington refuses to support LD's campaign to improve his (Aldington's) image and fortunes in England.

November 13. In New York, Random House publishes Faulkner's *The Mansion*, completing the Snopes trilogy (with *The Hamlet* and *The Town*).

c. November 15. Claude and LD decide to add several rooms to the rear of the Mazet to better house the children and certain guests.[13] LD begins

[13] The addition of the rooms elevated the property from a "mazet", a small Provençal country house, to a "mas", a larger house; and after GD and Lee began staying and eventually purchasing the place in 1982, they and LD referred to it as simply the "Mazet" or "mas Michel" (personal communication from Lee Durrell).

another verse play, *Acte*, about a Scythian princess who rebels against Rome.

November 22. Sappho, with Elizabeth Flickenschild as the girl and young Maximilian Schell in a supporting role, directed by Gustaf Gründgens, opens at the Deutsche Schauspielhaus in Hamburg with Claude and LD in attendance; Margaret Rawlings also attends: she praises the play but not this production.[14]

November 25. In Reinbek bei Hamburg, Rowohlt publishes the German edition of *Mountolive*.

End November. Faber and Dutton publish *Art and Outrage* (LD's correspondence with Alfred Perlès about Miller's work, including a letter from their old friend).

December. Heinemannn in London and New Directions in New York publish *The Best of Henry Miller* edited by LD (titled *The Henry Miller Reader* in the USA).

Mid-December. Suffering the results of media fame and infested with uninvited visitors, LD posts a sign at the road entrance to the Mazet's property reading "This is a workshop. If uninvited and unexpected, don't knock!" The sign is in English and LD himself thought it "churlish".[15] (Ten years later it might have read, "If you haven't been invited, fuck off!" but that is speculation.)

December 17. LD flies to London to pick up Sappho, who spends the holidays with Claude's children at the Mazet because Eve is in a hospital in England with an undisclosed malady.

1960

Flannery O'Connor's *The Violent Bear It Away*, Kingsley Amis' *Take a Girl Like You*, Jabra Ibrahim Jabra's *Hunters in a Narrow Street*, Harper Lee's *To Kill a Mocking Bird*, Anthony Powell's *Casanova's Chinese Restaurant*,

---

[14] GB, 278, has Claude and LD flying to Hamburg "for the opening of *Sappho* on November 2" — surely a typo.

[15] GB, 277, has this as "This is a workshop — please write."

Nancy Mitford's *Don't Tell Alfred* and Ian Fleming's *For Your Eyes Only* are published. Wole Soyinka's *A Dance of the Forests*, Jean Anouilh's *Becket* and Robert Bolt's *A Man for All Seasons* receive their première performances.

[1960]

Faber reissues LD's *Prospero's Cell* and *Reflections on a Marine Venus*. Andre Deutsch in London and The Overlook Press in the USA republish LD's translation of *Pope Joan* in a revised edition. Rowohlt publishes a German edition of *Art and Outrage* (correspondence between LD and Perlès). A new edition of E. M. Forster's *Alexandria: A History and a Guide* with an introduction by LD is published in London. The first volume of Olivia Manning's Balkan trilogy, *The Great Fortune*, is published in London. Heinemann in London publishes the novel *The Age of Bronze* by Rodis Roufos, who served in the Greek consulate on Cyprus during the time LD was director of the British public information office; the book is meant as a rebuttal of LD's *Bitter Lemons*.

January 2. Aldington backs out of an arrangement for him to be interviewed with LD by BBC television, a project LD has worked on for some time as part of the campaign to rehabilitate Aldington in England.

January 4. Albert Camus dies in an automobile crash driving from Lourmarin in the south to Paris, the first draft manuscript of his last novel in a briefcase; the man worth ten Sartres is gone in a flash of loud metal and burning rubber. The headline of *Combat* the following day reads: "ABSURD!"

January 8. The BBC-TV *Monitor* team arrives to spend three days filming an interview in the Nîmes arena and at the Mazet. The humourless and over-serious interviewer, Huw Wheldon,[16] showed himself indifferent to LD's work and asked clichéd questions to which LD answered whatever he wished, having learned the art of avoiding the answer to questions he did not want to or could not answer during his career as press and information manager for the British establishment, in Rhodes, Belgrade

[16] In the mid-1950s Wheldon produced a series of BBC television programmes called *The Orson Welles' Sketchbook* in which Welles improvised talk about various themes. Wheldon went on to become Managing Director of BBC Television,1968– 1975, and was knighted in 1976.

and Cyprus.

January 9. Jean-Paul Weber's long article viciously caricaturing LD appears in *Figaro Littéraire*, disturbing LD and Claude even more because they had lavished time and food and drink on the malicious hack.

January 12. Nevil Shute dies in Melbourne, Australia, at the age of 61 and his ashes are scattered in the Solent (the strip of water between the Isle of Wight and the southern coast of mainland England).

January 28. The novelist and anthropologist Zora Neale Hurston dies penniless in Fort Pierce, Florida, at the age of 69 and is buried in an unmarked grave there.

February 5. Clea, dedicated to the author's father, is published. *Books and Bookmen* publishes an interview with LD entitled, "Lawrence Durrell: Is he the Greatest Novelist of the Fifties?"

February 14. The BBC television programme *Monitor* broadcasts the interview filmed the previous month (see the entry for January 8).

February 27. LD is 48 years old, at the peak of all his powers.

Spring. LD travels to Geneva to write a travel piece for *Holiday*, where he meets the Russian-born Alexandr Blokh, a translator at the United Nations, who published poems under the name Jean Blot, and his wife Nadja, a painter, who become good friends.

March. LD sends two acts of *Acte* to Juliet O'Hea at Curtis Brown.

End March. Aldington visits with his Australian friends the Geoffrey Duttons, to whom LD sings some (unpublished) naughty songs which he ascribes to Scobie, the fictional quasi-comic character in *The Alexandria Quartet*.

c. April 2. In New York, Dutton publishes *Clea* to generally positive reviews.

Mid-April. Miller, at age 69, arrives in Europe without his wife Eve but with a waitress from Big Sur who caught his eye; Eve remains in Big Sur enjoying the peace and quiet.

Early May. Claude and LD are in Paris for ten days for the publication of *Mountolive* in French (to fine reviews). While there he works on the script for *Cleopatra*, which 20th Century Fox has hired Rouben Mamoulian to direct.[17] Faber publishes LD's *Collected Poems*.

[1960]

May 2. Miller and his new, and soon to be former, girlfriend are in Cannes where he serves as a judge at the Film Festival.

May 6. In Paris, LD signs copies of the English edition of *Clea* (published in early February) at the Mistral Bookstore, 37 rue de la Bûcherie, owned and operated by George Whitman, who in the late spring of 1964 will change the name of the shop to Shakespeare and Company in honour of Sylvia Beach, the proprietor of the original cultural centre of that name (1919–1941).

May 20. Miller and the girlfriend arrive in Sommières for a stay in a rented flat. The writer David Hughes and his wife, the actress Mai Zetterling, also visit at the same time.

May 27. The *TLS* prints LD's "No Clue to Living", an essay on the writer-artist as "a public Opinionator" in an age of uncertainty.[18]

May 30. Boris Pasternak, Nobel 1958, dies at the age of 70 and is buried in the Peredelkino Cemetery, outside Moscow.

June 2. LD appears on the BBC television programme *Tonight* discussing "Diplomats Abroad".

June 4. Kenneth Rexroth publishes his second article on LD in *The Nation* magazine in which he begins, "Sitting down to write this review of Durrell's *Clea*, I have little relish for the job." He goes on to disparage all of LD's post-*Justine* work in the most savage terms, except the poetry which he praises.

Mid-June. LD and Claude spend two weeks in London on the *Cleopatra* script. LD appears on radio and TV. When they return to the Mazet the mason has caused the well to run dry and they both come down with the

---

[17] Mamoulian had previously directed the musicals *High, Wide and Handsome* (1939), *Summer Holiday* (1952) and *Silk Stockings* (1957), in addition to several earlier inventive film dramas. See Thomson, *A Biographical Dictionary of Film*, 473–4, for a balanced overview of his career.

[18] Reprinted in LD, *From the Elephant's Back*, 37–43.

flu. The *Yale Review* publishes two appreciations of LD's work: positive (George Steiner) and negative (Martin Green).[19]

End June. Fake Durrell papers and paintings are on sale in a London book shop: he has "arrived".

July. The children arrive from England for the summer holiday; LD and Claude rent a cottage and pitch a big tent on the beach at Les Saintes-Maries-de-la-Mer for them all: the Blokhs and other friends join them throughout the summer. Nigel Dennis interviews LD for *Life*, and some days later two obnoxious photographers haul an unnecessarily large amount of equipment into the Mazet. Brassaï arrives with one camera and a recalcitrant tripod to photograph LD and makes curiously evocative images.

End July. Arthur Guirdham and his wife Mary visit briefly.

c. August 7. LD completes the 10th revision of the *Cleopatra* script despite the turmoil of the long, hot summer.

August 7. The BBC television programme *Monitor* broadcasts another interview with LD, filmed earlier.

September. Eve Durrell is working in Paris doing publicity for an art gallery. LD resumes work on *The Placebo*, starting a second draft "The Placebo: An Attic Comedy". (See the entry for Winter at the start of 1956, and the accompanying footnote.)

October. Faber publishes *The Dark Labyrinth* (formerly *Cefalû*), dedicated to Margaret, Gerald and Leslie. Unable to find a sympathetic writer to do a study of LD's work, Harry T. Moore begins collecting pieces on LD for an anthology he will edit. Rupert Hart-Davis in London publishes GD's *A Zoo in My Luggage*.

Early October. The Swedish Academy awards Saint-John Perse (France) the Nobel Prize in Literature. Dutton publishes LD's *The Black Book*, *Prospero's Cell* and *Reflections on a Marine Venus* in the USA.

November. In New York, the Readers' Subscription magazine, *The Griffin*, publishes Rexroth's review article on *The Black Book*; Rexroth proves to be ambiguous but generally negative and condescending (especially

[19] Both essays are reprinted in Moore, *The World of Lawrence Durrell*.

about the characters) in his reaction to the book.[20]

November 2. D. H. Lawrence's *Lady Chatterley's Lover* is cleared of obscenity charge in London without LD having to testify on its behalf, as he had offered to do.[21]

November 28. The Black American writer Richard Wright dies in Paris at the age of 52 under what might be suspicious circumstances and is buried in the Père Lachaise Cemetery there.[22]

December 10. Aldington comes south to visit his daughter Catha; they lunch with LD and Claude at the Oustaloun restaurant in Maussane.

End December. A Durrell Family Reunion takes place at GD's zoo on Jersey. The published photographs do not include Claude or Sappho, but do include Lulu the chimp. Louisa Durrell is now living with GD and Jacquie. Margo is there, but not Leslie who is in Africa. Another *Life* photographer shows up to immortalize the clan. LD and Claude move on to London to discuss *Cleopatra*, and also *Acte*, which Gründgens wants to put on the following autumn in Hamburg.

1961

Joseph Heller's *Catch-22*, John le Carré's *Call for the Dead*, J. D. Salinger's *Franny and Zooey*, Richard Hughes' *The Fox in the Attic*, V. S. Naipaul's *A House for Mr. Biswas*, Gabriel García Márquez' *No One Writes to the Colonel*, Walker Percy's *The Moviegoer*, Muriel Spark's *The Prime of Miss Jean Brodie*, Robert Heinlein's *Stranger in a Strange Land*, Marshall McLuhan's *The Gutenberg Galaxy* are published. Samuel Beckett's *Rough for Radio I* and *II* are broadcast. Max Frisch's *Andorra*, John Osborne's *Luther*, Tennessee Williams' *Night of the Iguana* and Heiner Müller's *Die Umsiedlerin* receive their première performances.

George Wickes is appointed to edit the Durrell–Miller correspondence

---

[20] The text is reprinted in Rexroth, *Assays*.

[21] LD did write a brief "Preface" to the edition of the book published in New York by Bantam Books in 1968 (reprinted in LD, *Endpapers and Inklings*).

[22] See Rowley, *Richard Wright: The Life and Times* and Webb, *Richard Wright: A Biography*.

for Dutton. Hamish Hamilton in London publishes GD's *Look at Zoos* and Rupert Hart-Davis brings out his *The Whispering Land*. Scorpion Press in Middlesex publishes Perlès' book *My Friend Lawrence Durrell*.

January 10. Dashiel Hammett dies in New York at the age of 67 and is buried in the Arlington National Cemetery in Virginia.

January 15. The *New York Times* prints LD's "A Traveler in Egypt", a brief appreciation of E. M. Forster's rich and well-written book *Alexandria: A History and a Guide*..

January 21. Blaise Cendrars dies in Paris at the age of 74 and is buried in the Batignolles Cemetery. In 1994 his remains are reinterred in the village of Tremblay-sur-Mauldre, Yvelines, where he had a country retreat for many years.

Mid-February. LD has written half of *An Irish Faustus* to meet Gründgens' request that he write a Faust with humour in it.

February 17. LD and Claude go to London to spend six weeks working with an experienced co-scriptor (Sidney Buchman) for a large amount of money on a new screenplay for the new director of *Cleopatra* (the Hollywood veteran, Joseph Mankiewicz, who had apparently already written a script of *The Alexandria Quartet* (the collective title of LD's four novels, *Justine, Balthazar, Mountolive* and *Clea*) for the producer Walter Wanger,[23] who, until the studio fired him, was also producing *Cleopatra*, a project he had been working on for forty years).[24]

---

[23] GB, 295.

[24] Typical of the Hollywood studio system, everything except the title changed before filming seriously got under way. Mamoulian had been fired and Mankiewicz rewrote the entire script making it very talky. LD's name does not appear in the credits of the film as released. It failed at the box office and with the critics, but our hero earned lots of dough while he worked on the script. For a scathing commentary on Mankiewicz's career and a sympathetic portrayal of Wanger's, especially their disastrous association with *Cleopatra*, see Thomson, *A Biographical Dictionary of Film*, 475–6, and 791–2. LD's early treatment for the filmscript and his memorandum on the subject to Wanger are reproduced in LD, *Endpapers and Inklings*. When he was asked, many years later, whether any of his work on *Cleopatra* had survived, LD said, "No, no, that's the point. [Mine] was the seventh treatment in a movie which ran to about, I think, thirty-two. How could there be anything left? [...] I would rather sell my child into prostitution than it [my books] go into movies" (Haller, "The Writer

[1961]

February 27. LD is 49 years old.

March 21. In London, BBC Radio Three broadcasts an interview with LD by Peter Duval Smith about the cinematic potential of Alexandria.

March 27. LD and Claude-Marie Vincendon Forde marry in London at the Chelsea Registry Office.[25]

Early April. The Durrells return to the Mazet via Paris where Fanchette throws a party for them; he'd sold the manuscript of *Mountolive* with LD's permission and bought his wife a washing machine. In Sommières they celebrate with Miller at the Auberge du Pont Roman, a rustic eatery being converted from a factory to a hotel/auberge.[26]

April 21. The Durrells meet Miller in Avignon for an elaborate lunch.

Summer. LD meets Denis de Rougemont in Geneva. The Durrells are in Paris for a party given by Curtis Cate, writer for *The Atlantic Monthly*.

June 11. The BBC television programme *Book Stand* broadcasts an interview with LD on *The Alexandria Quartet*.

June 24. In New York, Barney Rosset's Grove Press publishes Miller's *Tropic of Cancer* and faces a multitude of obscenity charges in various courts throughout the nation.

July. The children come south for a summer holiday.

July 2. Hemingway, Nobel 1954, commits suicide in Ketchum, Idaho, 19 days before his 62nd birthday and is buried in the local cemetery there.

August 13. The East Germans, with Soviet support, begin building the Berlin Wall, increasing the Cold War tensions, but stopping the haemorrhaging of their educated and skilled population.

in Hollywood"). For LD's work on the movie *Judith*, see the entry for September 1962 and the accompanying footnote.

[25] GB, 295. According to IMN, 523, they married at the Kensington Registry Office, where Joyce married Nora, D.H. Lawrence married Frieda and George and Pamela Wilkinson were married. The Chelsea location fits the fact that LD and Claude gave their address as the Basil Street Hotel.

[26] It is today a fine restaurant with a good wine list.

August 21. Sappho is produced at the Edinburgh Festival with Margaret Rawlings and Nigel Davenport, the opening night attended by LD, Claude, Mary Mollo Hadkinson, Alan and Ella Thomas, the physician Raymond Mills and his wife (friends from Rhodes 1945-47, who are now living in Edinburgh). The reviews are not very complimentary, but the house sells out each night and the costs are recovered.

August 22. The BBC television programme *Tonight* broadcasts an interview with LD about the *Sappho* production.

August 31. LD having run out of his two months' tax free sojourn in England, the Durrells leave in a hurry for France.

September. Stephanides writes from Corfu that he'd like to sell the letters LD wrote to him; Robin Fedden asks the same about the *Personal Landscape* letters.

Early October. The Swedish Academy awards Ivo Andrić (Yugoslavia) the Nobel Prize in Literature.[27]

November 12. Claude and LD are in Copenhagen to meet the reclusive Karen Blixen[28] for a day, after which they travel on to Hamburg for the première of *Acte/Actis*.[29]

November 24. Actis opens at the Deutsche Schauspielhaus to a generally positive critical response. While in Hamburg, LD meets Groddeck's widow on the occasion of the republication of *Das Buch vom Es* with an LD preface and the publication of LD's *Horizon* essay as a pamphlet.

December. The Atlantic Monthly has LD on its front cover accompanied by a lengthy essay by Curtis Cate. The Leigh Fermors visit the Mazet briefly

[27] According to Bowker, 299, Rowohlt informed LD that he had been only two votes short at the Swedish Academy from winning the prize; LD was not convinced and believed his anti-communism precluded him from receiving the prize.

[28] Karen Blixen, author of *Out of Africa*, is also known by the pseudonym Isak Dinesen, which she used for her short story collections, *Seven Gothic Tales* (1934) and *Winter's Tales* (1942).

[29] IMN, 526–7; GB, 299, has the Durrells travelling to Hamburg by way of Geneva to visit the Blokhs. Gründgens wanted a title change for the German performance because "Akte" in German is the word for "file" or "folder" and is close to the German word for coitus and nude, "Akt". After a struggle, they decided on *Actis*, which however only applies to the German version.

and a version of *Acte* is published in *Show* magazine.

December 25. Aldington visits for the holiday.

End December. The Durrells are settled in at the Mazet with colds in freezing temperatures and the mistral howling around the roof edges.

1962

James Baldwin's *Another Country*, Anthony Burgess' *A Clockwork Orange*, Barbara Tuchman's *The Guns of August* (titled *August 1914* in the UK), Kurt Vonnegut's *Mother Night*, Aleksandr Solzhenitsyn's *One Day in the Life of Ivan Denisovich*, Ken Kesey's *One Flew Over the Cuckoo's Nest*, Vladimir Nabokov's *Pale Fire*, James Jones' *The Thin Red Line*, Flannery O'Connor's *Wise Blood*, W. H. Auden's *The Dyer's Hand*, Rachel Carson's *Silent Spring*, V. S. Naipaul's *The Middle Passage* and Helen Gurley Brown's *Sex and the Single Girl* are published. Edward Albee's *Who's Afraid of Virginia Woolf?* and Friedrich Dürrenmatt's *Die Physiker* receive their première performances.

Faber publishes *The Alexandria Quartet* as a single volume. Collins in London publishes GD's *Island Zoo* and Lutterworth brings out his *My Favourite Animal Stories*. Olivia Manning's second Balkan trilogy novel, *The Spoilt City*, is published in London.

January. The University of Southern Illinois Press publishes *The World of Lawrence Durrell*, edited by Harry T. Moore. Moore has a publisher's contract to write a monograph on LD, but never does. Claude is translating Marc Peyre's *The Captive of Zour*.

Mid-January. LD visits Aldington in Aix-en-Provence for a night, then tramps about the countryside for several days.[30]

Mid-February. LD is having trouble finishing *An Irish Faustus*.

February 27. LD is 50 years old.

Early spring. Visits from Aldington, Temple, the writer Claude Seignolle, et al. interrupt work on *An Irish Faustus*. LD travels to Montpellier to

---

[30] GB, 301. Doyle, *Richard Aldington*, 313, tells some of the visit's amusing details, but naught about any "tramping". IMN doesn't mention it either.

record some of his lyric poems for Jupiter Records, run by his old friend Wallace Southam in London, whom he's known since the British Council days in Athens 1940–41. Seferis writes a note for the album cover.

April. Jupiter releases the album.

Late April. The Blokhs visit for a weekend from Paris, where they've moved to work at UNESCO.

May 2. Sir Walter Smart dies.[31]

First week in May. Claude's father dies in Paris.

Early May. A BBC team arrives in Nîmes to make two programmes on LD's works and records him reading several poems.

May 5. LD is interviewed on a Montpellier–Languedoc radio station.

End May – early June. LD is offered an OBE, which he turns down. Aldington is infuriated at the low level of the award, but LD doesn't seem to care very much.

June 4. In New York, Random House publishes Faulkner's *The Reivers*.

June 22. Aldington and his daughter Catha fly from Paris to Moscow on a "goodwill" tour sponsored by the Soviet government, ostensibly to celebrate his 70th birthday.

July 6. William Faulkner, Nobel 1949, dies in a hospital in Byhalia, Mississippi, at the age of 65 and is buried in the family plot in St Peter's Cemetery at Oxford, Mississippi.

July 10. The Aldingtons return to France from Moscow.

Mid-July. The Durrells' collected children arrive for the summer holidays. LD is spending much of his time painting watercolours and making desultory notes for the novel then called "The Placebo: An Attic Comedy".

July 27. Richard Aldington dies of a heart attack in Sury-en-Vaux at the age of 70 and is buried in the village's small cemetery.[32]

---

[31] The Braybrookes, *Olivia Manning*, 123, incorrectly write that Smart died in 1965.

[32] GB, 303, has this happening on July 26. LD wrote a warm tribute to his friend, "Richard Aldington", in Kershaw and Temple, *Richard Aldington*; reprinted in LD,

[1962]

August 9. Hermann Hesse, Nobel 1946, dies in Montagnola, Switzerland, at the age of 85 and is buried in the St Aggondio Curch cemetery there.

August 20. LD and Miller are in Edinburgh for the week-long International Writers' Conference where LD is introduced to a language computer at the university that would end up in *Tunc* and *Nunquam*. Norman Mailer, Mary McCarthy, William Burroughs, Rebecca West, Stephen Spender, Alexander Trocchi, Hugh MacDiarmid, et al. are also attending the conference.

August 21. LD and Miller speak as part of a panel at the conference.

August 24. LD reads two poems ("Ballad of the Oedipus Complex" and "La Rochefoucauld") on the BBC Home Service programme, *Readings on Record.*

Autumn. At the Mazet, LD begins to paint in oils.

September. The Durrells depart Marseille for Israel to research a film scenario, *Judith*, for a movie to feature Sophia Loren.[33]

September 3. The American poet e. e. cummings dies in North Conway, New Hampshire at the age of 69 and is buried in Forest Hills Cemetery, Jamaica Plain, Boston.

Early October. Despite renewed talk about LD receiving the prize, the Swedish Academy awards John Steinbeck (USA) the Nobel Prize in Literature. LD thinks this is because a Swedish communist on the

---

From the Elephant's Back, 271–4.

[33] The movie was released in 1966, LD is credited with the story, screenplay by John Michael Hayes, directed by Daniel Mann, produced by Kurt Ungar, cinematography by John Wilcox and Nicolas Roeg (who went on to direct a number of fine films such as *Don't Look Now*, *Walkabout*, and *The Man Who Fell to Earth*). Jack Hawkins and Peter Finch also acted in the movie. In the USA the video title is "Conflict". A version of LD's story was serialized in *Woman's Own* (February–April 1966) and in French in *Elle* the same year. There are, in fact, three versions: the serialization, a 38-page scenario and a 169-page typescript; the latter two are in the Durrell collection at Southern Illinois University at Carbondale. In June 2012, the Durrell School of Corfu published *Judith: A Novel*, in a limited edition edited and introduced by Richard Pine. Later that year a US edition was published by Open Road Media.

committee blackballed him.

October 8. The BBC Third Programme broadcasts a discussion of their writings by LD and Miller, moderated by D. G. Bridson, recorded at the Edinburgh Writers' Conference in August (see entry for August 20).

Mid-October. The Durrells travel from Israel to Athens where they meet Katsimbalis and Seferis, then travel to Mykonos to discuss *Sappho* as a possible opera with the composer Peggy Glanville-Hicks.[34]

December. LD agrees to edit the 1963 PEN Poetry Anthology (see the entry for November 1963).

December 8. LD makes haste to complete a draft of the *Judith* scenario.

December holidays. LD and Claude are on Jersey with other Durrells for a family holiday.

1963

John Fowles' *The Collector*, Sylvia Plath's *The Bell Jar*, Susan Sontag's *The Benefactor*, Kurt Vonnegut's *Cat's Cradle*, Pierre Boulle's *Planet of the Apes* (in Xan Fielding's translation), John Hawkes' *Second Skin*, Thomas Pynchon's *V* and John le Carré's *The Spy Who Came in from the Cold* are published.

January. The Durrells have a telephone installed at the Mazet Michel but only for outgoing calls; those incoming are taken by appointment at a local café.

January 21. The BBC Third Programme broadcasts the first part of the "Conversations with Lawrence Durrell", recorded with D. G. Bridson in France.

January 28. BBC Third Programme broadcasts the second part.

January 29. The American poet Robert Frost dies at the age of 89 and is buried in Old Bennington Cemetery (behind the Old First Congregational Church), Vermont. The BBC Third Programme broadcasts LD

---

[34] GB, 305, says that this is LD's first visit to Greece in ten years, though he had been there in 1955 (see entry for July 3); IMN doesn't mention this Athens sojourn.

reading a selection of his own poetry.

[1963]

February. In New York, Dutton publishes *Lawrence Durrell and Henry Miller: A Private Correspondence*, edited by George Wickes, to generally positive reviews. (See entry for May 1963 regarding the British reaction to the book.)

February 5. The BBC Third Programme broadcasts LD reading and discussing poems he likes.

February 11. The American poet Sylvia Plath commits suicide in England at the age of 31 and is buried in the St Thomas à Becket and St Thomas the Apostle churchyard at Heptonstall, West Yorkshire.

February 20. The BBC Third Programme broadcasts an extended version of the Edinburgh Writers' Conference discussion originally broadcast on October 8, 1962 (see entry for that date).

February 27. LD is 51 years old.

March. The Durrells are in Geneva for ten days where Claude is diagnosed with a fibroid condition.

March 4. The influential American poet William Carlos Williams dies in Rutherford, New Jersey at the age of 80 and is buried in the Hillside Cemetery, Lyndhurst.

Early-April. LD sends the manuscript of *An Irish Faustus* to Curtis Brown in London.

April 24. In Geneva, Claude undergoes a successful hysterectomy procedure.

April 26. LD flies from Geneva to Madrid to discuss the *Judith* script with Sophia Loren, who tells him she cannot play an "intellectual"; LD agrees to rewrite the story to fit Loren's "peasant" character.[35]

April 29. LD returns to Geneva, where he and Claude remain at the Hotel Touring-Balances for her post-operative care.

---

[35] GB, 307, has this happening in March. In the film, Loren's character Judith can hardly be described as a "peasant".

May: In London, Faber publishes *Lawrence Durrell – Henry Miller: A Private Correspondence* to generally dismissive and some scathing reviews.

May 14: The Durrells return to the Mazet.

May 21. The Durrells sail from Marseille on the *San Marcos* for Piraeus, then spend time in Spetses with Katsimbalis and the photographer Dimitris Papadimos, and a week on Mykonos, where Claude's liveliness and LD's infectious laughter catch the attention of an American couple, Horst (an immigrant from Germany) and Frances von Maltitz, with whom they briefly chat. Apparently the Americans recognize LD but no introductions are made. They meet again several weeks later on Rhodes where they become fast friends and later, after returning to Athens, they spend a weekend together at Delphi.

July 6. GD establishes the Jersey Wildlife Preservation Trust after ten years of planning.[36] (In 1999 "Conservation" replaced "Preservation".)

Mid-July. The Durrells are back at the Mazet. GD and Jacquie visit for about ten days.

September. The Durrells are in Greece visiting Peggy Glanville-Hicks at her home on Mykonos; Peggy has been commissioned by the San Francisco Opera, with a grant from the Ford Foundation, to write an opera based on LD's verse play *Sappho*.

September 5. The poet Louis MacNeice dies in Hertfordshire at the age of 56 and is buried in the Carrowdore Church of Ireland churchyard in Lisnevin, Co. Down, Northern Ireland.

September 11. Bernard Spencer is found dead on a railroad track in a suburb of Vienna, a possible suicide.

Early October. George Seferis wins the Nobel Prize in Literature, the first Greek to do so.

October 7. Gustaf Gründgens dies in a hotel room in Manila — the circumstances are not unsuspicious — and is buried at the Ohlsdorf Cemetery in Hamburg.

Mid-October. Ursula Schuh, wife of the new Schauspielhaus intendant in

---

[36] IMN, 542, misdates this as 1964.

Hamburg, finishes translating *An Irish Faustus* for the production planned by Gründgens.

[1963]

November. The PEN anthology that LD agreed to edit is published by Hutchinson in London as *New Poems 1963: A PEN Anthology of Contemporary Poetry.*[37]

November 11. In London, Faber publishes *An Irish Faustus.*

November 22. US President John F. Kennedy is assassinated in Dallas, Texas under still unexplained circumstances. Aldous Huxley dies in Los Angeles at the age of 69 under the influence of a heavy dose of LSD to help him on the way and to escape the pain ravaging him from throat cancer. The Irish author of the children's series *The Chronicles of Narnia*, C. S. Lewis, dies at the age of 65 in Oxford, England, and is buried there in the Holy Trinity Churchyard.

First week in December. Katsimbalis and the Fieldings visit the Mazet.

c. December 7. On the way to Hamburg the Durrells fly to Paris to visit the Blokhs where they come up with the name Oscar Epfs for the painter of LD's oils and watercolours for an exhibition that Nadia Blokh wants to organize. They also meet David Gascoyne, who is again down on his luck.

c. December 10. The Durrells are in Hamburg for revisions and rehearsals of *An Irish Faustus*;[38] LD refuses to change the name of the protagonist to Morienus, as he had been urged to do in order to forestall comparisons with Goethe's *Faust.*[39]

December 18. The Durrells are in Hamburg for the opening of *An Irish Faustus* at the Deutsche Schauspielhaus with Will Quadflieg as Faust.

---

[37] PEN International, founded in London in 1921, defends the interests and rights of authors, including journalists, and has numerous national branches around the world. The letters of the name are said to stand for Poets and Playwrights /Essayists and Editors/Novelists.

[38] This may be the visit that GB, 299, confuses with the 1961 trip to Hamburg (see the latter part of the entry for November 12, 1961, with accompanying note, and the entry for November 24).

[39] IMN, 536. GB, 309, has LD agreeing to the change.

Time magazine reports that LD is booed off the stage (January 3, 1964),[40] *The Times* (London) prints an enthusiastic review; *The New York Times* reports that despite a few catcalls the cast, director and author are cheered for 20 minutes.[41]

December 21. The General Director of the San Francisco Opera writes to Glanville-Hicks that the piano score of Sappho is unacceptable. Glanville-Hicks agreed to revise the score in an orchestra version, which she does dating the new version October 24 1965; it is almost identical to the piano score. Deteriorating eyesight resulting from an undiagnosed brain tumour precludes the composer from further work on the opera and it remains unperformed *in toto* until 2012. (See the entry for July 10– 20, 2012.)

December 25. With Alan and Ella Thomas the Durrells spend an "improvised" Christmas in Hamburg before flying to Paris.[42]

December 31. The Durrells are in Paris with Eléonore Hirt (actress) and Antonio Vargas (stage designer), both of the Jean-Louis Barrault company, to celebrate at Fauchon, one of the best-known restaurants in Paris.[43]

1964

Saul Bellow's *Herzog*, Gore Vidal's *Julian*, Ralph Ellison's *Shadow and Act* and Len Deighton's *Funeral in Berlin* are published. Brian Friel's play *Philadelphia, Here I Come!* is first performed in Dublin.

Faber publishes LD's *Acte: A Play*; later in the year Imo Moszkowicz directs a filmed version for West German television with LD credited as the writer and featuring Arno Assmann and Elizabeth Orth. Rupert Hart-Davis publishes GD's *Menagerie Manor* in London. Faber publishes

[40] Perhaps the *Time* editors confused LD with Henry James! James was booed when he came on the stage after the première London performance of his play, *Guy Domville*, in 1895; this discouraged James from writing plays for performance.

[41] Curiously, Quadflieg makes no mention of his role in his memoirs, *Wir spielen immer.*

[42] GB, 310–11, has the Durrells on Jersey for the annual family holiday.

[43] GB, 311, has Vargas as an actor.

LD's *Selected Poems 1935–1963*. The Cypriot poet Costas Montis publishes *Kleistes portes* (*Closed Doors*) with the subtitle "An Answer to Lawrence Durrell's *Bitter Lemons*". The Belgian French-language radio network broadcasts a programme on LD by Daniel Gillès and Jean Antoin in the series *L'Œil écoute*.

[1964]

January. *London Magazine* prints LD's homage to his recently dead friend from Cairo and Alexandria, Bernard Spencer.[44] LD continues work on *The Placebo*.

January–February. LD paints several oils for the Paris exhibition (see entry for c. December 7, 1963).

c. January 4. From Paris the Durrells return to the Mazet and a mistral-whipped snowstorm.

January 24. Louisa Durrell dies in a Bournemouth nursing home. Claude, LD, Jacquie and GD fly to England for the funeral, which Ella and Alan Thomas also attend.

January 31. Radio–Télévision Française, Canal I, broadcasts "Chez Lawrence Durrell" with a script by F.-J. Temple.

February 27. LD is 52 years old.

March 6. The Oscar Epfs exhibition of paintings opens at the Galerie Connaître at 36 rue des Saints-Pères (Paris). At the vernissage, Mary Mollo Hadkinson plays the role of the painter's sister, LD is there as himself to represent his good friend the artist, who was stuck deep in the darkest of Africas, or a shepherd in the hills of Greece, or any of several stories LD told. The show makes £60 and closes on March 21.

c. March 20. *Elle* magazine prints the news that Epfs is really LD, who suspects that Miriam Cendrars (daughter of Blaise), who works for the magazine, leaked the fact.

Late March. LD hears a rumour from Crete that he helped import arms to Cyprus for the Turks and that if he ever showed up on Crete he'd be taken care of by some of "the boys". He quickly writes a letter to *The*

---

[44] Reprinted in LD, *From the Elephants Back*, 247–53.

Times (London) in support of *Enosis* (*Union* of Cyprus with Greece).[45]

April 7. Alfred Perlès and his wife write to LD from Crete, where they are living, that there is nothing to the rumour of a threat to LD's life.

End April.[46] The Durrells drive the fairly new blue Opel van to the Brindisi ferry, where they meet Joan and Peter Bird, the latter on leave from his job as military attaché at the British Embassy in Oslo, and they arrive on Corfu as the first stop on a tour of Greece. At a seaside rental house in Paleokastritsa, escaping a drunken argument with her husband, Claude falls and fractures two ribs, whereupon they cancel the tour and remain on Corfu where they meet the Athinaios family at the White House in Kalami. LD, Anastasios ("Totsa") Athinaios and Niko the schoolteacher visit the Saint Arsenius shrine. LD spends a night in his old bedroom at the White House.

May 22. LD's letter supporting *Enosis* appears in *The Times* (London).

June. Jacquie and GD come to Corfu from Jersey for a week.

July. Judith is being filmed in Israel. LD refuses an invitation to be there, disgusted by the changes in the screenplay; but see the entry for August 16 below.

c. July 11. The Durrells go to Athens to pick up Sappho, and Claude's children, Barry and Diana (for their first holiday in Greece), and visit friends.

c. July 16. LD sees Seferis for what turns out to be the last time.[47]

July 18. The Durrells return to Corfu with the children.

August 16. LD flies to Israel to make a short TV programme for CBS with Sophia Loren to hype the movie *Judith*, despite his earlier misgivings.

[45] Reprinted in LD, *Endpapers and Inklings*.
[46] GB, 312. IMN, 539, has the departure as May 7, which seems impossible. DB, 319, notes that GD and Jacquie joined LD and Claude on Corfu but had returned to Jersey by May 2 when GD wrote a letter to Alan Thomas from there.
[47] IMN, 540, does not mention Seferis meeting LD. On July 19, Seferis wrote to LD, "It was good to see you the other day" (Beaton, *George Seferis*, 483). GB, 312–13, puts this meeting on Corfu, and therefore after July 18 (see next entry), but it took place in Athens.

End of summer. Daphne and Xan Fielding move into a rented house north of Uzès, some 15 miles up the Engances road from the Mazet.

Autumn. The current edition of *Two Cities* prints LD's letters to Jean Fanchette, upsetting some of LD's friends, who claim the young man is taking advantage of the writer's fame.[48]

September 18. The Irish playwright and autobiographer Seán O'Casey dies at the age of 80 and is buried at the Golders Green Crematorium.

Early October. The Swedish Academy awards Jean-Paul Sartre (France) Nobel Prize in Literature; he refuses to accept it.

c. November 1. The Durrells are in Paris to read the proofs of the French version of LD's *Selected Poems* published by Gallimard.

November 13. In Paris, LD lectures for twenty minutes at the opening session of a three-day UNESCO celebration of the 400th anniversary of the birth of Shakespeare, the invitation arranged by Alex Blokh, for which LD is paid $750.[49] The session also features Jorge Luis Borges and Giuseppe Ungaretti; other presenters at the event include Jean Vilar, Peter Brook, Ian Holm, Peggy Ashcroft, Christopher Fry, Kenneth Tynan, Akira Kurosawa, and Georges Sadoul.

December. The Christmas holidays are spent at the Mazet with Catha Aldington, Temple and the Fieldings.

December 31. Claude is rushed to a local hospital with a burst appendix.

1965

Jerzy Kosiński's *The Painted Bird* is published. John Osborne's *A Patriot for Me* and Samuel Beckett's *Come and Go* are given their first performances. Olivia Manning's third volume of the Balkan trilogy, *Friends and Heroes*, is published in London.

January 4. T. S. Eliot, Nobel 1948, dies of emphysema in London at the age of 77 and is buried in the village cemetery at St. Michael's Church in

---

[48] The letters were eventually published by Fanchette as LD, *Letters to Jean Fanchette.*
[49] What appear to be two different lectures are printed as one in English under the title "L'Amour, Clef du Mystère?" in *From the Elephant's Back*, 149–76.

East Coker, the village from which his ancestors had emigrated to America. At the memorial service in Westminster Abbey the frail and ill Ezra Pound unexpectedly appears from Italy.

January 24. Winston Churchill, Nobel 1953, dies at the age of 91and is buried in the family plot at St Martin's Church, Bladon, near Woodstock, not far from his birthplace at Blenheim Palace.

February 6. LD writes to Miller that he has begun a "novel of sorts" but doesn't know "where it is going yet", probably referring to "Dactyl" the third incomplete draft of what eventually became *Tunc.*[50]

February 27. LD is 53 years old.

Spring. Faber commissions G. S. Fraser (one of the Cairo rivals to Alexandria in the mock poetry duel[51]) to write a critical study of LD and suggests Alan Thomas might edit a volume of LD's travel letters.[52]

April. In Paris, *Preuves* prints LD's personal essay on T. S. Eliot.

May. The *Atlantic Monthly* prints LD's warm tribute to Eliot in English.[53]

May 1. LD estimates he's completed one third of *Tunc.*

Summer. The Durrells and the children live in a rented villa on the shore in Paleokastritsa, Corfu, as do Mary Mollo Hadkinson, her husband and children. LD meets Ghislaine de Boysson who is staying with Catha Aldington at a nearby hotel. The two women spend time with Claude, but not LD who is either sleeping or drunk.[54] LD travels to Athens to see Austen Harrison, his architect friend from Cyprus. Joan and Peter Bird visit Corfu. LD works with Ernle Bradford on the CBS-TV documentary "Search for Ulysses".[55]

---

[50] *DML*, 405–6.

[51] See the entry for January–February 1944.

[52] Fraser, *Lawrence Durrell: A Critical Study* (1968). Alan Thomas published his compilation of texts as LD, *Spirit of Place* (1969).

[53] Reprinted in *From the Elephant's Back*, 257–67.

[54] GB, 315.

[55] The approximately-50-minute film is available on You-Tube with James Mason reading from the *Odyssey* and Bradford reading the narration, broadcast in 1966. In it LD is shown being interviewed by Bradford on a rocky Corfu coastline claiming

[1965]

Autumn. In the USA, Twayne publishes John A. Weigel's critical analysis, *Lawrence Durrell.* Dutton publishes a paperback edition in 1966.

September. Alan and Ella Thomas are now living in London (Chelsea) and gathering LD materials for the travel book (see entry for 1965, Spring).

Early October. The Swedish Academy awards Mikhail Sholokhov (USSR) the Nobel Prize in Literature.

October 15. The American poet Randall Jarrell dies under suspicious circumstances at the age of 51 and is buried at the New Garden Friends Cemetery, Greensboro, North Carolina.

October 19. The BBC TV programme *Intimations,* produced by Margaret McCall, broadcasts Malcolm Muggeridge's interview with LD.[56] McCall and LD become good friends and she later produces a documentary film with him.

c. October 20. LD meets the trapeze artist and friend of painters and poets (Paul Éluard's companion in the late 1940s), Diane Deriaz, on the flight to Paris and invites her to dine at the Closerie des Lilas. In her memoirs, she notes that, having resisted an invitation to spend the night at the Hôtel Royale, they remain "platonic" friends for the rest of his life.[57]

October 27. The BBC radio program *Midday Dialogue* broadcasts an interview with LD on his poetry, recorded earlier in the Mazet by Margaret McCall.

November. Katsimbalis and his wife visit the Mazet.

November 15. Alan Ross in London offers to publish Claude's translation of Marc Peyre's *The Captive of Zour.*

December. LD finally sees the direction for the new novel (*Tunc*) and

Ulysses landed there before going on to his home on Ithaca.

[56] An extract from the interview can be heard on the BBC–British Library CD "The Spoken Word: Lawrence Durrell" (2012).

[57] Deriaz, *La Tête à l'envers.* See also Cowling, *Visiting Picasso,* 73–6, 101, 347. As Richard Pine has pointed out to me, Deriaz offered a rather different scenario in her interview on the BBC "Smile in the Mind's Eye" in which she gave strong indication that she slept with him: "He wasn't playing cards in bed!" (personal communication).

begins writing it for the fourth time. Yehudi and Diana Menuhin visit the Mazet.

December 16. W. Somerset Maugham dies at the age of 91 in Nice on the Côte d'Azur and his ashes are scattered near the Maugham Library, at The King's School, Canterbury.

December 19. Charles de Gaulle defeats François Mitterrand in the French presidential elections.

1966

Thomas Pynchon's *The Crying of Lot 49*, Friedrich Dürrenmatt's *Der Meteor*, Margaret Atwood's *The Circle Game*, Bernard Malamud's *The Fixer*, Truman Capote's *In Cold Blood*, Marcel Pagnol's *Jean de Florette* and *Manon des Sources*, Mikhail Bulgakov's *The Master and Margarita* and Jean Rhys' *Wide Sargasso Sea* are published.

Faber publishes LD's *The Ikons and Other Poems* and *Sauve Qui Peut*. In London, Collins brings out GD's *Two in the Bush* and Alan Ross publishes Claude's translation of Marc Peyre's *The Captive of Zour*, with a preface by LD. John Fowles publishes the first version of his novel *The Magus*, said by some critics to be influenced by LD's writings, most especially *The Alexandria Quartet*.

February 11. LD contributes to a programme on "Roy Campbell et la Provence" on a Marseille–Provence radio station.

February 27. LD is 54 years old.

Spring. At an auction in Paris, Claude buys Mme Tarte's house in Sommières for £6,000; it is located a short walk from the river Vidourle and across the water from the walled town.[58]

March 10. The Irish writer, Frank O'Connor, dies in Dublin from a heart attack at the age of 61 and is buried in Deansgrange Cemetery there.

April 1. Appropriate to the day, the Irish writer Flann O'Brien (Brian Ó Nualláin) dies in Dublin at the age of 55 and is buried at Deansgrange

---

[58] GB, 314, implies this took place in the spring of 1965.

Cemetery there.

[1966]

April 10. Evelyn Waugh dies at the age of 62 of heart failure at his Combe Florey home in Somerset, and is buried in the grounds of what was then his own home, Combe Florey House, in the village of Combe Florey, next to the boundary with the Anglican churchyard of St Peter and St Paul.

May. Abandoning the fourth attempt at the novel *Tunc*, LD begins anew.

May 18. After dining privately with LD in Paris the previous week to discuss the matter of the 1962 Commonwealth Immigrants Act's effect on LD's citizenship (the Act made him a UK Subject but not a Citizen of the UK), which in turn meant he would have to apply for a visa each time he wished to enter the UK. LD's friend the Ambassador Sir Patrick Reilly writes to the Foreign Office and the Home Secretary protesting the application of the Act's provisions to LD. After consulting with the Home Office, the FO informs Reilly that no exception can be made in LD's case, but that LD could become a Citizen by residing in the UK for five consecutive years. The Marseille consulate offers him a situation that would require his occasional appearance there over a five year period obviating the necessity for UK residence. LD declines and, in fact, the situation causes him no problems in the future.[59]

Summer. The Durrells have central heating installed and organize significant renovations on the Sommières house under Claude's direction. Sappho visits for the summer. GD and Jacquie on Corfu are appalled by the effects of mass tourism; they sign a two-year lease with LD for the Mazet Michel. LD and Claude drive the new VW microbus, named L'Escargot, to Brindisi and ferry across to Corfu for several weeks, where they are visited by Frances and Horst von Maltitz, whom they had met on Rhodes in 1963, and Joan and Peter Bird. LD becomes seriously attracted to Joan.[60]

---

[59] For excerpts from Reilly's letter to the FO, see John Ezard, "Durrell fell foul of migrant law" in *The Guardian*, April 28, 2002. Michael Haag provided the details of the matter as above (private communication).

[60] GB, 324, has the purchase of the camper being made in May 1967.

June 14. LD attends a dinner in his honour at the British Embassy in Paris, hosted by his old friend Sir Patrick Reilly; the dinner celebrates the publication of a French translation of LD's poems and is attended by the Duke of Windsor (the former British king, Edward VIII), and other dignitaries.

July 15. The Durrells now officially change their address to Mme Tarte's house at 15 route de Saussine, Sommières.

End July. Eve McClure Miller, Henry's lovely fourth ex-wife, dies at the age of 35 after an unsuccessful battle with alcohol in California.

August. LD is now seriously working on *Tunc.*

September. The Durrells move into their Sommières house.

September 28. In Paris, the Pope of Surrealism André Breton dies at the age of 70 and is buried in the Cimetières des Batignolles.

Early October. The Swedish Academy jointly awards Nelly Sachs (a German Jew in exile in Sweden) and S. Y. Agnon (Israel) the Nobel Prize in Literature.

Mid-November. LD writes to Miller that he has reached the halfway mark with *Tunc* but is clearly having trouble with the text.

Late November. LD and Claude make grand plans for "a real English Christmas" at their home in Sommières with the Thomases, Catha Aldington, Mary Mollo Hadkinson and her family, GD and Jacquie, and Theodore Stephanides.

November 26. The Thomases and Stephanides plan to drive together from London to Sommières.

December 5. Anaïs Nin writes at length to LD about her relationship with him, Miller and Perlès, and threatens to tell all when her diary is published. It is not clear why she thinks it is necessary to make what appears to be this threat.

Early December. Penelope marries the actor, Peter Ellis Jones, but tells her father and GD about it too late for them to travel to England to attend the ceremony. In any case LD is too preoccupied to pay much attention to the event.

December 9. LD cancels the holiday celebration and takes Claude, who has been in ill health for months, to Geneva to see specialists. She has cancer and does not leave the Swiss city alive.

December 22. LD writes to Alan Thomas that Claude is improving.

1967

Cecil Day-Lewis is appointed Poet Laureate of the United Kingdom. William Styron's *The Confessions of Nat Turner*, Naguib Mahfouz' *Miramar* (giving a decidedly non-Durrellian view of Alexandria), Gabriel García Márquez' *One Hundred Years of Solitude* and Chaim Potok's *The Chosen* are published. Tom Stoppard's *Rosencrantz and Gildenstern Are Dead* is given its première performance.

Oxford University Press publishes Wallace Southam's musical setting of LD's poem "Lesbos", adapted for voice and piano by Patrick (Pat) Smythe, a four-page broadsheet publication.

George Weidenfeld and Nicholson in London and Putnam in New York publish Alan Thomas's book, *Fine Books*, dedicated to Ella.

January 1. Claude-Marie Vincendon Durrell dies in the Geneva hospital at the age of 42. LD is devastated. He keeps Claude's ashes in a bedroom at the Sommières house until 1975.[61] He refuses to allow his daughters to come to Geneva or Sommières for the funeral. He stops the hands of the wall clock in the house at 7:10, the time of Claude's death, and does not reset them.

February 22. A 35-minute British TV show called *Stiff Upper Lip* directed by Michael Mills, with Giles Cooper listed as writer and LD credited with the "story", is broadcast by BBC in its *The Sound of Laughter* series.

February 23. LD closes the Sommières house and goes to London to stay with Alan Thomas whose wife has gone missing earlier in the month (she is never found and, after a period of time, is presumed dead). They console each other and work.

---

[61] See LD's brief elegy on Claude's death written some fifteen years later in *A Smile in the Mind's Eye*, 32–3; and see the entry for December 1975.

146

February 27. The widower LD is 55 years old.

Early March. LD travels from London to Paris to stay with the Blokhs.

April. Sappho and Claude's son Barry arrive in Sommières for longer visits and Diana visits on weekends from Geneva, where she is working. The Fieldings come over from Uzès often. In Athens a group of colonels inflicts a coup d'état on the Greek people and installs a repressive military dictatorship.

May. LD drives L'Escargot to Corfu with Margaret McCall after sending the completed manuscript of *Tunc* with Peter and Joan Bird to Juliet O'Hea in London. In Athens, McCall discusses making a film with Katsimbalis and LD, including Henry Miller should he be in Greece.

May 12. The former British poet laureate John Masefield dies at the age of 89 from a gangrene infection and his ashes are placed in Poets' Corner in Westminster Abbey.

Summer. On Corfu, LD stays at the Zefiros Beach Hotel and tours the island; he learns that Athinaios has committed suicide and his widow has left Kalami. GD and Jacquie also register at the hotel, while making the film *The Garden of the Gods* with Stephanides. LD paints pictures of Corfu scenes. McCall and LD return to Athens to talk to Katsimbalis about the film.

September. Plans are made for another Oscar Epfs exhibition in a Paris gallery.

September 10. The 78-year-old Miller marries his fifth wife, the 28-year old Hiroko (Hoki) Tokuda, a piano player and bar singer with an extensive family in California. They make an agreement that specifies that they do not sleep together.

September 20. An exhibition of Miller's watercolours opens in Paris attended by the artist and his new platonic wife, LD, the Blokhs and McCall. Joan and Peter Bird are also in Paris where Joan's refusal to allow LD to father a child with her results in a break in the friendship of several years. LD, Brassaï and Perlès participate in filming a documentary directed by Robert Snyder called *The Henry Miller Odyssey* along the streets and in the cafés of Paris. The film, in which both LD and Perlès play very small roles, is released in 1969 and is now available on YouTube.

[1967]

October. Miller, Hoki, Jean Renoir, Miriam Cendrars and the Perlèses meet in Sommières for a grand reunion, filmed by the team making the *Odyssey.* The proofs of *Tunc* arrive with word that Juliet O'Hea at Curtis Brown has sold the book in seven countries. During the filming in Nîmes, they meet Simone Perier, a pretty admirer of Miller's who becomes LD's good friend. Hoki rather blatantly pursues LD, who returns to Paris with the Millers, where he sees Miriam Cendrars and stays with the Blokhs in their Parc Montsouris apartment, reminding him of the days in that quarter with Nancy in 1937–38.

Early October. The Swedish Academy awards Miguel Angel Asturias (Guatemala) the Nobel Prize in Literature.

October 9. William Styron's *The Confessions of Nat Turner* is published to great acclaim and intense controversy.

November. Visits by the Fieldings, the Temples, and Miriam Cendrars give LD a social life in Sommières as he works on *Nunquam.*

December. LD tells Miller he is writing the text for a musical called *Smoke* and plans to send it to Hoki to score.[62] Sappho, Penelope, Barry and Diana are in Sommières for the holidays.

---

[62] *DML,* 423. The relation, if any, between this project and the musical *Ulysses Come Back* is unclear (see the entries for May 7 and Summer, 1968).

FRANCE ALONE : 1968–1971

1968

Norman Mailer's *Armies of the Night*, Aleksandr Solzhenitsyn's *The Cancer Ward* and *The First Circle* and Philip K. Dick's *Do Androids Dream of Electric Sheep?* are published.

Faber publishes a revised edition of LD's *Collected Poems*. Collins in London brings out GD's *The Donkey Rustlers* and *Rosie is My Relative*. Collins also brings out Jacquie Durrell's memoir, *Beasts in My Bed*.

January 1. LD reads the proofs of G. S. Fraser's book on his oeuvre and is happy with the text.

February 27. LD is 56 years old.

End February–early March. LD is in London for PR work anticipating the publication of *Tunc*. He stays with Alan Thomas with whom he drives from London to Leicester to attend an Arts Festival organized by Fraser (who is teaching at the university there) where LD appears on a panel "Poets in Person" with Richard Hughes.

March 10. LD flies to Montreal for interviews and other public relations work.[1]

March 14. LD lands in Los Angeles on his first visit to the USA and is driven to Pacific Palisades to visit Miller for two weeks, during which time he sees the Forest Lawn Cemetery and cuckholds Miller with Hoki.[2]

March 20. LD visits Disneyland with Hoki and several others.

March 28. LD flies to New York to promote *Tunc* where he meets Tambimuttu, now living in Manhattan. He stays at the Algonquin Hotel, meets Marianne Moore at the Gotham Bookstore and has a reunion with Thérèse Epstein Marberry whom he hasn't seen since Paris before the

---

[1] GB, 330, has him leaving London for the USA on March 12 and makes no mention of the Montreal stop.
[2] According to GB, 331.

War when they had a brief but intense love affair.

[1968]

April. In London, Faber publishes *Tunc: A Novel*, dedicated to Claude, to mixed reviews.

April 1. LD gives a reading at the 92nd Street Young Men's Hebrew Association (YMHA).

April 4. A paid assassin murders Martin Luther King Jr. in Memphis, Tennessee.

April 9. Riots in American cities take place following King's assassination.

April 12. LD is back in London.

May 7. Student riots begin in Paris and spread beyond the city limits; the "days of rage" begin that will threaten the de Gaulle government. LD begins work on a musical play called *Ulysses Come Back*.[3]

Mid-May. Hoki visits Sommières for additional cuckolding, but refuses to write the music to LD's play.[4]

May 17. Another 30-minute British TV show called *Stiff Upper Lip*, based on LD's Antrobus stories, written by Barry Took, and directed by Michael Mills, is shown on BBC TV, in its *Comedy Playhouse* season.[5]

Summer. LD remains in Sommières to work on *Nunquam*.[6] Margaret McCall visits to plan a BBC film entitled "Lawrence Durrell's Paris", and takes care of household business formerly dealt with by Claude. LD meets Claudine Brelet, an anthropologist-photographer, whose charm and enthusiasm lift his spirits. After work on *Nunquam* in the mornings,

[3] GB, 335, calls it "Ulysses Comes Home."

[4] GB, 334. IMN makes no mention of this visit.

[5] Richard Vernon as Sir Reginald Polk-Mowbray, Michael Bates as Antrobus and Bernard Bresslaw as the embassy footman. Took was a veteran TV writer who organized the team that produced *Monty Python's Flying Circus* (1969–74).

[6] DB, 345, has LD visiting his brother on Corfu during the late summer, along with Alan and "Shirley Thomas" (DB should have said "Shirley Calentano", as she and Alan did not marry until 1970), David Hughes and Mai Zetterling, Xan and Daphne Fielding, and LD's sister, Margo.

LD continues work on the *Ulysses* musical in the afternoons.

June. Diane Deriaz visits Sommières and they remain friends despite her rejection of his offer of a job as secretary and bed-partner.

June 6. A deranged assassin murders Democratic Party presidential candidate, New York U. S. Senator, Robert F. Kennedy, in Los Angeles.

July 7. Diana Menuhin writes a highly critical letter to LD about *Tunc*.[7]

Last week in July. GD and Jacquie set off by car for Corfu, where they spend the next two months, entertaining friends and writing a draft screenplay for *My Family and Other Animals* with Peter Bull (an LD actor friend from before the War in London). Albert Finney had expressed interest in making the movie, but it is never produced.

Autumn. LD travels to London to see Arthur Guirdham. When he returns to Sommières he finds the house has been burgled and books and paintings (but not his own, as he ruefully admits) have been stolen. He obtains a pistol to protect his property.[8] On Corfu GD experiences a mental and emotional breakdown brought on by the pressures of the zoo, his heavy drinking and depression about what development has done to Corfu, for which he feels partly to blame.[9]

September. Patrick and Joan Leigh Fermor visit Sommières.

September 23. LD and McCall are in Paris to work on the BBC film.

Early October. The Swedish Academy awards Yasunari Kawabata (Japan) the Nobel Prize in Literature. LD is again in Paris for the BBC film.

December 20. John Steinbeck, Nobel 1962, dies in New York aged 66.

Late December. LD spends Christmas in London helping McCall edit the BBC film, staying with Alan Thomas and his new companion, the American Shirley Calentano.

---

[7] GB, 335. The letter is in the Durrell Collection at Southern Illinois University at Carbondale. In it she tells him he is essentially running in neutral and that the characters in no way matched the depths and breadths of the Alexandrians. He needs to refresh his well of creativity and reinvigorate his soul.

[8] IMN, 567; GB, 350, has this happening in 1972.

[9] There is every reason to believe, and little to doubt, that the word "developer" should more accurately be spelled "devil-oper."

1969

Vladimir Nabokov's *Ada or Ardor: A Family Chronicle*, John Fowles' *The French Lieutenant's Woman*, Mario Puzo's *The Godfather* and Philip Roth's *Portnoy's Complaint* are published.

Collins in London brings out GD's *Birds, Beasts and Relatives*. Early in the year GD is quietly admitted to a private clinic in Roehampton, London, to treat his depression.

February. Claudine Brelet visits LD in Sommières and together they see similarities between her and Claude.

February 16. LD writes to Miller that he has moved *Nunquam* to within 50 pages of completion.

February 27. LD is 57 years old.

March 27. The German writer known as B. Traven dies somewhere in Mexico and at unknown age.

April 4. LD pronounces *Nunquam* finished.

Easter Sunday. LD and Sappho, with Claude's children Barry and Diana Forde, ride horses in the Camargue.

Mid-April. LD travels to Geneva to have a cyst removed from his ear.

April 28. De Gaulle resigns as president of France as a result of the social turmoil in the country stemming from the May 1968 riots.

End April. Alan Thomas and Shirley Calentano travel to Sommières for a visit; they return to London with LD's archives and the manuscript of *Nunquam* for Juliet O'Hea at Curtis Brown.

May. The French version of *Tunc* appears in a translation by Roger Giroux. In London Faber publishes LD's *Spirit of Place: Letters and Essays on Travel* (edited by Alan Thomas with his commentary).

May 11. Margaret McCall's "Lawrence Durrell's Paris" is shown on BBC television in the *Omnibus* series (which ran from 1967 until 2003).

May 25. With Margaret McCall, LD leaves Sommières for Greece to see if a film about the country would be feasible. In the end they decide against it, possibly due to the colonels' repressive dictatorship.

Summer. The French actress Jeanne Moreau is in the USA to shoot the movie *Monte Walsh*; she dines with Anaïs Nin and Henry Miller, and later tells a biographer, "Regrettably I never met his friend Lawrence Durrell. I was a great admirer of his books. In fact, so much that I nicknamed my Rolls 'Justine', after one of the women in his *Alexandria Quartet*."[10]

June. In New York, Dutton publishes *Spirit of Place*.

August 6. The unfortunate Hollywoodized movie *Justine* opens to appropriate blasts from the critics. The fine actor Dirk Bogarde, who plays Pursewarden in this travesty, later called it a "disasterous [*sic*] mess they made of Durrell's *Justine*, in which I was, sadly, involved".[11]

Mid-August. Thérèse Epstein Mayberry visits Sommières for a week. She warns LD not to see the film, and he doesn't — fortunate fellow!

August 14. Leonard Woolf dies in London at the age of 89.

September 1. McCall and Diane Deriaz arrive in Sommières to make a short documentary, *The Lonely Roads*, for the BBC and Bavarian television networks, with LD and Deriaz discussing various matters more or less relating to the concept of freedom exemplified by the life of a local tramp called Blanco. Deriaz interviews LD about various matters including *Tunc*. He responds with a convoluted explanation of his concerns expressed in the book, such as the destruction of Western culture, the

---

[10] Quoted in Gray, *La Moreau*, 126.

[11] Coldstream, *Ever, Dirk*, 221. See also Henry Miller's response in the entry for September 3, 1969. Bogarde also complained about Anouk Aimée, who played Justine: "I worked with her on a disaster called 'Justine'. She pissed off and left us floundering for the final three weeks: we used double and 'outakes' to get through and neither Cukor nor I ever forgave her. Nor did Mr Durrell, as I recall" (Bogarde to Lee Langley, September 9, 1991, in Coldstream, *Ever, Dirk*, 414). LD too spoke disparagingly about the movie version of *Justine*, a year after it appeared, and about his work on the script for the movie *Cleopatra*. Asked if he had been consulted about the script for *Justine*, he replied, "No. There's no point in that. They changed it so frequently I would have had to waste my time reading all that jibberish [*sic*]. It is jibberish, film scripts, you know. It is work for a semi-literate, and often these scripts they send you might have been done by some mentally demented infant" (Haller, "The writer and Hollywood").

notion of freedom as an illusion, etc.[12] The filming goes on throughout the month.[13]

September 3. Henry Miller writes from California that the movie *Justine* is incomprehensible — a judgement with which it is difficult to disagree.

Early October. The Swedish Academy awards Samuel Beckett (Ireland) the Nobel Prize in Literature.

October 21. The influential novelist and poet Jack Kerouac dies at the age of 47 of alcohol and ennui; he is buried in Lowell, Massachusetts.

December 11. LD's old friend from the Corfu days, Constant Zarian dies at the age of 84 in Yerevan, Armenia, USSR.

Mid-December. LD and Alan Thomas produce a limited signed edition of *An Irish Faustus.*

December 31. LD is in Paris to spend the old year's ending with Eléonore Hirt, where they drink a toast to Miller at the Café du Dôme.

1970

Albert Camus' *La mort heureuse*, Anna Kavan's *Julia and the Bazooka* and Graham Greene's *Travels with My Aunt* are published.

At some point, Anaïs Nin lunches with Edmund Wilson at the Princeton Club in New York to show him the passages of her soon-to-be-published diary which concern him. In his own diary he noted, "We talked about current French and English books and agreed about many things — notably Lawrence Durrell: that the good thing in *The Alexandria Quartet* was his lavish and colorful word-painting. She thought that he had gone over so well in America because this kind of rather lush writing was a relief from the plainness and bleakness of the Hemingway kind of thing."[14]

Early in the year. Shirley Calentano's husband sues Alan Thomas for

---

[12] LD's explanation is excerpted in Pine's introduction to LD, *The Placebo*, 68.

[13] See also the entry for March 21, 1970.

[14] Wilson, *The Sixties*, 864.

alienating the affections of his wife; the court clears Thomas of all charges and grants Shirley a divorce, shortly after which Alan and Shirley marry. LD sells the bulk of his papers to Southern Illinois University at Carbondale; with the funds from the sale he has a swimming pool installed at the foot of the garden behind the Sommières house.

January–February. Wallace Southam visits Sommières for a week to write the music to LD's lyrics for the *Ulysses* musical.

January 10. The American poet and teacher Charles Olson dies of liver cancer and alcohol at the age of 59 in New York and is buried in the Beechbrook Cemetery at Gloucester, Massachusetts.

February 2. Bertrand Russell, Nobel 1950, dies in Penrhyndeudrath, Wales, at the age of 98.

February 17. S. Y. Agnon, Nobel co-winner 1966, dies in Jerusalem at the age of 82.

February 27. LD is 58 years old. Miller writes that he and Hoki have separated.

End February. LD flies from Marseille to London for a few weeks' public relations work on the publication of *Nunquam.* He stays with Alan and Shirley Thomas and sees much of the now aging Stephanides.

Early March. In London, Faber publishes *Nunquam: A Novel,* dedicated to Claude, to mixed reviews. LD appears on several radio programmes hawking the book.

March 17. LD flies to New York to do more public relations events, stays at the Algonquin Hotel, gives interviews and hangs out at the Grand Central Station Oyster Bar. He meets Miller's actress-singer friend, Fiddle Viracola, who falls in love with him; she squires him around Manhattan as well as Brooklyn and Staten Island. Together they fly to Chicago for interviews and book signings and listen to the city's special brand of the blues in clubs, after which they return to Manhattan.[15]

March 21. BBC TV broadcasts *The Lonely Roads.*[16]

---

[15] IMN, 574–5. GB, 342, has the meeting with Fiddle taking place in Chicago.

[16] Margaret McCall's notes on the script were published in the Lawrence Durrell

[1970]

March 23. Dutton publishes the American edition of *Nunquam*, the last of LD's works from this publisher. Viking Press will publish most of his future books in the USA.

March 25. LD appears on the BBC TV programme *The Arts This Week*, filmed while he was in London.

Late March – early April. LD returns to Sommières from the USA.

Late April. Fiddle visits Sommières for a week, an event LD tells Miller was "a perfect experience".[17]

May. LD flies to England to take Sappho to visit Derwent College, University of York, where she wishes to enroll. He is interviewed by the student newspaper, *Nouse.*[18]

May 12. The exiled German Jewish poet, Nelly Sachs, Nobel co-winner 1966, dies in Stockholm.

Summer. LD returns to London to record excerpts from *Ulysses Come Back* for an LP of 99 copies produced by Bernard Stone as a demo to send to agents and producers, including Fiddle in New York; nothing comes of this.[19] From London he moves on to Paris to make a film with Michèle Arnaud, a singer turned producer, *Spéciale sur Durrell*, broadcast by ORTF in February the following year. Arnaud convinces LD to write texts for pop songs in French. GD arrives in Sommières for a visit.

June 7. Edward Morgan Forster dies at the age of 91 in Coventry, Warwickshire, England, and is buried in the Canley Garden Cemetery and Crematorium there.[20]

---

special issue of *Twentieth Century Literature* 33/4 (1987).

[17] Letter dated May 12, 1970, *DML*, 440.

[18] "Osric Allen Talks to Lawrence Durrell," *Nouse* (May 28, 1970). Sappho matriculated at York the following autumn.

[19] GB, 342, has this happening on LD's way home from the USA at the end of March or early April. The Durrell Library of Corfu web site has a rehearsal recording for the disk made the day previously with Durrell himself singing the recitative, Belle Gonzalez singing the female parts, Pat Smythe on piano and Jeff Clyne on bass.

[20] Those interested in Forster, Cavafy and Alexandria should see Jeffreys, *The Forster–*

July 9. The BBC broadcasts the documentary film *John Gawsworth: Poet and Editor*, which features LD, Alan Thomas, Kate O'Brien and others.[21]

Summer–Autumn. The Fieldings, Mai Zetterling and James Stern arrive at Sommières together for a visit. Miriam Cendrars films an interview with LD. McCall stops by on her way to Italy, as do Simone Perier and Claude's son Barry, now a naval officer. LD writes songs for Annie Verneuil, a local singer.

Early September. Fiddle arrives in Sommières to help pack Epfs paintings and after a week they drive to Paris for an exhibition at Marthe Nochy's bookshop at 93, rue de Seine.

September 1. François Mauriac, Nobel 1952, dies in Paris at the age of 85 and is buried in the Cimetière de Vemars, Déparatement Val-d'Oise.

Mid-September. After he squires Fiddle around his old haunts and tells her he wants to marry her but is too old, she flies back to New York.[22] With Michèle Arnaud LD discusses making a film to be called *Les amis de Henry Miller*.

September 23. LD's old friend John Gawsworth (b. Terence Ian Fytton Armstrong) dies in London at the age of 58.

September 28. John Dos Passos dies at the age of 74 and is buried in the Yeocomico Episcopal Churchyard, Kinsale, Westmoreland County, Virgina.

September 29. Gilbert Seldes, the influential American editor, cultural critic and historian, dies of heart failure in New York at the age of 77.

Early October. The Swedish Academy awards Aleksandr Solzhenitsyn (Soviet Union) the Nobel Prize in Literature. The Oscar Epfs exhibition

Cavafy Letters, and the relevant chapters in Haag, *Alexandria*..

[21] The version of the film without credits is available on the Durrell Library of Corfu website. In the film, listed as made in 1970, LD tells Alan Thomas that he is going to write an essay on Gawsworth. This is an anachronism, to say the least, because LD published the Gawsworth piece in 1962 (see *Spirit of Place*, 17–23). Perhaps the producers thought it would be a good idea and LD and Alan Thomas agreed, or the producers used footage filmed much earlier, although when Gawsworth appears to greet LD and Thomas he is dressed exactly as he is in the rest of the documentary.

[22] GB, 343, has her flying to Japan for a singing tour.

opens in Paris.

November 25. In Japan, Yukio Mishima commits hara-kiri and is buried in the Tama Cemetery, Fuchu City, Tokyo.

December 25. Sappho and Penelope visit their father in Sommières for Christmas.

1971

Wallace Stegner's *Angel of Repose*, Jerzy Kosiński's *Being There*, E. L. Doctorow's *The Book of Daniel* and V. S. Naipaul's *In a Free State* are published.

Collins in London publishes GD's short stories, *Fillets of Plaice*, the title a sly reference to LD's *Spirit of Place*.

January. LD slides into a depression, trying to organise his thoughts for a new novel.

January 11. The Times (London) publishes LD's review of Curtis Cate's biography of Antoine de Saint-Exupéry.

January 28. LD writes to Miller that he has recently begun "a queer sort of novel about the Gnostic heresies, the Templars etc etc", which he has tentatively entitled "Le Monsieur".

End January. LD travels to Paris to see Michèle Arnaud, the Blokhs and Claudine Brelet, with whom he discusses marriage, though she is already married and has a small daughter. His health continues to deteriorate (eczema, asthma) and depression does not lift.

February 27. LD is 59 years old.

Late February. LD travels to Geneva to have a bad eczema examined. While there he discusses Gnosticism and the Templars with Denis de Rougemont, for whom he arranges a meeting with Arnaud.

Spring-summer. Marc Alyn, a poet and essayist in Uzès, continues a series of interviews with LD he began the previous year, which will appear the following year in French and in 1973 in English as *The Big Supposer*. LD joins a lunch club (in reality a sort of lonely hearts club) in Avignon to learn about the region and its history.[23] He visits Catha Aldington in Les Saintes-Maries-de-la-Mer and is reintroduced to Ghislaine de Boysson. Joan Bird reappears briefly to see him on her way to England from Israel (where her husband Peter is finishing his final tour as military attaché); she worries about LD's drinking.

April. GD and Jacquie move into the Mazet Michel for the summer.

May. GD rents the Mazet for a year and the brothers see each other regularly. LD would like to sell the Mazet. Yoga helps LD give up smoking, but not the excessive drinking. The eczema disappears temporarily.

June. LD travels to London for the publication of *The Red Limbo Lingo: A Poetry Notebook*, not particularly liked by the critics. He visits the Menuhins in Highgate.[24]

June 11. GD tells his brother he cannot afford the asking price to purchase the Mazet Michel but would like to rent it for an additional four years.

June 22. LD travels to York where Sappho is now a student at the University and they create a strange limited edition book called, *On The Suchness of the Old Boy*, poetic text by the father, drawings by the daughter.

End June. LD is in Paris staying with Arnaud where he meets Jacques Lacarrière, a writer on the Gnostics, author of *La cendre et les étoiles.*

July. LD is in Sommières for a month-long visit from Margaret McCall.

August. Eléonore Hirt comes to stay for ten days.

Mid-August. LD travels to Geneva to write a magazine article and discuss the Templars with de Rougemont; meets the beautiful Claude Kiefer, French wife of a Swiss physician and begins a long-term affair.[25]

---

[23] "Imagine lunching twice a fortnight outdoors under a tree with Raimu, Fernandel and company [...] and playing boules afterwards in a beret" (LD to Miller, *DML*, 448).

[24] GB, 345; IMN doesn't mention this.

[25] GB, 344, has this happening during the February visit and the later visit taking place in September.

[1971]

September 20. George Seferis dies in Athens at the age of 71 and is buried at the First Cemetery there.

September 22. At Seferis' funeral, amidst great gusts of weeping and wailing, parts of the crowd spontaneously begins to sing the forbidden music of Theodorakis' setting of Seferis's poem *Arnisi* ("Denial" or "Rejection") until the streets ring with hundreds of voices swelling upward in sadness, denial and resistance.[26] The scene is eerily reminiscent of Katsimbalis singing the Greek national anthem at the funeral of the poet Kostis Palamas during the German occupation in February 1943 (see the entry for that month).

September 23. Having rented an apartment on the shore of Lake Orta, a lovely spot in the northern Italian subalpine lake district west of Lago Maggiore and associated with Robert Browning and Nietzsche, LD reads the obituary of Seferis and sadly writes to Miller, "People have no right to do this to their friends", too many of whom were dying.

September 24. Claude Kiefer arrives for a tryst with LD at Lake Orta, that spot where Nietzsche first talked to Lou Salomé; LD begins to obsessively identify Claude with Lou and himself with the mad German and in part with the poet Rainer Maria Rilke.

Early October. The Swedish Academy awards Pablo Neruda (Chile) the Nobel Prize in Literature.

Late-December. LD and Margaret McCall fly to California for the celebration of Miller's 80th birthday at the UCLA Research Library.

[26] On June 1, 1967, the military Junta banned Theodorakis's music from public performance — even listening to it was forbidden — because of his vehement opposition to the Colonels' regime and association with the Greek Communist Party. The Junta jailed and banished him and his family, then put him in a concentration camp before an international protest movement led to his release and exile in France. He returned to Greece in July 1974 after the Junta was overthrown.

FRANCE WITH GHISLAINE
AND AFTER : 1972–1983

1972

Aleksandr Solzhenitsyn's *August 1914*, Hunter S. Thompson's *Fear and Loathing in Las Vegas* are published. Alan Ayckbourn's *Absurd Person Singular* receives its première performance.

Collins in London publishes GD's *Catch Me a Colobus*.

January. McCall and LD fly from California to Dublin to attend a session on LD organized by Richard Pine at Trinity College and to visit the capital of the country to which LD always claimed a familial relationship.

January 23. They visit Joyce's Martello Tower. The relationship between McCall and LD falls apart when he tells her she's too old for him and that he needs an artist as a lover, while she refuses to divorce her husband and marry him.[1]

End January. They visit the Thomases in Chelsea and continue arguing about themselves.

Mid-February. The Vidourle river floods, filling LD's cellar and damaging part of his library; the electricity is out for several days. Claude Kiefer comes to visit and takes the depressed writer off to the Hôtel Europe in Avignon and then further into the Vaucluse for rehabilitating sensual pleasures.

February 27. LD is 60 years old. To celebrate, he invites friends for champagne and food to help assuage his loneliness. Having given up smoking he finds moderating his alcohol intake difficult and his eczema continues to plague him.

---

[1] The fact that this conundrum makes no sense does not of course preclude its reality: she is too old for him and not an artist, but he wants her to divorce her husband and marry him. This is neither the first nor the last time LD places himself in such a situation. Richard Pine's account of the visit was published as "Lawrence Durrell: A Personal Portrait" in *Deus Loci* NS 13 (2012–2013), 204–8.

[1972]

Spring. Another of LD's French lovers, known to the public only as Buttons (Janine "Jany" Brun), visits; she is 30 years old and apparently employed by the Department of Antiquities at the Sorbonne. LD continues to see Margaret McCall, despite his unforgiveable behaviour toward her in Dublin.

Mid-March. LD is in Paris to visit Alain Bosquet who is translating the *Collected Poems* into French. He meets Eugène Ionesco, whom he finds funnier than his plays, and Simone Lestoquard, a painter from the Languedoc, whom he invites to Sommières. She is knowledgable about the Cathars and at some point they tour the region gathering information for the novel *Monsieur*, the first volume of *The Avignon Quintet*.

End March. LD meets Ludo Chardenon, the expert in the healing properties of herbs, in the Arles market, beginning a warm friendship. Chardenon's herb mixture cures LD's eczema, at least temporarily.

April. Bernard Stone's Turret Books in London publishes *On the Suchness of the Old Boy* in an edition of 226 copies (see the entry for June 22, 1971). Fiddle is touring the Camargue with a friend and stops in Sommières.

April 16. In Zushi, Kanafawa Prefecture, Japan, Yasunari Kawabata, Nobel 1968, perhaps best known in the Anglophone world as the author of *Snow Country* (1937), commits suicide at the age of 73.

May 2. LD is again at Lake Orta awaiting the arrival of Claude Kiefer; they meet at Stresa on Lago Maggiore. LD rents an apartment above a boathouse on Lake Orta, from where they make a trip to the Sacro Monte, another Nietzsche location. When Kiefer returns to Geneva, LD stays on reading, swimming and making notes for *Monsieur*.

May 22. Cecil Day-Lewis dies of pancreatic cancer at the age of 68 and is buried in St Michael's Churchyard, Stinsford, Dorset, at his wish to be interred as close to Thomas Hardy as possible.

Summer. LD visits Catha Aldington at her home in Les Saintes-Maries-de-la-Mer and once again makes the acquaintance of Ghislaine de Boysson.

July. LD's article "The Plant-Magic Man" appears in the Paris edition of the *New York Herald Tribune*, changing Chardenon's fortunes, but not his life style. Temple translates it for publication in the *Midi-Libre*, the daily newspaper of the Gard, the *département* in which Sommières is located.

Autumn. Travel and Leisure magazine publishes "The Poetic Obsession of Dublin", LD's account of his visit to Dublin.[2]

c. September 9. LD is in Paris to meet Alfred and Anne Perlès on their way back to Cyprus. He introduces them to Michèle Arnaud, who he thought might be helpful in getting Perlès's work published in France. LD spends lavishly on the couple for several days, but Anne is contemptuous of Miller and has no use for LD; the feelings are royally returned. After the Perlèses leave Paris, LD spends a few days in the company of Miriam Cendrars.

September 13. LD writes to Miller that he hopes to finish the new novel by the end of the year.

October. James and Tania Stern visit LD in Sommières.

Early October. The Swedish Academy awards Heinrich Böll (Federal Republic of Germany) the Nobel Prize in Literature.

November. Fellow yoga exerciser Yehudi Menuhin visits Sommières and when LD proudly says he can stand on his head in the lotus position for five minutes each morning, the violinist stands on his head in that position *and* plays his fiddle.

First week in December. Claude Kiefer pays a week-long visit to Sommières.

December 11. LD writes to Miller that he has only been able to reach 125 pages of the book, but he has stopped drinking for two extended periods with the help of yoga.

Mid-December. LD works correcting the proofs of *The Black Book* that Faber finally decided to publish in the spring of the following year, 35 years after its first Paris edition.

December 13. The prolific British novelist and essayist, L. P. Hartley dies in London at the age of 77 and is buried in Golders Green Crematorium.

Winter. LD has entertained Ghislaine de Boysson occasionally since

---

[2] Reprinted in LD, *From the Elephant's Back*, 337–45.

1971, but now with increasing frequency as she openly lusts after him, which must please him no end. He accepts a visiting lecturer contract for January-March 1974 at the California Institute of Technology (Caltech) in Pasadena, California.

1973

Thomas Pynchon's *Gravity's Rainbow*, Graham Greene's *The Honorary Consul*, Kurt Vonnegut's *Breakfast of Champions*, Iris Murdoch's *The Black Prince* and Hunter S. Thompson's *Fear and Loathing on the Campaign Trail '72* are published.

Collins in London publishes GD's *Beasts in My Belfry*. Amy Nimr Smart and Aspasia Katsimbali die. Temple's magazine *Entretiens* publishes an issue devoted to essays on LD.

January 21. The *New York Times Book Review* prints LD's "A Real Heart Transplant into English".[3]

February 10. Michèle Arnaud and LD fly to California to film Miller and LD for French television. LD is drinking copious daily amounts of champagne; Miller warns him this regime is suicidal. Disregarding logic, LD claims the drink helps with his eczema, which returned despite Chardenon's best remedies.

February 21. On the return trip a French strike allows LD to re-route his flight from London to Geneva, where he spends the day with Claude Kiefer, and the next day takes the express train to Nîmes. A cold mistral blows through the garrigues but the house is warm and the kitchen stocked.

February 27. LD is 61 years old.

February–March. Penguin publishes *Wordsworth Selected by Lawrence Durrell*, with a typical LD introduction (emphasising sibling incest), in the Poet to Poet series.

March 26. Noël Coward dies of a heart attack at the age of 74 and is

---

[3] Reprinted in LD, *From the Elephant's Back*, 129–32.

buried at Firefly Estate, Montego Bay, Saint James, Jamaica.

April 8. Pablo Picasso dies at the age of 92 in Mougins and is buried at his chateau in Vauvenargues near Aix-en-Provence.

Late April. LD and Ghislaine travel to London for the British publication of *The Black Book* and *Vega and Other Poems* (dedicated to Claude Kiefer).[4] LD is ubiquitous on the television and in the newspapers.

April 27. LD signs 220 copies of *The Black Book* at Hatchard's bookstore in London.

April 28. LD and Ghislaine leave London for Cannes, where LD serves as a judge at the Film Festival with Ingrid Bergman and Sidney Pollack.[5] Fiddle Viracola and Michèle Arnaud are also in Cannes. During an argument he slaps Ghislaine and she says she's leaving for Paris; he is tearfully contrite the next day and asks her to marry him, so she stays in Cannes. When LD returns to Sommières, Ghislaine moves in with him. Before leaving for Cannes, LD gives an interview to Philip Howard of the London *Times* during which he notes, "I'm becoming an elder of the established church." He no doubt grinned whilst making this statement.[6]

Summer. Alan and Shirley Thomas come for a visit. Sappho has graduated from college and is living in London with a boyfriend while working for the publishers Weidenfeld and Nicholson.

September 11. In Chile a military coup d'état, supported by the American Central Intelligence Agency, murders the elected president, Salvador Allende, and establishes a vicious dictatorship.

September 23. Pablo Neruda, Nobel 1971, dies at the age of 69 of leukemia in Santiago de Chile, after which his home is ransacked by the minions

---

[4] GB, 351, has this happening in May.

[5] Bergman needs no introduction. Pollack was an actor and television director in the late 1950s and early 1960s before he turned to directing Hollywood movies, the most memorable of which include *This Property is Condemned* (1966), *Castle Keep* (1968), *The Way We Were* (1973), which he ruined in the editing stage because he could not bear to have Robert Redford's character remain the son-of-a-bitch he was, and *Bobby Deerfield* (1977). His more recent film, *The Interpreter* (2005) almost redeems his flat work over the previoius 20 years. He died in 2008.

[6] The interview was published in *The Times* on April 28.

of the military dictatorship; he is buried on the Isla Negra, Santiago.

September 29. W. H. Auden dies in a Vienna hotel at the age of 66 and is buried in Kirchstetten, a nearby village where he and Chester Kallman have a summer home.

Early October. The Swedish Academy awards Patrick White (Australia) the Nobel Prize in Literature.

October 2. LD writes to Miller that *Monsieur* is finished; but it isn't.

November. LD and Ghislaine de Boysson are married in Sommières with a local hooker and a local drunk as witnesses.[7]

Mid-December. LD and Ghislaine fly to Los Angeles to visit Miller and take up the visiting professorship at the California Institute of Technology in Pasadena.[8]

December 30. The Durrells drive to San Diego to see the world-class zoo.

1974

John Fowles' *The Ebony Tower*, Erica Jong's *Fear of Flying*, Carl Bernstein and Bob Woodward's *All the President's Men*, John Hawkes' *Death, Sleep and the Traveler*, Vladimir Nabokov's *Look at the Harlequins* and Joseph Heller's *Something Happened* are published.

Faber publishes LD's *The Revolt of Aphrodite* combining *Tunc* and *Nunquam*. *100 Great Books: Masterpieces of All Time*, edited by John Canning, with an introduction by LD is published. Collins in London publishes GD's *The Talking Parcel*.

January 1. The Durrells watch the Rose Parade in Los Angeles.

January–March. LD begins lecturing at Caltech, where they stay at the Athenaeum Club. LD starts grilling steaks on the balcony of their suite against house rules and is asked to desist, greatly frustrating him. The Durrells visit with Miller and Anaïs Nin, and walk through the Forest

---

[7] GB, 353.

[8] GB, 355, has them leaving France on Christmas day.

Lawn cemetery.[9] While visiting Miller at his house LD slaps Ghislaine in the course of an argument. Miller tells LD if anything like that happens again he will no longer see him.

Mid-February. Finally LD feels so claustrophobic at the Athenaeum Club that the Durrells move to Malibu into a house owned by film director William Wyler (an acquaintance of Ghislaine's) who generously loans it to them. Burt Lancaster helps Ghislaine in the supermarket.

February 27. LD is 62 years old, an event he celebrates with Miller, Anaïs Nin and Ghislaine.

March. LD gives two public lectures, one at Caltech and one at Claremont College in Pomona. Anaïs Nin attends his final class meeting devoted to D. H. Lawrence's *Sons and Lovers.*

End March. The Durrells leave California to return to Sommières. LD never returns to the American west coast; his behaviour has strained the old friendship with Miller, but not to the breaking point.

End April. LD travels to Paris for the publication of the French version of *Pope Joan.* Upon his return to Sommières he is sick with the flu and announces he'll reduce his wine intake to one bottle a day for the summer so he can work on *Monsieur.* This admirable resolution is not long kept. He also takes up painting again to prepare for another Epfs exhibition in the autumn.

May. LD begins to have seizures he thinks are epileptic fits, but which were clearly related to his drinking. Ghislaine tries to get him to stop the excessive intake and he verbally abuses her in front of others. They frequently visit GD and Jacquie at the Mazet Michel.

Early June. LD sends the typescript of *Monsieur* to Faber.[10]

June 9. Guatamalan author Miguel Asturias, Nobel 1967, dies in Madrid at the age of 75 and is buried in the Père Lachaise Cemetery, Paris.

c. June–July. Sappho comes to Sommières for a lengthy stay.

---

[9] GB, 330, has this occurring during the March 1968 visit.

[10] GB, 357, has this happening "by the time they returned to France"; that is, at the end of March or early April.

[1974]

July 24. The military junta in Greece is deposed and democracy is restored.

August 22. The Daily Mail prints LD's "This Magnetic, Bedevilled Island that Tugs at My Heart", about the continuing situation in Cyprus.[11]

September. Advance copies of *Monsieur* are available; Miller writes that he has difficulty following the narrative after the Macabru section. He is not alone. Viking Press sends a $50,000 advance for the novel.

Mid-September. LD and Ghislaine are fighting more than ever, including mutual physical abuse; she writes to Miller that the situation is "dur".

September 28. The Times (London) carries a lengthy extract from the soon-to-be-published *Monsieur.*

October. LD tells friends the marriage will break up at the end of the year.

Early October. The Swedish Academy awards Eyvind Johnson and Harry Martinson (both Sweden) jointly the Nobel Prize in Literature.

Mid-October. LD and Ghislaine are in London for the publication of *Monsieur or the Prince of Darkness*, dedicated to Ghislaine, which receives generally negative reviews. On their way back to France they stop in Jersey to visit GD's zoo.

November. Another Oscar Epfs exhibition mainly of watercolours opens at Marthe Nochy's bookstore in the rue de Seine in Paris, attended by both Durrells. LD meets Françoise Kestsman at the store.

December. In Sommières, the Durrells' relationship appears tranquil to outsiders, but it isn't. Paul Scott in *The Times* (London) includes *Monsieur* among the best books of 1974.

December 31. The Durrells celebrate the end of the year with the de Rougemonts in Geneva.

[11] Reprinted in LD, *From the Elephant's Back*, 47–50.

1975

Saul Bellow's *Humboldt's Gift*, E. L. Doctorow's *Ragtime*, Malcolm Bradbury's *The History Man*, Ruth Prawer Jhabvala's *Heat and Dust* and Jacob Bronowski's *The Ascent of Man* are published.

Miller is so impressed with LD's California public lectures he arranges to have them published by the Capra Press in Santa Barbara as *Blue Thirst*.[12]

January–February. LD withdraws into himself, ignoring Ghislaine's attempts to make the marriage work. He continues to add to the manuscript of *Livia*, the second of the Avignon series, sometimes confusing Livia with Ghislaine. He tells her he wants a divorce because she is a lesbian. She retreats to her Paris apartment, returning on some weekends.

January. In New York, Viking Press publishes *Monsieur* to generally lukewarm reviews.

February 4. Ian MacNiven is in Sommières to present a copy of his dissertation ("A Descriptive Catalogue of the Lawrence Durrell Collection at Southern Illinois University") to LD. They enjoy a well-watered five-hour lunch at the Pont Roman restaurant. It has been raining, and as they leave the restaurant LD drops the dissertation in a parking lot puddle, twice. Fortunately the volume is in a plastic bag.

February 27. LD is 63 years old.

Spring. Ghislaine continues to live most of the time in Paris, effectively ending the marriage that has now become impossible. This arrangement seems to bring about a cessation of hostilities and at some point she returns to Sommières for several months. LD hires a cook (Mme Mignon) who also cleans when Marcelle, his former *femme de ménage*, leaves to marry.

March. LD is awarded the James Tait Black Memorial Prize, for *Monsieur or the Prince of Darkness*.

March 13. Ivo Andrić, Nobel 1961, dies at the age of 83.

---

[12] Reprinted in LD, *Endpapers and Inklings*.

[1975]

End March. *Livia* has reached just over 100 pages.

April. In America, the Literary Guild chooses *Monsieur* as a monthly book choice. Diana Menuhin writes to question why his women characters are so humourless.

May. Ian MacNiven is awarded a PhD for his dissertation.

Summer. LD decides not to sell the Mazet Michel to his brother for tax reasons and asks him to move out.[13]

July. LD travels alone to Sicily to write an article for *Travel and Leisure* magazine. During the next twelve months he expands this into the travel book, *Sicilian Carousel,* neglecting the *Livia* manuscript.

July 22. Marie Millington-Drake, an old LD flame from the Cyprus period, dies at the age of 49 in Naxos, Sicily, and is buried in a cemetery there.[14]

August. Having divorced Peter Jones the actor, Penelope Durrell marries Roger Walker, a potter, and moves to Cornwall.

September. LD and Michèle Arnaud spend a couple of weeks on Corfu to make a film for French television.

September 20. Saint-John Perse, Nobel 1960, dies at the age of 88 in Presqu'île de Giens, Provence and is buried nearby.

October. LD is back on Corfu and in other Greek locales to make a film, *Spirit of Place: Lawrence Durrell's Greece* with the director Peter Adam and the photographer Dimitri Papadimos for BBC TV.[15] He agrees to write the text for the coffee table book *The Greek Islands* and takes time from

[13] According to IMN, 558, Jacquie believed that LD loathed her to the extent that he refused to sell the Mazet to GD

[14] Two manuscripts of her unpublished novels are in the LD collection at Southern Illinois University at Carbondale. In *Caesar's Vast Ghost*, 175–6, LD writes a curious eulogy to her including the story of her coming to see him long after midnight in a taxi with flowers and champagne to announce, "Darling, Anaïs is dead. I didn't want you to hear the news from anyone but me." Anaïs Nin died in 1977, two years after Marie.

[15] In 2019 this film is still available on YouTube.

Livia to do so. Paul Gotch, on holiday in Kassiopi on Corfu, reconciles Joan and Peter Bird with LD. In Athens, LD spends several nights with Katsimbalis, now an invalid, one of his few old Greek friends who has not cut himself off from LD due to the latter's work on Cyprus.

Early October. The Swedish Academy awards Eugenio Montale (Italy) the Nobel Prize in Literature. LD travels alone to London for the unveiling of a plaque at the house in Bayswater where Cavafy lived from 1873 to 1876. He meets Alan Ross to discuss a new edition of his selected poems, two days after telling a journalist that his publisher "is letting my poetry go out of print", by which he may have meant Faber rather than Ross.

Late November. GD, Jacquie and some of their friends move their effects out of the Mazet Michel and transfer them to a house they've found in Le Tignet near Grasse.

December. At Ghislaine's urging, LD takes Claude's ashes, up to this point located in a bedroom at the Sommières house, for a proper burial in his own plot in the graveyard of the Saint Julien de Salinelles church some kilometres down the road from Sommières.

December 4. The controversial philosopher-historian Hannah Arendt dies in Manhattan at the age of 69 and is buried in the Bard College Cemetery, Annandale-on-Hudson, New York.

1976

Alex Haley's *Roots*, Gore Vidal's *1876*, Manuel Puig's *El beso de la mujer araña*, Melvin Van Peebles' *Just an Old Sweet Song* and Muriel Spark's *The Takeover* are published.

Collins in London publishes GD's *The Stationary Ark* and in New York Schocken Books publishes Robert Liddell's *Cavafy: A Biography*. Simone Lestoquard visits Sommières to paint LD's portrait.

January–March. GD and Jacquie separate, the marriage over; she spends the time at the house near Grasse and he in Bournemouth, part of the time in a nursing home because of his drinking and a slide into deep depression, then on Jersey, until he departs for Mauritius for a six-week field trip.

171

[1976]

January. Jolan Chang, a "Taoist-gerontologist" and sexologist, visits for a long weekend from Stockholm.[16] LD has Chang visit Ghislaine in Paris on his way back to Stockholm. Peter Adam visits to add more interview footage for the Greek film and LD shows him around the town.

February. The BBC's *Radio Times* sends a journalist to interview LD.

February 27. LD is 64 years old.

March 13. The BBC airs the film *Spirit of Place: Lawrence Durrell's Greece.*

April. The BBC broadcasts a dramatization of *The Dark Labyrinth.* Ghislaine attempts to organize a film version of Anaïs Nin's *House of Incest* with a script by LD, a project that has the full approval of Nin, who is now terminally ill with cancer.

Summer. Ghislaine visits Sommières at some length, as do Sappho and her live-in companion, Simon Tompsett, whom LD studiously ignores. Sappho tells Ghislaine to leave her father.

September. In London, Weidenfeld and Nicolson publish the first volume of Olivia Manning's Levant trilogy, *The Danger Tree*, one episode in which is considered by some as libelling Amy and Sir Walter Smart.[17]

Early October. The Swedish Academy awards Saul Bellow (USA) the Nobel Prize in Literature.

December. LD sends off the typescript of *Sicilian Carousel* to Curtis Brown.

---

[16] See LD's description of their meeting in *A Smile in the Mind's Eye.*

[17] On September 20, 1978, the Smart estate sued Manning and her publishers to remove the characters alleged to be based on the Smarts from the book and future volumes. The author and publishers ignored the threat successfully (Braybrookes, 123). Some have indicated that Manning's poet, William Castlebar, is based on LD, but the more accurate identification is Bernard Spencer (ibid.). Manning did not like LD and he returned the sentiment.

1977

John Fowles' *Daniel Martin*, John le Carré's *The Honourable Schoolboy*, Robert Coover's *The Public Burning*, Iris Murdoch's *The Sea, the Sea*, Richard Adams' *The Plague Dogs* and Mark Helprin's *Refiner's Fire* are published.

Faber publishes LD's *Sicilian Carousel*, dedicated to Diana and Yehudi Menuhin. Collins in London publishes GD's *Golden Bats and Pink Pigeons*. LD works on *The Greek Islands*. Alan Pringle and Lord Kinross die.

January 14. Anaïs Nin dies of cancer at the Cedars of Lebanon hospital in Los Angeles at 74. Her ashes are scattered over Santa Monica Bay. LD writes a eulogy to be read at her funeral but it arrives too late.

February. LD visits the Tibetan Buddhist centre at Dagho Kagyu Ling in the Château de Plaige, south of Autun, to celebrate the Tibetan New Year.[18]

February 27. LD is 65 years old.

March. Robin Fedden dies of cancer after a final mountain hike with Patrick Leigh Fermor and Xan Fielding.

April. LD reviews the manuscript of *Literary Lifelines*, his correspondence with Richard Aldington, edited by Harry Moore and Ian MacNiven.

April 11. The poet Jacques Prévert dies at the age of 77 in Omonville-la-Petite (Normandy) and is buried in the cemetery there.

Late April–early May. The 52-year-old GD is in the USA on a fundraising tour; he meets the 27-year-old zoology graduate student, Lee McGeorge, at Duke University.

May 6. Having read the first chapter of *Livia* in the *Malahat Review*, Diana Menhuin writes a critical letter with suggestions (e.g. that he leave the myths of Provence and return to those of Greece which are healthier).

May 16. Yale University confers an honorary degree on GD.

End May. LD finally agrees to sell GD the Mazet at a price the latter can

---

[18] GB, 397, has LD's first visit to the Buddhist Centre apparently taking place in the winter of 1982–83. He also spells the place "Kangû-Ling".

afford, and GD offers to rent the middle flat at the Sommières house.

[1977]

June. LD rents a small apartment in Le Grau-du-Roi near the Mediterranean, not far from Aigues-Mortes, to escape social and business calls and get on with the two-thirds finished *Livia* as well as escape Ghislaine who is in Sommières for the summer. She suspects he is taking a woman to the apartment.

June 25. LD rents the middle floor of the Sommières house to a German family for a month.[19]

June 26. LD finishes *The Greek Islands* in Le Grau-du-Roi.

July. In London, Faber publishes *Sicilian Carousel* to poor reviews.

July 2. The novelist and lepidopterist Vladimir Nabokov dies in Montreux, Switzerland, at the age of 78 and is buried at the Cimetière de Clarens.

August 7. LD writes to Miller that he has approximately 40 pages left to reach the end of *Livia*.

End August. Having agreed on the terms in June, Ghislaine and LD proceed with the divorce.[20]

September 10. LD writes to Miller that Ghislaine is insisting on a "fortune" in alimony.

October. Faber publishes *Selected Poems of Lawrence Durrell*, edited by Alan Ross.

Early October. The Swedish Academy awards Vicente Aleixandre (Spain) the Nobel Prize in Literature.

October 7. LD travels to London to visit Alan and Shirley Thomas and make final arrangements with Peter Adam and the photographer, Dimitri

---

[19] This would indicate that GD did not rent the middle flat.

[20] GB, 374, states that LD, who visited Sommières on weekends to collect mail and pay his housekeeper, left a letter for Ghislaine telling her he wanted a divorce, implying that this happened at the end of the summer. Apparently this story and other details of the several months they spent together in silence (because LD refused to speak to her) GB got from Ghislaine.

Papadimos, for a new documentary film to be called *Spirit of Place: Lawrence Durrell's Egypt.*

October 16. LD watches the Greek film he made with Adam and notes, "My god, what a lot of drivel".

October 17–November 11. A cranky LD reluctantly returns to Egypt with Adam and a crew to shoot the new film.

November 27. Ghislaine departs Sommières for Paris.

November 30. The playwright Terence Rattigan dies in Bermuda at the age of 66 and is buried in the Kensal Green Cemetery, London.

End December. LD finishes *Livia* and sends it to Faber.

1978

John Updike's *The Coup*, Richard Yates' *A Good School*, Don Delillo's *Running Dogs*, Martin Amis' *Success* and Ernest J. Gaines' *In My Father's House* are published.

Collins in London brings out GD's *Garden of the Gods*. The second volume of Olivia Manning's Levant Trilogy, *The Battle Lost and Won*, is published in London. LD's friend in Argentina Bebita Ferreyra dies. Lee McGeorge obtains her PhD at Duke University for her thesis on the communication of mammals and birds.

February 27. LD is 66 years old.

March. A French court fixes the amount of alimony LD is to pay Ghislaine, the level of which makes him weep.[21]

April. GD and his assistant John Hartley travel to the Mazet Michel to work on a collection of short prose pieces called *The Picnic and Suchlike Pandemonium.*

April 14. In Cambridge, the academic critic F. R. Leavis dies at the age of 82 and is buried in a corner of his garden where his wife Queenie (the critic Q. D. Leavis) will join him in 1981.

---

[21] At least this is the story Ghislaine told GB, 380.

[1978]

May. LD is in London for ten days reading the proofs of *Livia*.

May 12. LD meets James Brigham at Alan Thomas's house to discuss the *Collected Poems* that Faber agreed to publish. In Port Jefferson, New York, the influential American poet Louis Zukofsky dies at the age of 74 and is buried in the New Montefiore Cemetery, West Babylon, New York.

June 4. LD writes to Miller that he will begin the next volume of the Quinx (as he called what became *The Avignon Quintet*) "soon".

June 11. The New York Times prints LD's "With Durrell in Egypt".[22]

Mid-June. GD and Lee spend a month at the Mazet. They will spend summers there for most of the rest of his life.

August. LD still has not started writing the third volume, *Constance*.

September. In London, Faber publishes *Livia or Buried Alive* (the second volume of *The Avignon Quintet*) dedicated to Denis and Nanik de Rougemont.

Mid-September. LD stays with the Thomases in Chelsea where he is visited by a young Alexandrian university student whom he ignores in favour of Margaret McCall. The student threatens to kill herself but is talked out of this rash act by Shirley Thomas' daughter.

September 21. Faber publishes *The Greek Islands*. LD has a successful signing at Hatchard's in London.

September 22. LD is in Paris for a signing at Galignagni. While there, LD meets with Keith Brown, a professor of literature at the University of Oslo, to discuss the structure of *Tunc* and *Nunquam*. The meeting takes place in a small café and runs from eight in the morning to five in the evening. They go for a walk to meet a friend of LD's who turns out to be the Alexandrian student who followed him to Paris.

October. LD meets Claude Kiefer in Orta and finishes *A Smile in the Mind's Eye*. He still cannot seem to get a handle on *Constance*. George Katsimbalis (Miller's "Colossus of Maroussi") dies in Athens at the age

---

[22] A version of this essay is printed in LD, *From the Elephant's Back*, 359–76.

of 79.

Early October. The Swedish Academy awards Isaac Bashevis Singer (USA) the Nobel Prize in Literature.

November. In Paris, a reporter from the *International Herald Tribune* interviews LD at length at the Café du Dôme.[23]

November 20. LD writes to MacNiven in no uncertain terms that he wishes no biography to be written as was contemplated by another academic who had contacted MacNiven for information. But, understanding that a determined biographer could not really be stopped, LD asks MacNiven if he would be the "authorized" biographer and publish the book only after LD dies.

Christmas. LD spends the holiday with GD and Lee at the zoo's compound on Jersey.

December 26. Henry Miller is 86-years old, and deeply involved in a platonic relationship with a young woman called Brenda Venus. He writes to LD with sympathy about the latter's melancholy and obsession with death.

New Year's Eve. LD is in Paris at the Coupole with Ghislaine drinking champagne and, after he sends her home, spends the rest of the night with Buttons, age 35, at the Hotel Royal, Room 13.

1979

V. S. Naipaul's *A Bend in the River*, Norman Mailer's *The Executioner's Song*, Philip Roth's *The Ghost Writer*, Kurt Vonnegut's *Jailbird*, John Fowles' *The Tree*, and Kingsley Amis' *Collected Poems* are published.

Collins in London publishes GD's *The Picnic and Suchlike Pandemonium*. Thérèse Epstein Marberry dies. In England, Bran's Head Labrys Edition publishes *Lawrence Durrell: A Symposium* with contributions by David Gascoyne, Gerald Durrell, George Seferis, Diana Menuhin and others.

Early January. LD is in Geneva to have two cysts removed from his back,

23 "Lawrence Durrell Takes Stock", *International Herald Tribune* (Paris, November 7, 1978).

then travels to Paris to meet a young concert pianist named Françoise who also visits him in Sommières.

[1979]

February 23. Brian Friel's play *Faith Healer* opens in Boston before moving to New York.

February 27. LD is 67 years old and seeing the pianist, Buttons and two other young women, but not writing *Constance.*

Spring. A British divorce court grants GD and Jacquie a divorce on the grounds of "irreconcilable breakdown" after 25 years of marriage.

Mid-March. LD finally gets down to work on the novel, writing regularly from 6.00 to 9.00 a.m. each day and drinking only several glasses of wine daily. He reads Jay Martin's biography of Miller, which he deplores, and Brassaï's *Henry Miller: grandeur nature,* which he defends against Miller's complaints.

April. The British Council invites LD to Vienna for ten days to do readings.

April 5. Sappho begins therapy with a psychoanalyst in London to help her examine her relationship with her father, whose treatment of her is ever more erratic. For her part, she has attacked LD for years about such matters as his drinking, his conservative politics, and his treatment of women. In New York at the Longacre Theater, Brian Friel's play *Faith Healer* opens to negative responses, despite the presence of James Mason in the main role.

May. The British elect the Conservative Party headed by Margaret Thatcher who becomes Prime Minister.

May 9. Sappho records in her diary that she has just had a miscarriage.

May 14. In Exeter, Devon, the under-rated novelist Jean Rhys dies at the age of 85.

May 2. GD and Lee McGeorge are married in her hometown, Memphis, Tennessee.

June 11. William Styron's novel *Sophie's Choice* is published in New York causing controversy, but less than his *The Confessions of Nat Turner* evoked.

September. Sappho apparently has a nervous breakdown.

October. Sappho drafts her will, stating she wishes to be buried in the Steep churchyard, a small village near the Bedales School in Hampshire which she attended when Eve worked there, and begins intensive reading about incest. LD, Raymond Mills and Anthea Morton-Saner, his new agent at Curtis Brown, drive L'Escargot to Corfu.[24]

Early October. The Swedish Academy awards Odysseas Elytis (Greece) the Nobel Prize in Literature.

December. LD continues to experience problems with getting the book, *Constance,* down on paper despite the fact that he says he's got it written in his head.

c. December 15. Sappho visits Sommières for a brief stay, but her father is preoccupied with the recalcitrant novel.

December 25. LD is in Paris with a 31-year-old French woman psychiatrist named Nicole; he claims he is doing research for the character Constance, also a psychiatrist.

1980

Samuel Beckett's *Company,* E. L. Doctorow's *Loon Lake,* Umberto Eco's *The Name of the Rose,* Mordecai Richler's *Joshua Then and Now* and Madeleine L'Engel's *A Ring of Endless Light* are published. Brian Friel's play *Translations* is first performed in Londonderry, Northern Ireland.

The final volume of Olivia Manning's *The Levant Trilogy, The Sum of Things,* is published in London.

January 3. G. S. Fraser dies at the age of 65.

February 27. LD is 68 years old.

End February. LD is in Paris with the young psychiatrist.

March. LD goes back to Vienna for several days.

March 26. LD agrees to the establishment in the USA of what becomes

---

[24] GB, 383, has the trip taking place in the spring.

the International Lawrence Durrell Society (ILDS), an academic fan club with serious intent. In Paris, Roland Barthes, French obscurantist, structuralist, deconstructionist semiotician dies from injuries suffered in an automobile accident and is buried in the Cimetière d'Urt, Département des Pyrénées-Atlantiques.[25]

[1980]

April 5. The first ILDS academic conference devoted to LD's work (each of which is called "On Miracle Ground" from LD's 1937 poem "On Ithaca Standing") is held at the State University of New York's Maritime College, where Ian and Susan MacNiven are lecturers.

April 13. Jean-Paul Sartre dies in Paris at the age of 75 and is buried with great to-do in the Père Lachaise Cemetery in Montparnasse.

June 7. At Pacific Palisades, Henry Miller dies at the age of 88, ending a 45-year-old friendship and opening a void in LD's life.

June 9. J. Y. Smith's obituary of Henry Miller in the *Washington Post* cites LD's opinion that Miller's novels have an "Elizabethan quality, a rare tonic vitality which comes from the savage health of its creator" and that the novels are "one of the greatest liberating confessions of our age".

June 27. From his home in Provence, the great British cinema actor Dirk Bogarde, having severely cut back his acting jobs to become a successful novelist and memoirist, writes a letter to the managing director of the Chatto and Windus publishing house, Sarah Smallwood, in response to her suggestion that he write a book about Provence in the vein of LD, in which he notes that the idea is interesting, but that "God knows I am not the right chap to do it. I am most woefully ignorant of my history, my Arts, and all the other things which go up to the making of that kind of book. Durrell is a scholar. I am an amateur-actor-writer. There is a difference."[26]

July 23. Olivia Manning dies on the Isle of Wight at the age of 72 and her

[25] See the "Barthesian" obituary by the extraordinary Hugh Kenner, "Decoding Roland Barthes", with its reference to Roy Campbell, the rightwing poet friend of Aldington and LD (originally published in *Harper's*, August 1980, and republished in Kenner, *Mazes*, 270ff).

[26] Coldstream, *Ever, Dirk*, 213.

ashes are interred in Billingham Manor there.

August. LD arrives in Athens and stays for more than a month.[27]

September 13. Sappho and Simon Tompsett are married at Islington town hall; neither of her parents attends the ceremony.

September 16. The National Greek Tourist Organisation awards LD's *The Greek Islands* its prize for the best book of 1979.

September 18. From Athens, LD flies to London, and stays with Celia and Rose Voelcker, neighbours of Anthea Morton-Saner, wisely refusing the offer of a room in the house owned by Sappho and Simon (for which he had given them £5,000). He is there for the publication of his *Collected Poems 1931–1974* (edited by James A. Brigham) and *A Smile in the Mind's Eye,* "Dedicated to Chantal De Legume wherever and whoever she might be" (published by Wildwood House in England and later by Universe Books in the USA). He visits with the Perlèses, still disliking Anne but putting on a good front for his old pal Alf. From London he flies to Edinburgh to undergo medical examination for his severe asthma, supervised by his old Rhodes friend, Raymond Mills, with whom he stays.

Early October. The Swedish Academy awards Czesław Miłosz (Poland/USA) the Nobel Prize in Literature. From Edinburgh LD flies to Paris and sees Buttons.

October 10. LD returns to Sommières to work on *Constance.*

December. LD remains in Sommières, where Joan and Patrick Leigh Fermor come for a visit.

December 2. In Paris, the French novelist and diplomat Romain Gary (né Roman Kacew, born in Vilnius, Lithuania) dies by shooting himself at the age of 66; after cremation in the Père Lachaise Cemetery, his ashes are scattered in the Mediterranean Sea near Roquebrune-Cap-Martin.[28]

---

[27] GB, 387, has LD returning to Sommières "by summer".

[28] Romain Gary has the distinction of being the only author to win the Prix Goncourt twice: the jury awarded him the prize, which can only be given once to an author, in 1956 for *Les racines du ciel* and in 1975 for *La vie devant soi*, which he published under the pseudonym of Émile Ajar. The truth did not become public until the posthumous publication of his book *La vie et mort d'Émile Ajar* in 1981.

1981

Samuel Beckett's *Ill Seen Ill Said*, Naguib Mahfouz' *Arabian Nights and Days*, Salman Rushdie's *Midnight's Children*, John Irving's *Hotel New Hampshire* and Martin Cruz Smith's Russian thriller *Gorky Park* are published.

Collins in London brings out GD's *The Mockery Bird*.

Early January. LD falls victim to an illness diagnosed as aspirin poisoning, leaving him temporarily unable to use his hands and with a stiffening of his joints.

Early February. Sappho visits Sommières.

February 23. LD writes to MacNiven that Sappho will soon be in New York and will talk to him about LD's life for the biography.

February 27. LD is 69 years old.

March 8. LD reports he is 50 or 60 pages from the end of *Constance*.

April 1. After an introduction by Jean Fanchette, LD delivers a slide lecture about his life and work at the Centre Pompidou in Paris and appears on the 1.00 p.m. news broadcast.[29] Ghislaine attends and meets him as the crowd disperses; he is not pleased at her presence.

c. April 5. LD returns home to continue *Constance*.

April 23. The first draft of *Constance* is finished, lacking only the conclusion.

May. In New York, Viking Press publishes *Literary Lifelines: The Richard Aldington–Lawrence Durrell Correspondence* (edited by Ian S. MacNiven & Harry T. Moore) to generally positive reviews.

May 3. Sappho flies to New York for almost a month and, among other things, talks with MacNiven.

May 15–30. LD dawdles in the Corfu Club Méditerranée for a rest, before wrestling with the novel's conclusion. During this visit he meets

---

[29] Published in English as "From the Elephant's Back" in *Poetry London/Apple Magazine* 2 (1982) and reprinted in LD, *From the Elephant's Back*, 1–16.

the mysterious Sourayya Frick and is very much attracted to her.

June. Faber publishes the English edition of *Literary Lifelines* to (unsurprisingly) less than enthusiastic reviews.

Late June–early July. Sappho visits Sommières.

August. LD is in Paris for the French publication of *Livia*, where a reporter from *L'Express* interviews him at the Café du Dôme.[30]

September 12. In Milan, the poet Eugenio Montale, Nobel 1975, dies a month short of his 85th birthday and is buried in the churchyard of the Chiesa di San Felice in Florence.

October. LD travels to Edinburgh for medical examinations due to his asthma and is diagnosed with emphysema. After treatment he flies to Corfu to continue working on *Constance.* He stays at a hotel on the old port (possibly the Konstantinoupolis), visits Sourayya Frick at her house at Pirgi, and is deeply affected by her beauty, spirituality and otherworldliness; indeed he seems to fall in love with her. Under her influence he stops drinking alcohol. They meet almost every day until she leaves Corfu on December 15.[31]

Early October. The Swedish Academy awards Elias Canetti (Bulgaria/Great Britain) the Nobel Prize in Literature.

End December. LD returns from Corfu to Sommières via Paris, where he spends a lonely Christmas at the Hôtel Royale, boulevard Raspail, before reaching home on New Year's Eve to find the house freezing. The North Hollywood California radio station, KPFA, plays seven days of materials on LD and *The Alexandria Quartet.*

1982

Alice Walker's *The Color Purple*, Isabel Allende's *La casa de los espiritus*, Graham Greene's *Monsignor Quixote*, Thomas Kenneally's *Schindler's Ark*

---

[30] Eric Ollivier, "Lawrence Durrell: un Européen bien tranquille", *L'Express* (August 27, 1981).

[31] IMN, 654, who did not meet her, describes her as the "grave Saroyya [*sic*]". Not much is known about the lady's origins or background.

and James Merrill and David Jackson's *The Changing Light at Sandover* are published.

[1982]

Hamish Hamilton brings out Gerald and Lee Durrell's *The Amateur Naturalist* and Collins publishes GD's *Ark on the Move*. GD is awarded the OBE. GD finally purchases the Mazet from LD.[32]

January 20. Sourayya Frick arrives in Sommières for a two-week visit.

February 24. Sappho arrives for a ten-day visit.

February 27. LD is 70 years old.

March 3. LD mails the typescript of *Constance* to Faber in London.

April 24. The ILDS holds its 2nd On Miracle Ground conference at the University of Baltimore.

Summer. LD travels to Corfu to stay with the Birds, but his return to drinking causes Joan Bird to toss him out. He moves to the Club Méditerranée to concentrate on writing *Sebastian* (the fourth volume of *The Avignon Quintet*) and, under the influence of Sourayya, stops drinking. Over the summer he writes several thousand words of *Sebastian*.

August. LD is writing "a little telly script", "Notions de Femme", for Laure Casteil, "the pretty actress": "it's really woman's magazine material" he writes to Sourayya.[33]

August 7. LD has written 20 pages of *Sebastian*.

August 13. Leslie Durrell dies in a Notting Hill pub of a heart attack at the age of 65.[34]

August 30. The typescript of *Sebastian* has reached 20,000 words.

September 1. Brigitte Salkin, the actress who played Sappho at the Liège Festival arrives in Sommières for a short visit to discuss her ambition to set up as an astrologer in Montpellier.

---

[32] Lee Durrell in Shimwell, *Dining with the Durrells*, xiv.

[33] LD's letters to Sourayya Frick are in the Durrell Library of Corfu.

[34] GB, 394–5, and DB, 512; IMN, 654, seems to imply that this happened sometime in the previous year.

September 10. LD seriously considers returning to Corfu (and Sourayya) with the composition of *Quinx*, the final volume of *The Avignon Quintet* in mind. But he is realistic about his health and compositional ability at this point. He writes to Sourayya, "The food problem is a psychological torment [...] Even God is overweight," and about completing the Avignon novels, "it may take several years which I mayn't have in hand."

September 20. LD travels to Paris for discussions with Laure Casteil (see the entry for August above); there is no evidence that the project ever got beyond the talking stage, but much later Casteil did write an appreciation of LD to commemorate the 100th anniversary of his birth.[35]

October. Faber in London publishes *Constance or Solitary Practices*, dedicated to Anaïs, Henry and Joey [Alfred Perlès]. In Britain it is shortlisted for the Booker Prize but does not win it. LD sits for his portrait by Barbara Robinson at her studio in Quissac, ten miles distant from Sommières. His appreciation of her work appears two years later as the preface to a book about her painting.[36]

Early October. The Swedish Academy awards Gabriel García Márquez (Columbia) the Nobel Prize in Literature.

November 15. Responding to a request from Ara Baliozian for information about his friendship with Constant Zarian, LD writes, "my own little essay in the Poetry Review [of] London was based entirely on his conversations — for two winters we dined almost every day and had long chats. I understood from them how gifted a writer and a humanist he was [...] I have no letters from him alas — when we were chased out of Greece we lost all our papers."[37]

First week in December. LD has brought *Sebastian* to about 60,000 words.

---

[35] "Les cent ans de Lawrence Durrell", published in *Midi-Libre*. February 26, 2012.
[36] "Barbara Robinson vue par Lawrence Durrell" in *Lumières de Barbara Robinson* (Toulouse: Tierra, 1985). IMN, 657, writes that the portrait has LD "looking rather like a sunburned Winston Churchill". In 2008 one of her portraits of LD hung on the reception foyer wall of the Auberge du Pont Roman restaurant in Sommières, a favourite LD eatery.
[37] Quoted in VM, 77 and 78.

1983

William Kennedy's *Ironweed,* J. M. Coetzee's *Life and Times of Michael K,* John le Carré's *The Little Drummer Girl,* Salman Rushdie's *Shame,* Isaac Asimov's *The Robot of Dawn* and Samuel Beckett's *Worstward Ho* are published.

Early in the year. Sappho is briefly in a hospital with a nervous breakdown. Penelope stays with her at her London house. Southern Illinois University pays $6,000 for seven LD letters.

February. The UK television programme *This is Your Life* features GD with an appearance by Theodore Stephanides.

February 7. LD sends the manuscript of *Sebastian* to Faber in London.

February 15. LD tells Sourayya Frick that he is expecting the final proofs of *Sebastian.*

February 23. Penelope arrives for a four-day visit. LD tells Sourayya, "Her situation is sad with the divorce [from Roger Walker] and the obviously approaching death of her mother."

February 25. Tennessee Williams dies in a New York hotel room at the age of 72 under suspicious circumstances and is buried in the family tomb in the Calvary Cemetery, St. Louis, Missouri, his ashes not scattered in the Caribbean as he requested.

February 27. LD is 71 years old.

March 3. LD travels to Paris to discuss his introduction to the Miller-Venus letters with Brenda Venus.[38]

March 25. LD leaves Sommières for a holiday in Greece.

March 31. He arrives on Corfu where he stays until May 19. His relationship with Sourayya Frick comes to an end.

April. A gallery in Lyon mounts a "Hommage à Lawrence Durrell", including Epfs' paintings, photographs and paintings by other artists

---

[38] The book, containing approximately 1,500 letters Miller wrote to Venus was published in 1986 as Miller, *Dear, Dear Brenda* with LD's introduction. The introduction is reprinted in LD, *Endpapers and Inklings.*

inspired by LD's works.

April 13. Theodore Stephanides dies at the age of 87 in London.

Summer. LD accepts the presidency of a committee devoted to raising funds to build a Buddhist temple at Kagyu-Ling.

June. Tambimuttu dies in London, falling off the fire escape he used to enter his third floor flat.[39]

June 8. In Milton Abbas (Dorset) Nancy Myers Durrell Hodgkin dies at the age of 71 of cancer in the presence of her family and Margo. LD is visibly distraught at the news. Her ashes are interred somewhat later at the local cemetery attended by her husband and her daughters Penelope and Joanna Hodgkin.

Autumn. Faber publishes *Sebastian or Ruling Passions*, dedicated to Simone Perier. It is well received by British critics.

October. Sappho, severely affected by Nancy's death and her own demons, attempts suicide with sleeping pills, but calls Eve in time to have her stomach pumped.

Early October. The Swedish Academy awards William Golding (Great Britain) the Nobel Prize in Literature, which must have galled LD as it did his admirers.

Mid-December. LD is well into *Quinx*, the fifth volume of *The Avignon Quintet.*

---

[39] LD wrote an appreciation of his old friend and publisher, "Poets Under the Bed", in Williams, *Tambimuttu*; reprinted in LD, *From the Elephant's Back*, 281–2.

FRANCE WITH FRANÇOISE
1984–1990

1984

Marguerite Duras' *L'Amant*, J. G. Ballard's *Empire of the Sun*, Anita Brookner's *Hotel du Lac*, Don Delillo's *White Noise* and John Updike's *The Witches of Eastwick* are published.

Françoise Kestsman, a friend of Sappho's, mother of five children and owner and operator of a failed restaurant in Sommières (her partner absconded with the takings), takes over as LD's *femme de ménage*, but soon is organizing his life and protecting him from intrusions. He has a book about Provence in mind as his next project.

February 21. Mikhail Sholokhov, Nobel 1965, dies at the age of 79 and is buried on his farm in Veshenskaya, USSR (now Russian Federation).

February 27. LD is 72 years old.

Spring. LD succumbs to a serious case of hepatitis.

April. In Paris, LD falls down and passes out and is taken to the American Hospital in Neuilly, where he is urged to stop drinking. For some years he has been subject to these falling episodes but usually regains consciousness in a short time. GD is also suffering from similar episodes. The International Lawrence Durrell Society holds its 3rd On Miracle Ground conference on LD's works in Muskingum College, Ohio.

May–June. LD is interviewed by Michel Braudeau for *L'Égoïst*, which maliciously prints the writer's half-drunken meanderings.[1]

June 1. LD seriously goes on the wagon having realized that alcohol is detrimental not only to his health but to his art as well.

June 11. LD finishes *Quinx*, he dedicates the book to Stela A. Ghetie, a young Romanian woman writer with whom he corresponds passionately but never meets.

---

[1] "Après ça j'aurai tout dit", *L'Égoïst* (June 1984).

August 1–8. Sappho and Penelope are in Sommières for a week's visit.

September. Sappho travels to Australia with funds provided by her father.

September 12. LD is seriously considering a long-cherished desire to move permanently to Corfu, and writes to Sourayya, "My old yearn to try it out again is coming back because of the fearful spread of urbanism happening here. Provence is gone. The principal cities — glorious Avignon, Aix, Arles, Nîmes, Montpellier, Toulouse, Beziers, Perpignan, completely disembowelled by autoroutes! It's the end of a whole epoch." He continues to express his love and admiration for Sourayya.

October. In Paris, Gallimard publishes Paule Guivarch's translation *Constance ou les pratiques solitaires.*

Early October. The Swedish Academy awards Jaroslav Seifert (Czechoslovakia) the Nobel Prize in Literature. LD is contemplating selling the remainder of his papers and books.

November 18. The *Telegraph Magazine* prints LD's "Lamas in a French Forest" about the Budhist centre at Château de Plaige near Dijon.[2]

December. Sappho returns to London to spend Christmas with her mother. The newspaper *Libération* brings LD and the Perlèses together for a reunion and tour of their former haunts. They have dinner one night with David Gascoyne and his wife at the Coupole. LD continues bravely to eschew alcohol.

1985

Margaret Atwood's *The Handmaid's Tale*, Anne Tyler's *The Accidental Tourist*, John Irving's *The Ciderhouse Rules* and Larry McMurtry's *Lonesome Dove* are published.

LD's *Antrobus Complete* is published. Collins in London brings out GD's *How to Shoot an Amateur Naturalist.*

January 24. Sappho writes a suicide note to Eve.

February 1. Friends find LD's daughter Sappho hanging by her neck in

[2] Reprinted in LD, *From the Elephant's Back*, 53–8.

her London house, a suicide. LD flies to London for the funeral.

February 8. Sappho's remains are buried in the Trent Park cemetery in Cockfosters, London.

February 9. A brief memorial service is held at Saint Luke's Church in Chelsea. Eve stands next to LD. Afterwards, LD, Penelope, Shirley and Alan Thomas, Diana Forde Mitchell and some others walk to Edward Hodgkin's flat. LD never fully recovers from his daughter's suicide (his character Livia, with whom Sappho identified, believing Livia was modelled on herself, also committed suicide by hanging), but Sappho's death does not drive him back to drinking.

February 27. LD is 73 years old.

May. The French edition of *Sebastian* is published.

May 20. LD travels to London for the publication of *Quinx or The Ripper's Tale.* During the visit he returns to drinking after a year of no alcohol. The novel receives divided reviews in England and quite positive ones in France and Germany. In London he meets Richard Lumley, now the Earl of Scarborough, to whom he had let a room in Nicosia, and reunites with Alan Thomas and Bernard Stone at a book-signing at Turret Books. He submits to a raft of interviews for the press, radio and television. The reviews are generally positive.

June 4. LD returns to France.

June. The French *fisc* (L'Administration fiscale) serves LD a writ for £250,000 in unpaid French taxes. He contemplates suicide and selling the Sommières house. Françoise is of great help as she takes over the administration of his life and home and fills the house with her energy and passion. With her three youngest children she moves into a small house across the Route de Saussine from LD's house to be closer to her job.

June 14. LD appears on Bernard Pivot's Paris literary television programme *Apostrophe*.

July 7. The *Sunday Telegraph* has *Quinx* at number three on the bestseller list.

Early October. The Swedish Academy awards Claude Simon (France) the

Nobel Prize in Literature.

December 7. Robert Graves dies at the age of 90 at Deià, Majorca, and is buried the next morning in the small churchyard on a hill at Deià on the site of a shrine which had once been sacred to The White Goddess of Pelion.

1986

Reynolds Price's *Kate Vaiden*, Pat Conroy's *The Prince of Tides* and Anthony Powell's *The Fisher King* are published.

Macdonald in London publishes Gerald and Lee Durrell's *Durrell in Russia*.

January 4. Christopher Isherwood dies in Los Angeles at the age of 82 and his corpse is donated to the Medical School of the University of California at Los Angeles.

January 10. Jaroslav Seifert, Nobel 1984, dies at the age of 85 and is buried in the Kralupy nad Vlatavou cemetery, Czechoslovakia (now Czech Republic).

February 27. LD is 74 years old.

March 4. LD flies to London to stay with Anthea Morton-Saner in Shepherd's Bush.

March 18. The American novelist Bernard Malamud dies at the age of 72 and is buried in the Mount Auburn Cemetery, Cambridge, Massachusetts.

April 8. Morton-Saner requires her house to be repaired and LD joins a London club for a week, where they will not let him into the bar without a tie. This turns out to be LD's last visit to England.

c. April 15.[3] LD reluctantly flies to New York to attend the 4th ILDS On Miracle Ground conference, at Pennsylvania State University, College Station, Pennsylvania, where he lectures and engages in a podium

---

[3] GB, 415, has Viking Press hosting a party for LD at the Gotham Book Mart on April 14.

discussion with the American novelist, John Hawkes, about life and literature.[4] This is LD's last visit to USA. He is visited by Claudine Brelet and stays overnight in Connecticut with Horst and Frances von Maltitz where he suffers a seizure. Fiddle Viracola visits him in the Bronx, where he is staying with the MacNivens; she unsuccessfully tries hard to make him feel better. While he is in the USA, a French court rejects his appeal against the tax levy.

April 15. Simone de Beauvoir dies in Paris at the age of 78 and is interred at the Père Lachaise cemetery in Montparnasse.

May 20. Chili Hawes comes to Sommières for three days to interview LD for the film *Quiet Days in Sommières*; he is exhausted and the filming does not go very well. On this date, the mayor of Sommières, standing in for the Minister of Culture, awards LD the title of Commandeur de l'Ordre des Arts et des Lettres in a public ceremony.

June 14. Jorge Luis Borges dies in Geneva at the age of 87 and is buried in the Cimetière des Rois there.

July. The radio station France Culture sends a team to interview LD. Having divorced her potter husband, Roger Walker, Penelope marries the artist John Hope in Scotland.

July 16. Heinrich Böll, Nobel 1972, dies in Eifelort-Langenbroich, Germany, at the age of 68 and is buried in the Old Bornheim-Merte Cemetery, Bornheim, Nordrhein-Westfalen.

October. The result of months of working on the mass of material on Provence for what becomes *Caesar's Vast Ghost* is only 50 typed pages. Frustrated, LD complains there is too much material and he is having serious trouble organizing it.

Early October. The Swedish Academy awards Wole Soyinka (Nigeria) the Nobel Prize in Literature.

---

[4] LD's speech and his brief dialogue with Hawkes are reprinted in *Endpapers and Inklings*.

1987

Martin Amis' *Einstein's Monsters*, Michael Ondaatje's *In the Skin of a Lion*, Garrison Keillor's *Leaving Home*, and Betty Mahmoody's *Not Without My Daughter* are published.

The German television station ZDF broadcasts the one-and-a-half-hour interview Chili Hawes conducted with LD, entitled "Stille Tage in Sommières" (*Quiet Days in Sommières* — Henry Miller's book *Quiet Days in Clichy* is called *Stille Tage in Clichy* in German). Conran Octopus in London publishes GD's childrens' adventure, *The Fantastic Flying Journey*.

January 6. LD considers the Provence book finished, but Faber editors think otherwise and return the manuscript for additional work.

February. Suffering the worst medical crisis of his life, influenza and respiratory complications, he forges ahead with work on the manuscript.

February 27. LD is 75 years old.

Summer. The writer Robin Rook and the painter Paul Hogarth visit Sommières to discuss a volume to contain brief excerpts from LD's books, a text by Rook and sketches and paintings by Hogarth, to be called *The Mediterranean Shore*. Penelope visits to look at the collection of books her father plans to give her as a belated wedding present. While there she sorts through his papers and manuscripts with a view toward selling them.

June 1. LD becomes an official resident of England to take advantage of the Thatcher government's tax laws favouring the rich; in France he is now a tourist in residence "as a member of the European Economic Community on a British passport".

August. LD believes he has only 20 pages left before finishing the Provence book. Artemis Cooper visits to interview LD for her study on Cairo during the war.

August 22. LD and Françoise attend the consecration of the Buddhist temple at Daghpo Kagyu Ling as guests of honour.[5]

---

[5] GB, 418, has LD and Françoise participating in a Buddhist "marriage" ceremony after LD has been given a dispensation to consume alcohol on the premises. IMN

September 25. Emlyn Williams dies at the age of 82 and is buried in the Evergreen Cemetery, Santa Cruz, California.

October. The BBC begins broadcasting the series based on GD's *My Family and Other Animals*, filmed on Corfu; GD attends some of the filming.

Early October. The Swedish Academy awards Joseph Brodsky (USSR/USA) the Nobel Prize in Literature.

November 9. LD and Françoise drive to Lyon for the opening performance of *An Irish Faustus*, starring Eléonore Hirt, at the Théâtre des Célestins.[6]

December 1. James Baldwin dies at his home in Saint-Paul-de-Vence in the South of France at the age of 63 and is buried in the Ferncliff Cemetery and Mausoleum, Hartsdale, New York.

December 24. Terence Tiller, LD's friend and fellow poet from the war days in Cairo and Alexandria, dies in London at the age of 71.

1988

Stephen Hawking's *A Brief History of Time*, Paulo Coelho's *The Alchemist*, Margaret Atwood's *Cat's Eye*, Umberto Eco's *Foucault's Pendulum* and Gabriel García Márquez's *Love in the Time of Cholera* are published.

The Durrell-Miller Letters: 1935–1980, edited by Ian MacNiven, is published

does not mention this. GB probably got the story from Françoise herself. In no legal sense were they married. There is a lovely but undated photograph of Penelope Hope at a Daghpo Kagyu Ling event in JH, 325. The resemblance to her mother Nancy is striking.

6 IMN, 679, states that Penelope Durrell Hope edited the play based on an acting version that resulted from the 1984 ILDS conference at Muskingum College in Ohio and that this served as the text for the French production, not mentioning whether the play was performed in French or English. GB, 418, states that the text was the 1976 translation by Frédéric-Jacques Temple. Penelope Durrell Hope confirms that the Lyon performance was Temple's translation, and notes that her version has to her knowledge never been performed. (Communication to the author, January 20, 2006.) Penelope Durrell Hope's version was published in a limited edition by The Delos Press in 1987.

in London by Faber/Michael Haag (in the USA by New Directions). Fanchette publishes LD's letters to him. Diane Deriaz publishes her memoirs, *La Tête à l'envers: souvenirs d'un trapéziste chez les poètes*, with a preface by LD.[7] Georges Hoffman and a French TV crew visit Sommières to film LD, having already filmed Perlès; the final production used existing footage of Miller and Anaïs Nin. Richard Pine's *The Dandy and the Herald: Manners, Mind and Morals from Brummell to Durrell* is published.

[1988]

February 27. LD is 76 years old.

March. Robin Rook returns to Sommières to show LD Hogarth's pictures and go over last minute revisions to the texts for *The Mediterranean Shore*.

March 13. GD brings lunch to his brother, limping with a hip replacement; each is troubled by the other's appearance.

April. LD suffers a seizure. The ILDS holds its 5th On Miracle Ground conference at Southern Illinois University, but LD cannot attend due to his deteriorating health. He notes that were it not for Françoise he would have "croaked" already.

Summer. Christophe, Françoise' eldest son, moves his photographic studio into the top floor of LD's house, so that, when Françoise is out, there will be someone else in the place with the writer whose seizures continue. LD resents the time Françoise spends with her youngest children whom he doesn't want in the house. He asks her to marry him and she refuses; nonetheless he adds a codicil in her favour to his will.

July. Sotheby's opens LD's papers to the auction public causing a small scandal when his letters to Miller's wife Hoki indicate their sexual relations. The lot is withdrawn when the bidding does not reach the asking price.[8]

October. *The Mediterranean Shore: Travels in Lawrence Durrell Country* is published in London by Pavilion.

---

[7] Reprinted in *Endpapers and Inklings*.

[8] Southern Illinois University later purchased the lot to add to its already large collection of Durrelliana.

Early October. The Swedish Academy awards Naguib Mahfouz (Egypt) the Nobel Prize in Literature. Richard Pine brings a copy of his recently published book, *The Dandy and the Herald*, to Sommières and spends time with LD and Françoise, who guards LD's time and watches over the amount imbibed; LD seems exhausted, but is watching closely to know the recipient of the Nobel award, in the belief that he was a nominee.

Winter. Friends continue to visit the ageing writer in Sommières, but his loneliness increases and he withdraws further into himself: the Birds, Barbara Robinson, Raymond Mills, Mary Mollo Hadkinson, Penelope and John Hope also visit with some regularity; Françoise's friends are also in and out of the house from time to time. LD refuses to go to the Mazet to see GD and Lee.

1989

Bharati Mukherjee's *Jasmine*, Amy Tan's *The Joy Luck Club*, Martin Amis' *London Fields*, John Irving's *A Prayer for Owen Meany* and Salman Rushdie's *Satanic Verses* are published.

Conran Octopus in London publishes GD's children's adventure story, *The Fantastic Dinosaur Adventure*. Simone Lestoquard stops in Sommières to see LD, who rouses himself out of his usual torpor to entertain her, but this costs him considerable effort. LD asks Françoise's friend Mary Byrne, who lives nearby, to see what she can do with the mass of material for *Caesar's Vast Ghost* which he cannot seem to put into a coherent order for Faber; she does this with a word processor. With this flexibility he moves the volume to completion. Françoise gives him a puppy dog for protection.

January. LD's old poet friend Audrey Beecham, whom he met in 1937, dies at the age of 72.

February 27. LD is 77 years old.

August. Le Figaro publishes a piece on LD entitled "Le Vieux Sage".

September. Perlès is 92 years old.

October. The town of Antibes awards LD its first Grand Prix Littéraire;

Françoise and Anthea Morton-Saner accept it for him.

Early October. The Swedish Academy awards Camilo José Cela (Spain) the Nobel Prize in Literature. Georges Hoffman comes to Sommières to make a short film about LD. David Gascoyne visits LD.

December 11. The third French television channel (FR3) broadcasts Einar Moos' film *Une amitié parisienne* dealing with Henry Miller's life in Paris during the 1930s, containing an interview conducted with Miller in 1980 shortly before he died as well as interviews with LD, Betty Ryan and Perlès.

December 22. Samuel Beckett, Nobel 1969, dies at the age of 83 in Paris and is buried in the Montparnasse Cemetery.

1990

Elmore Leonard's *Get Shorty*, Ray Bradbury's *A Graveyard for Lunatics* and Thomas Pynchon's *Vineland* are published. Brian Friel's *Dancing at Lughnasa* receives its première performance at the Abbey Theatre in Dublin.

In London Collins brings out GD's *The Ark's Anniversary* and Michael O'Mara Books publishes his *Keeper*.

Erica Jong brings her blonde energy and laughter to Sommières to talk to LD about her book on Miller. Surgeons remove a cataract from one of LD's eyes.

January 27. Alfred Perlès dies in Wells, Somerset at the age of 92 and his ashes are scattered in Bath.

February 27. LD is 78 years old.

April 9–21. The ILDS holds its 6th biennial On Miracle Ground conference in Statesboro, Georgia.

Summer. Faber in London and Arcade in New York publish *Caesar's Vast Ghost*, dedicated to Françoise Kestsman.

June. Jean Fanchette tells MacNiven that LD is drinking himself to death.

June 8. The city of Sommières converts part of a former Ursuline convent into a cultural centre called L'Espace Lawrence Durrell.

June 15. In Sydney, the Australian composer, Peggy Glanville-Hicks, dies at the age of 78.

July 3. In Paris, the old *pornographe*, Maurice Girodias dies of a heart attack at the age of 71.[9]

September 24. Peter and Joan Bird arrive for a visit to find Raymond Mills there, but despite outbreaks of wit and laughter, LD is fading toward death, his words slurred but not from drink. They drive to Aigues Mortes for lunch at one of LD's favourite restaurants.

September 30. In Sydney, the Australian writer Patrick White, 1973 Nobel, dies at the age of 78.

October. The Antibes literature award is given to LD's friend, Jacques Lacarrière, the ceremony attended by LD and Françoise.

Early October. The Swedish Academy awards Octavio Paz (Mexico) the Nobel Prize in Literature.

October 18. Following Françoise' urging, Penelope arrives for five days in Sommières and finds her father tranquil and apparently ready to accept death. They discuss Françoise' notion of creating a Durrell study centre in the house after he dies.

November 6. LD telephones Morton-Saner sounding tipsy but happy, telling her that Françoise had finally agreed to marry him.

November 7. LD dies of cerebral haemorrhage/pulmonary embolism at his house in Sommières.[10]

November 9. LD is cremated in Orange; the cremation is attended by Françoise, her son Christophe, Penelope, Anthea Morton-Saner, Mary Byrne and her husband Jean-Claude Vidal, and Georges Hoffman. Later

[9] In the early 1960s, Girodias appeared at the annual Frankfurt Book Fair wearing a badge that read "Girodias Pornographe" when the author of this chronology met him.

[10] IMN, 688, has Françoise's son Pierre hearing LD collapse in the toilet and, finding him unconscious, running across the street to his mother's house to fetch her, while GB, 423, has Françoise herself discovering the body after returning from an errand. *¿Quien sabe?*

in the day some of his ashes are put in the ground above Claude's unmarked burial plot in the Sommières cemetery of Saint Julien de Salinelles. The rest of the ashes apparently remain in the possession of Françoise Kestsman.

[1990]

November. *The Independent* prints David Gascoyne's memoir "Lawrence Durrell".

AFTERMATH : 1991–2019

1991

Harper Collins in London publishes GD's *Marrying Off Mother* and Michael O'Mara brings out GD's *Toby the Tortoise*.

May 26. The front page of the *Sunday Telegraph* publishes Barbara Robson's story of LD's alleged incestuous relations with Sappho. This was the beginning of a press feeding frenzy about the story with Robson, a neighbour of Sappho's, claiming the daughter had told her about this.

July 7. A tribute is held in Stratford-upon-Avon honouring LD in the presence of Penelope, Eve and Françoise.

July 24. Isaac Bashevis Singer, Nobel 1978, dies at the age of 87 or 89 and is buried in the Beth-El Cemetery, Paramus, New Jersey.

August 19. In Paris, LD's old friend, Xan Fielding dies at the age of 73 and his ashes are scattered in the White Mountains of Crete where he served during the war.

Autumn. The magazine *Granta* publishes Sappho's journals and letters.

September 18. GD unveils a plaque on the wall by the entrance to the Sommières property announcing the existence of the Centre d'Études et de Recherches Lawrence Durrell.

November. Françoise Kestsman opens the Centre to scholars and begins translating *Caesar's Vast Ghost* into French.[1]

1992

In London Harper Collins publishes GD's *The Aye-Aye and I.* LD's *The Avignon Quintet* is published by Faber as a single volume.

June. The International Lawrence Durrell Society convenes its 7th

---

[1] GB, 429, notes that Françoise "found herself in charge of the Pléiade edition of Durrell". This does not seem to have been the case.

biennial On Miracle Ground conference at the Palace of the Popes in Avignon, at which Susan MacNiven, the young Emilie Pine and Brewster Chamberlin serve as bartenders, handing out jars of wine organized from local vintners by the energetic Denis Constancias. Among the notable speakers is David Gascoyne. Françoise Kestsman allows the conference participants to hold a party at the Sommières house. Ghislaine de Boysson Durrell attends the conference dinner at Le Bain Marie restaurant.

1993

David Gascoyne publishes his memoir, *Lawrence Durrell*, as a slim volume in 75 numbered and signed copies (privately printed for Alan Clodd at The Tragara Press, Edinburgh).

June 19. William Golding, Nobel 1983, dies in Perranarworthal, Cornwall at the age of 82 and is buried in the Holy Trinity Churchyard, Bowerchalke, Wiltshire, England under a huge yew tree.

1994

March 17. The actress Mai Zetterling dies in London at the age of 68 and her ashes are given to a friend.

May 11. Gallimard in Paris publishes Françoise Kestsman's translation of *Caesar's Vast Ghost* as *L'Ombre infinie de César: Regards sur la Provence.*

June. Macmillan in London and St. Martin's Press in New York publish Richard Pine's *Lawrence Durrell: The Mindscape.*

June 24–28. The ILDS holds its 8th biennial On Miracle Ground conference in San Diego, California.

August 14. Elias Canetti, Nobel 1981, dies at the age of 85 in Zurich and is buried adjacent to James Joyce in the Fluntern cemetery in the hills above the city.

1995

André Deutsch in London publishes Margo Durrell's *Whatever Happened to Margo?*[2]

LD's house in Sommières is sold; the contents of the Centre d'Études et de Recherches Lawrence Durrell are sold to the University of Paris X (Nanterre).[3]

January 30. Gerald Durrell dies in St. Helier on the island of Jersey at the age of 70.

March 9. GD's ashes are laid to rest beneath a small marble plinth in the garden at his home and zoo, Les Augrès Manor on Jersey.

May 30. Philip Sherrard, author of many Greek-related books including *Edward Lear: The Corfu Years* and co-translations with Edmund Keeley of Cavafy's and Seferis' poems, dies at the age of 72 and is buried near the Orthodox chapel he had had built on his property in Evvia, Greece.

1996

Harper Collins publishes *The Best of Gerald Durrell* edited by Lee Durrell. In London, Sinclair Stevenson publishes Gordon Bowker's *Through the Dark Labyrinth: A Biography of Lawrence Durrell*.[4] The third French television channel broadcasts an episode on LD in its *Un siècle d'écrivain* series with Frédéric-Jacques Temple, Corinne Alexandre-Garner and Daniel Costelle.

January 28. Joseph Brodsky, Nobel 1987, dies at the age of 56 and is buried in the Protestant cemetery on the Isola di San Michele, Venice, near the graves of Ezra Pound, Igor Stravinsky and Sergei Diaghilev.

March 18. Odysseas Elytis, Nobel 1979, dies at the age of 85 and is buried

---

[2] GB, 429, notes that Margo wrote the book "in the early 1960s" and that it was published in 1994.

[3] GB, 429, has this happening in 1997.

[4] GB was refused permission to quote from LD's works before IMN's authorized biography appeared.

in the First Cemetery, Athens.

June. The ILDS convenes its 9th biennial On Miracle Ground conference, in Alexandria, Egypt, with the organizational cooperation and efforts of Professor Soad Sobhy and her colleagues at the University of Alexandria. The ILDS sends a letter to the city authorities urging the restoration of the Ambron villa, where LD lived during the War for sixteen months before he was transferred to Rhodes in February 1945.

1998

In London, Faber publishes Ian MacNiven's authorized *Lawrence Durrell: A Biography* and Pimlico publishes Gordon Bowker's revised edition of *Through the Dark Labyrinth.*

February 8. Halldór Laxness, Nobel 1955, dies at the age of 96 and is buried in the cemetery Fossvogskirkjugarður, Reykjavik.

April 15. Stephen Kinzer's article, "Bitter Memories of a Love Affair with Cyprus" appears in the *New York Times*, noting the plaque on the wall of the Bellapaix house ("Bitter Lemons: Lawrence Durrell Lived Here 1953–56") and that one of Sabri Tahir's legs had been shot off by a business rival, though he was still willing to talk to reporters about LD's time on the island.

April 19. Octavio Paz, Nobel 1990, dies at the age of 82 and his ashes are scattered to the winds.

May 15. John Hawkes dies at the age of 73.

May 20–24. The ILDS holds its 10th biennial On Miracle Ground conference in Cincinatti, Ohio.

August 18. The BBC 2 TV programme, *Bookmark*, broadcasts *Lawrence Durrell: A Smile in the Mind's Eye* a documentary on LD's life and work featuring interviews with Richard Pine, Ian MacNiven and Margaret McCall, who co-produced the programme with Nadia Haggar.[5]

---

[5] The film is available commercially, oddly enough, for $225!! Grove Koger reviewed it in *Deus Loci*, NS 8 (2001–2002), 210–11.

1999

In New York, Carroll and Graf publishes Douglas Botting's *Gerald Durrell: The Authorized Biography*.

2000

May 8. The Turkish Cypriot "real estate agent", Sabri Tahir, is shot dead at 76 by a former bodyguard.[6]

July 2–7. The ILDS convenes its 11th biennial On Miracle Ground conference, on Corfu (with the participation of Margo Durrell and Penelope Durrell Hope). The proceedings include a performance of an abridged version of LD's *Bromo Bombastes: A Fragment from a Laconic Drama* by a troupe of thespian academics and a performance of H. R. Stoneback's work in progress "Meet Me at the Existential Café, Huck Honey" with various Durrellians playing the roles.[7] While enjoying a glass of wine on the Esplanade in the warmth of the early evening, Richard Pine conceives of a Socratic school on Corfu dedicated to the works of the Durrell brothers and the themes important to them.

2001

Richard Pine works to establish the Durrell School of Corfu to fulfill his vision and appoints Alexina Ashcroft as Administrative Director.

October. The French Cultural Centre in Alexandria, Egypt (Institut Française d'Égypte à Alexandrie), mounts an exhibition devoted to LD.

November 25. LD's friend, the poet David Gascoyne dies at the age of 85 on the Isle of Wight.

---

[6] Stephen Kinzer, "Sabri Tahir, 76, Slain; Cypriot in Durrell Book", *The New York Times* (May 10, 2000).

[7] The title is a pun on a controversial essay by the American literary critic and teacher, Leslie Fiedler, called "Come Back to the Raft Ag'in, Huck Honey!" printed in Fiedler, *Collected Essays*.

2002

January 17. Camilo José Cela, Nobel 1989, dies at the age of 86 and is buried in the Cementario de Iria Flavia, La Coruña, Galicia, Spain, under an olive tree.

May 26–June 7. The Durrell School of Corfu opens its library and teaching facilities in an old building in Corfu Town with its inaugural two-week session, covering subjects such as Post-Colonialism, Travel Writing, Mystery Cults and Modernity, and Translation, prefaced by a two-day symposium entitled "Understanding Misunderstanding", moderated by Brewster Chamberlin, held in the Ionian Cultural Centre at the Phaliraki, Corfu Town.

July. The ILDS holds its 12th biennial On Miracle Ground conference in Ottawa, Canada.

July 20. The Association Lawrence Durrell en Languedoc and the Promusica et Algo Concept present "Duo pour un Quatuor", a vocal and instrumental performance by Christina Delume and Bernard Wystraëte using extracts from *Spirit of Place* and *Caesar's Vast Ghost*, at the Chapelle Saint Julien de Salinelles outside Sommières.

2003

June 4. Joan Leigh Fermor dies at the age of 91 and is buried in the graveyard of the Church of St Peter in the Village of Dumbleton.

June 18–24. The DSC holds its second annual session devoted to such subjects as Translation, The Writer as Exile, Corfu Cultural Landscapes, and Globalization and Nationalism.

October 14. Ghislaine de Boysson Durrell dies in Paris at the age of 75.

November 13. Susan MacNiven, the founding editor of The International Lawrence Durrell Society's newsletter *The Herald*, dies at the age of 65 from cancer, which she has fought like a tiger for many years, depriving the world of a grand spirit and a lively intellect.

2004

Yale University Press publishes Michael Haag's *Alexandria: City of Memory*, containing lengthy chapters on E. M. Forster, C. P. Cavafy and LD.

January 15. The French Canal 5 television special on Alexandria, *Double Je*, hosted by Bernard Pivot, discusses LD and *The Alexandria Quartet*.

April 20. Patrick Besson discusses the recently published French edition of the Durrell-Miller correspondence on the TF1 program *Vol de nuit*.

April 23. The French radio station Canal 3 (Sud) broadcasts a brief interview with F.-J. Temple about LD and Miller.

June 12–25. The DSC holds its third annual two-week session with the participation of Lee Durrell, Gayatri C. Spivak, Harish Trivedi, Eve Patten, Terry Eagleton, Nuala ni Dhomhnail, among others, preceded by a two-day symposium entitled "Globalisation and Nationalism" moderated by Richard Pine and Brewster Chamberlin.

June 28 – July 2. The ILDS convenes its 13th biennial On Miracle Ground conference on Rhodes (attended by Penelope Durrell Hope, John Hope and Eve Cohen Durrell).

August 14. Czesław Miłosz, Nobel 1980, dies at the age of 93 and is buried in the Skalka Sanctuary, Kraków.

December 19. Eve Cohen Durrell dies in London at the age of 86 and is buried next to her daughter Sappho in the Trent Park Cemetery, Cockfosters.

2005

February 27. In a sudden surge of excitement the author of this chronology reaches for the glass and a pencil simultaneously and spills red wine on the manuscript.

March 28. Brewster Chamberlin publishes *Mediterranean Sketches* in which LD, the DSC and the ILDS conferences in Alexandria, Corfu and Rhodes are prominently featured.

April 5. Saul Bellow, Nobel 1976, dies in Boston at the age of 90 and is buried in the Morningside Cemetery, Brattleboro, Vermont.

April 11. The novelist and GD's friend David Hughes dies in London at the age of 74.

May 23–27. The DSC holds a one-week seminar on the subject of "Madness and Creativity", during which Richard Pine offers a paper asking if LD was mad. The DSC publishes the revised second edition of Richard Pine's *Lawrence Durrell: The Mindscape.*

June–July. The BBC sends a production team to Corfu to film a second, shorter version of GD's *My Family and Other Animals*, scheduled for airing in Britain during the Christmas holidays.

July 6. Claude Simon, Nobel 1985, dies in Paris at the age of 91.

September 25–30. The DSC holds a one-week seminar on "Borders and Borderlands" in the DSC library in Corfu Town.

October. In London, the Carcanet Press publishes *The Tenth Muse*, an anthology of poems by various British writers edited by Anthony Astbury, with nine poems by LD selected and with a foreword by Françoise Kestsman Durrell.[8]

November 5. John Fowles, whose massive novel, *The Magus*, is said to have been greatly influenced by LD, dies in Lyme Regis at the age of 79; apparently his ashes are scattered.

2006

May 21–26. The DSC holds the year's first summer seminar, "The Emergence of Modern Greece".

June 5–9. The DSC holds its second summer seminar, "Empire and Aftermath: Core and Periphery".

June 25–29. The ILDS holds its 14th biennial On Miracle Ground conference in Victoria, Canada.

---

[8] There is no evidence that LD and Françoise were ever legally married, but see the entry for August 22, 1987, and the footnote relating to it.

September 6. Edward Hodgkin dies of natural causes at the age of 93 and the following year his ashes are interred at the Milton Abbas cemetery with his wife Nancy's remains.

September 24. The municipality of Corfu unveils plaques honouring Lawrence and Gerald Durrell at the entrance to a public garden adjacent to the Old Fortress causeway facing the Esplanade (Spianada) in Corfu Town, in the presence of Lee Durrell and Penelope Durrell Hope. The garden is thereafter officially called Bosketto Durrell.

September 25–30. The DSC holds its third seminar of the year, "Tradition and Change in Rural Society".

2007

Cambridge Scholars Publishing publishes *Creativity, Madness and Civilisation* edited by Richard Pine, the proceedings of the DSC seminar held in May 2005.

January 16. Margo Durrell, the last of LD's siblings, dies in Bournemouth at the age of 87 and is buried in the cemetery there.

May 20–25. The DSC holds a seminar entitled "The Literatures of War".

June 3–8. The DSC holds a seminar entitled "The Writer's Reputation: Gender, Time, Geography".

September 14–19. The DSC organizes a week of events around the interests of the botanist GD during his years on the island during the 1930s entitled "The Amateur Naturalist".

September 24–28. The DSC holds a seminar entitled "Cleaning Up the Mediterranean".

2008

The DSC publishes *Nostos: Proceedings 1: 2002–2005*, edited by Richard Pine.

In London, Arrow Books publishes Deborah Lawrenson's novel loosely based on LD and Nancy's life on Corfu, *Songs of Blue and Gold.*

In Canada, ELS Editions re-publishes LD's *Pied Piper of Lovers* (with an introduction by James Gifford), originally published in 1935, and LD's *Panic Spring: A Romance* (with an introduction by Richard Pine), originally published in 1936.

Cambridge Scholars Publishing publishes *Literatures of War* edited by Richard Pine and Eve Patten, the proceedings of the DSC seminar held in May 2007.

The American University in Cairo Press publishes Michael Haag's *Vintage Alexandria: Photographs of the City 1860–1960.*

Mary Alexander Stephanides, widow of Theodore, dies in London at the age of 103.

May 17. LD's old friend from the beginning of the War, in Athens then in Egypt and Palestine, Paul Gotch, dies.[9]

May 18–22. The DSC holds a seminar entitled "An Investigation of Modern Love".

June 1–6. The DSC holds a seminar entitled "Travel Writing, Spirit of Place and the Discovery of the Self".

July 1–5. The ILDS holds its 15th biennial On Miracle Ground conference "Lawrence Durrell: A Writer at the Crossroads of Arts and Sciences" at the Université Paris X (Nanterre).

2009

May 24–29. The DSC holds a seminar, "The Garden of the Gods".

---

[9] An editorial note to Gotch's reminiscence of his friend LD incorrectly has Gotch dying on July 2 (*Deus Loci: The Lawrence Durrell Journal*, NS13 (2012–2013), 183); this is the date his obituary appeared in the London *Times.*

2010

May 16–21. The DSC holds a seminar entitled "The History and Culture of the Ionian Islands", moderated by Peter Mackridge.

July 7–10. The ILDS holds its 16th biennial On Miracle Ground conference "Durrell and the City: Reconstructing the Urban Landscape" at the Louisiana Tech University in New Orleans.

October 21. Penelope Durrell Hope dies peacefully at the age of 70 at her home, The Garden House, Whitney-on-Wye.

2011

The DSC and the ILDS jointly publish Theodore Stephanides' *Autumn Gleanings: Corfu Memoirs and Poems,* edited by Richard Pine, Lindsay Parker, James Gifford and Anthony Hirst.

May 16–23. The DSC holds an event entitled "Gerald Durrell's Corfu", a week-long programme of visits to sites of natural interest associated with GD's childhood in Corfu.

2012

The DSC publishes LD's novel *Judith* edited and with an introduction by Richard Pine.

Virago Press publishes Joanna Hodgkin's *Amateurs in Eden. The Story of a Bohemian Marriage: Nancy and Lawrence Durrell.* Hodgkin is the daughter of Nancy and her second husband Edward Hodgkin.

February 26. The daily newspaper of the Gard, *Midi-Libre,* publishes a laudatory article by Laure Casteil for the 100th anniversary of LD's birth, "Les cent ans de Lawrence Durrell".

May 11–18. Given the success of the previous year's event, the DSC organizes the second "Gerald Durrell's Corfu". Known informally as "The Gerald Durrell Week", it becomes from now on an annual event. When the DSC closes in 2014, the organizers Alex and Dave Ashcroft arrange for the Durrell Wildlife Conservation Trust in Jersey to take over the sponsorship of this event, with the participation of Lee Durrell.

June 13–18. The ILDS holds its 17th biennial On Miracle Ground conference "Durrell 2012: The Lawrence Durrell Centenary" in London, celebrating the hundredth anniversary of LD's birth.

June 20–27. The DSC holds a similar seminar entitled "Lawrence Durrell in Corfu: A Centenary Reappraisal".

July 10–20. In Lisbon, at the Grande Audiório, Fundação Calouste Gulbenkian, Jennifer Condon conducts the Orquestra Gulbenkian in the first full version of Peggy Glanville-Hicks' opera based on LD's verse play *Sappho* for the Toccata Classics record label, with Deborah Polaski (Sappho), Martin Homrich (Phaon), and Scott MacAllister (Pittakos). The recording is available on a two-CD set.

September 17–21. The DSC in conjunction with the Ionian University on Corfu holds a seminar entitled "The Music, Dance and Drama of the Ionian Islands".

2013

After eleven years of splendid work in mounting many seminars on subjects related to the Durrell brothers and their interests, the Durrell School of Corfu ceases activities for pecuniary reasons and formally closes in early 2014. It is succeeded by the annual ongoing "Gerald Durrell's Corfu" and, in 2016, by the Durrell Library of Corfu established by Richard Pine.

2014

Cambridge Scholars Publishing publishes *The Ionian Islands: Aspects of Their History and Culture* edited by Anthony Hirst and Patrick Sammon, based on the proceedings of the 2010 DSC seminar with a similar title.

May 14–17. The ILDS holds its 18th biennial On Miracle Ground conference "Durrell & Place: Translation, Migration, Location" at Fairleigh Dickenson University, Vancouver, Canada.

2015

The University of Alberta Press publishes LD's *From the Elephant's Back. Collected Essays and Travel Writings*, edited by James Gifford.

2016

*June 26–30.*The ILDS holds its 19th biennial On Miracle Ground conference, "Threading the Labyrinth: Durrell, Greece, and World War II" at the University of Crete in Rethymnon, Greece.

2017

October 18–20. The Durrell Library of Corfu, in conjunction with the Ionian University, holds a symposium "Novel Encounters", celebrating Greek and Irish fiction, at the Ionian Academy and the Solomos Museum in Corfu Town.

2018

May. In London Colenso Books and The Delos Press publish LD's *The Fruitful Discontent of the Word: A Further Collection of Poems*, edited by Peter Baldwin.

July 4–7. The ILDS holds its 20th biennial On Miracle Ground conference "Exile, Survival and Dissent" in Chicago.

August. In London Colenso Books, for the Durrell Library of Corfu, publishes LD's *The Placebo* (three drafts of what eventually became *Tunc*), edited with extensive introductions by Richard Pine and David Roessel.

October 28. Alexia Stephanides-Mercouri, daughter of Theodore and Mary Stephanides, dies in Athens at the age of 91; her husband Spyros Mercouris died at the end of August.

2019

June 23–28. The Durrell Library of Corfu holds a symposium "Islands of the Mind" at the Solomos Museum in Corfu Town.

INDEX OF PERSONS

An asterisk after the page number indicates that the person in question is referred to in more than one entry on that page.

Where a page number is followed by "n", it means the person in question is referred to in a footnote on that page.

Brackets around a page number indicate that the person in question is referred to on that page but without their name being mentioned (e.g. a husband and wife referred to jointly by their surname in the plural, or persons referred to only by their relationship to others).

A page range (e.g. 17–20) means that the person in question is referred to on each of the pages within the range (a minimum of four consecutive pages), with multiple references on one or more pages (including footnotes).

Where two consecutive page numbers are separated by a forward slash (e.g. 73/4) it means the person's name is split across a page break.

Lightning Source UK Ltd.
Milton Keynes UK
UKHW010219140121
376750UK00001B/4